East by Sea

and

West by Rail

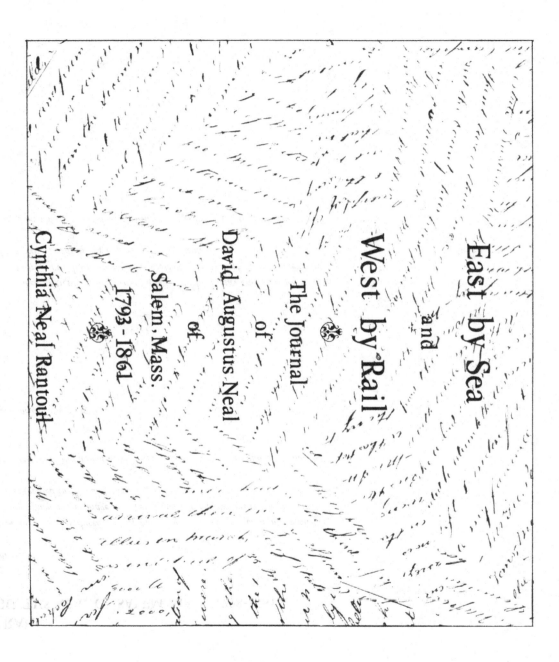

The Journal

of

David Augustus Neal

of

Salem, Mass.

1793 - 1861

Cynthia Neal Rantoul

iUniverse, Inc.
Bloomington

EAST BY SEA AND WEST BY RAIL
THE JOURNAL OF DAVID AUGUSTUS NEAL OF SALEM, MASS. 1798-1861

iUniverse books may be ordered through booksellers or by contacting:

iUniverse
1663 Liberty Drive
Bloomington, IN 47403
www.iuniverse.com
1-800-Authors (1-800-288-4677)

ISBN: 978-1-4620-3513-7 (sc)

Printed in the United States of America

iUniverse rev. date: 07/18/2011

This Book
is Presented to

_____

on the _____ day of _____ ,19_____

This Book
is Number

_____

of a Limited Edition.

Signed,_____

_____ day of _____ , 19_____ .

First Edition,June,1979

Typefaces:
        Captions: Script,12 pica
        Cover Design:Lectura Bold,42 & 28 pica
        Journal: Courier,10 pica
        Numbers: Helvetica Med.,18 pica
        Research: Prestige Elite,12 pica
        Other: Advocate,10 pica

Original Typed Translation:
        Norma Rantoul

Final Typing:
        Heather Burke Word Processing Ltd.
        Toronto,Ont.

Reproduction:
        Artistat (Canada) Ltd.
        Toronto,Ont.

1

East by Sea

and

West by Rail

The Journal
of
David Augustus Neal
of
Salem,Mass.

1793-1861

Research,Editing and Layout Design
by
Cynthia Neal Rantoul

Introduction

This Journal contains the life of David A.
Neal written in his own hand sometime
before his death in 1861. It is my belief
that he maintained notebooks during the
events described since the dates,names
and places are too carefully detailed to
have been based on memory alone.

As he set sail on his first voyage in
1810, he embarked on a career that would
not only take him to the four corners
of the world but include the opening
of the midwestern United States with
the advent of their first railroad.

Until now it is unlikely that you have
ever heard of this man. It is my hope
that by the end of this book, you'll
have felt you've lived it with him.

Signed

Cynthia N. Rantoul

Cynthia N. Rantoul
June 7,1979

Neal Family Crest

Published by:
        Elvidge Printing Company Limited
        Toronto,Ontario

First Printing:
        June,1979

Acknowledgements

I would like to extend my thanks to the
following Archives for permission to
reproduce excerpts from documents in
their collections:

Essex Institute, Salem, Mass.
Peabody Museum, Salem, Mass.
Newbury Library, Chicago, Illinois
Maritime Museum, Greenwich, England
Historical & Genealogical Society, Boston,
            Mass.

Also I would like to thank Dr. Josephine
Lee Murray of Topsfield, Mass. and Mrs.
Charlotte Rantoul-Bonner of Boston for
their hospitality during my research
expeditions.

Dedication

To Aunt Hat, whose maternal Grandfather
wrote the Journal on which this book
is based; for her pride in our family
heritage that she passed on.

This book is affectionately dedicated
to her memory.

4

Journal Contents

******

Blood.

Auto biography is seldom interesting except in cases where the incidents of the writer's life have been associated with great events or his own acts have been of such a character as to minister to the honest pride of his posterity or add a bright page to the history of his country. But such can be the fortune of but few. The interest in the lives of ordinary men dies with them. Even their immediate descendants are usually too much involved in the cares of rising fam-ilies or absolved in new connections to give much thought to the memories and still less to the acts of those who have passed away and left no sign. Nor is this a matter of reproach. It is the inevitable result of daily duties and daily wants, pressing on the mind, and compelling to look forward to the performance of the one and the other, rather than back to works completed.

trees is a

The Journal of David A. Neal

Autobiography is seldom interesting except in cases where
the incidents of the writer's life have been associated with
great events or his own acts have been of such a character
as to minister to the honest pride of his posterity or add a
bright page to the history of his country. Such can be the
fortune of but few. The interest in the lives of ordinary
men dies with them. Even their immediate descendents are
usually too much involved in the cares of rising families or
absorbed in new connections to give much thought to the
memories and still less to the acts of those who have passed
away and left no sign. Nor is this a matter of reproach.
It is the inevitable result of daily duties and daily events
pressing on the mind, and compelling it to look forward to
the performance of the one and the supply of the other,
rather than back to works completed and friends at rest.

Blood

Ancestry therefore under ordinary circumstances is a matter
of secondary importance. "Act well your part, there all the
honor lies." Mankind are so constituted and the relations
of society are so varied, that no man can expect to find
behind him a long line in which virtues and accomplishments
have always predominated. That there is much in blood,
whether in men or in the lower animals is undeniably true.
But among the former there is nothing but inclination or
fancy to control their intermixtures and consequently
nothing that would be likely to improve its results. Among
some of the latter a power over individuals or kinds may be
exercised as to extirpate the inferior portion and connect
what remained so as to produce a vastly superior race. The
pedigree of our domestic animals would therefore seem to be
of more consequence than our own, for from it we may obtain
a reasonable assurance of their qualities. It is not so
with man. Those who can trace back their progenitors for
two or three centuries will seldom come from the search
fully satisfied with their discoveries. Those who can do so
have good cause for self congratulation.

Neal Family Genealogy
[Continued from the "Neal Record" by Theodore A. Neal, Henry W. Dutton & Son, Printers, Boston, 1856]

7th Generation

Jonathan Neal   Born: Jan. 15,1759, Salem   Died: Oct. 9, 1837   Aged 78 yrs.

     First Wife: Mehetable Eden   Born: 1757   Died: Sept. 29, 1786   Aged 25 yrs.
            Date Married:

     Issue: Mehetable   Born: Nov. 1783   Died: Oct. 20, 1856   Aged 73 yrs.
            Married: Amos Choate ----- - 1844   Date of Marriage: Issue: None

     Second Wife: Hannah Ward   Born: 1775   Died: Jan. 26, 1814   Aged 39 yrs.
            Date Married: 1791   Aged 16 yrs. (Jona Neal aged 32 yrs.)

     Issue: Twins   Born: Died: In infancy, dates unknown
         David Augustus   Born: June 7, 1793   Died: Aug. 5, 1861   Aged 68 yrs.
            Married: Harriet Charlotte Price 1794-1865 Date: July 26, 1818
            Issue: 2 sons, 3 daughters

         Nathan Ward   Born: Aug. 27, 1797   Died: Nov. 17, 1850   Aged 53 yrs.
            Married: No

         William Henry   Born: March 8, 1799   Died: Jan. 1851   Aged 52 yrs.
            Married: Sarah Ropes ---- - May,1851   Date of Marriage: Issue: None

         Theodore Frederick   Born: Nov. 3, 1802   Died: June 14, 1821, Havana   Aged 19 yrs.
            Married: No

8th Generation

David Augustus Neal m. Harriet Charlotte Price

     Issue: Theodore Frederick   Born: December 18, 1822   Died: Under 1 yr. old
         Theodore Augustus   Born: March 23, 1827   Died Oct. 26, 1881   Aged 54 yrs.
            Married: Elizabeth Boardman Whittredge   Date: Issue:

         Harriet Charlotte   Born: Feb. 1, 1831   Died: March 17,1837   Aged 6 yrs.
         Margaret Maria   Born: June 15, 1832   Died March 28, 1903   Aged 70 yrs.
            Married: No

         Harriet Charlotte   Born: July 8, 1837   Died: May 26, 1899   Aged 62 yrs.
            Married: Robert S. Rantoul   Date of Marriage:
            Issue: 3 daughters, 5 sons

Lineage

I confess I have never felt any great curiosity in regard to
my distant lineage, but my son has a fancy for such
researches and has compiled a genealogical table of the Neal
family which he traces to an englishman and one of the early
settlers of New England and his wife an englishwoman who
came to this country and located in Salem sometime prior to
1642 in which year or before he married Mary Lawes who was
(probably) the only child of Francis Lawes who came from
England and at the time of his death was possessed of
considerable landed property in Salem which through his
daughter descended in the Neal family by whom some portions
of it is yet held. Within my recollection a very
considerable part of it belonged to my Father viz. that on
which my house on corner Cambridge and Chestnut the South
Church on the opposite corner and all the grounds then to
Summer St. and all the lots on Chestnut Street opposite the
above including those on which Hamilton Hall is built.

Family History

My Father was born on the 15 of January 1759. He went to
sea when quite young, probably some time before the
commencement of the American Revolution. On the breaking
out of the war or shortly after he enlisted in the Army and
was among those who were taken prisoner at the capture of
Fort Washington on the Hudson. He was confined in the
prison ships at New York, but escaped or was exchanged. He
made his way through Connecticut on foot, and on arriving
home he embarked in privateering, at first as an officer and
afterwards as Commander. He was on a cruise in the ship
'Cicero', of 26 guns, at the time peace was signed, but a
little after that event, and before it was known, he was
captured by an English Frigate and sent into Bermuda. On
his arrival he was of course liberated, but his ship was not
given up. He returned home and took charge of a vessel in
the Merchant Service and made voyages to the West Indies and
to Europe.

William Henry Neal

Nathan Ward Neal

His first wife was Mehitable, daughter of Thoman Eden, who
died Sept. 29th 1786, leaving one daughter Mehitable who was
born Nov. 1783. He afterwards married Hannah, daughter of
Miles and Experience Ward (by her) leaving four sons, myself
born June 7th 1793, Nathan Ward born Aug. 27th 1797, William
Henry born March 1799, and Theodore Frederick born Nov. 3rd
1802. My sister Mehitable married Amos Choate who died in
1844 without children, and she after a protracted and severe
illness of a catharral affection died in her house No. 10
Chestnut St. on the 20th Oct. 1856.

My brother Nathan graduated in Cambridge in the class of
1816, subsequently engaged in commerce and died unmarried of
anemia, or bloodlessness Nov. 17th 1850.

My Brother William made his first voyage with me after the
peace of 1815 in the Alexander, and subsequently commanded
several vessels in E.I. voyages; - then engaged in commerce
at home and died of exhaustion from Rheumatism Jan. 17 '51.
He had married Sarah, daughter of John (Joseph) Ropes who
survives. He left no children.

My Brother Theordore died on his first voyage at Havana, on
the 14th June 1821.

They were all highly respected during their lives, and
deeply regretted at their deaths.

Maternal Ancestry

In regard to my Maternal Ancestry I have a portion of its
history from a paper in the Historical collections of the
Essex Institute for August 1860, contributed by Benj. F.
Brown, Esq. and add some facts in relation to members of the
family within my own knowledge.

My Mother was the daughter of Miles Ward, who resided in the
house on the north side of High Street, and corner of that
and Mill Streets, which estate and the wharf opposite
belonged to him. She was born in 1775, was married in 1791,

Early Recollections.

My own life has not been an eventful one, but it "
passed in probably the most eventful period of the
world's history, whether considered in a political or
a scientific point of view. My birth took place
at the most convulsed period of the French Revo-
-lution. Louis XVI had just fallen a victim to its
fury and Maria Antoinette. than whom said Burke,
never lighted on this orb a more delightful vision,
was in prison awaiting the same fate.

The year 1793 is probably the most bloody on record.
From that time until Napoleon Buonaparte closed
the great tragedy by assuming the whole power of
government as First Consul, the number of lives
sacrificed in the eternal wars for defense, or in the internal feuds for supremacy, is counted by millions.

...ere I was too young to notice the current
...d ...n the news of the dispersion
...nd the consequent
...ne faint ...

at the early age of 16 years, and died on the 26th of January 1814, after a long and distressing illness of a dropsical character.

Early Recollections

My own life has not been an eventful one but it has been passed in probably the most eventful period of the world's history, whether considered in a political or a scientific point of view. My birth took place at the most convulsed period of the French Revolution. Louis XVI had first fallen a victim to its fury and Maria Antoinette than whom said Burke, "never lighted on this orb a more delightful vision," was in prison awaiting the same fate.

The year 1793 is probably the most bloody on record. From that time until Napoleon Buonaparte closed the great tragedy by assuming the whole power of government at First Consul, the number of lives sacrificed in the external wars for defense, or in the internal feuds for supremacy, is counted by millions, but of these I was too young to notice the current advices as received.

But of the excitement on the news of the dispersion of the Council of Five Hundred and the consequent accession of Buonaparte to power, I have some faint impression. The short peace of 1802 is clearly within my recollection. The general interest excited by the elevation of Napoleon to the Imperial throne in 1804, the battles of Austerlitz in 1805, and the Jena and Friedland in 1806 and the treaty of Tilsit in 1807 was fully shared by me for I had then attained an age when I could form some opinions of the merits and the consequences of acts and events that were then agitating the whole civilized world. From this time I took a deep interest in the politics both of my own country and of Europe. In the former the withdrawl from the ocean of all American shipping by the embargo of 1807 with a view to avoid the necessity of defending it by war against the hostile acts of the two great belligerants in europe created intense excitement. It completed what the British Orders in

---

Dropsical Character: Cause: Unkown. Symptoms: swelling of the whole body occasioned by a collection of watery tumours, four types of dropsy are of the bowels, skin, breast or head (Smith, E. "The American Physican and Family Assistant, B. True Publishers, Boston, 1837, P. 173)

Council of Five Hundred: (France) Sept. 4, 1797; Napoleon ousted the government of France in Paris comprised of the Council of 500 and took control. (EWH)

Treaty of Amiens, March 27, 1802: Concluded between England and France thus achieving a complete pacification of Europe. (EWH)

Napoleon I Dec. 2, 1804: was proclaimed Emperor by the French, and was consecrated by Pope Pius VII. (EWH)

Battle of Austerlitz: Dec. 2, 1804: one of the greatest victories of Napoleon. When the combined armies of Austria and Russia were defeated, the Austrians hastily agreed to a truce and the Russians retreated. (EWH)

War with Prussia and Russia Battles of Jena and Auerstadt: Oct. 14, 1806: The main Prussian armies were completely routed by Napoleon and quickly fell to pieces. (EWH)

Battle of Friedland: June 14, 1807: France versus Russia; French were victorious and the Russians fell back. Napoleon then occupied Lonigsberg and all the country as far as the Niemen River. After the conclusion of a truce Napoleon met with Alexander I (Russia) and Frederick William III (Prussia) on a raft on the Niemen and concluded the Treaty of Tilsit. (EWH)

Treaty of Tilsit: July 7 - 9, 1807: Between France and Russia and France and Prussia ending the war. (EWH)

Fox's Order: (England) May 16, 1806: Declared the coast of Europe from Brest to the Elbe River to be in a state of blockade, except between Ostend and the mouth of the Seine, where neutral vessels were admitted provided they were not coming from or bound to an enemy port. (EWH)

Berlin Decree: Nov. 21, 1806: Napoleon retaliates with his Berlin Decree declaring a paper blockade of the British Isles (EWH) (Note: Paper blockade means he did not have his government's support so it was a threat not a reality)

An Order of Council: (England) Nov. 11, 1807: Another blockading the coast from Copenhagen to Trieste against Neutrals unless they had first entered or been cleared from a British port and paid duties there. (EWH)

Milan Decree: December, 1807: (France) Napoleon's reply was that ships lost their neutral status if they obeyed the British Order of Council of Nov. 11 or if they submitted to a search on the high seas by British Officers. (EWH)

The Embargo Act: Dec. 22, 1807: (United States) President Jefferson, still averse to war with Britain or France resolved on commercial coercion as a means of forcing France and England to withdraw their restriction on American trade. This act forbade the departure of ships for foreign ports, except foreign vessels in port at the time the act was passed. coasting vessels were required to give bond to land their cargoes at American ports. (EWH)

Repeal of the Embargo Act: March 15, 1809: (United States) James Madison is the new President. The Embargo had not brought England and France to terms but instead had weighed heavily upon American shipping. (EWH)

The Non-Intercourse Law: May 20, 1809: (United States) It permitted commerce with all countries except France and England. (EWH)

Rambouillet Decree: May 23, 1810: (France) Napoleon ordered the sale of all American ships which had been siezed for violation of French Decrees. (EWH)

Battle of Trafalger: Oct. 21, 1805: a combined victory of Nelson (England) over the combined French and Spanish fleets. This victory broke the naval power of France and established Britain as the mistress of the seas throughout the 19th Century. (EWH)

Napoleon invades Russia: June, 1812: Niemen River (EWH)

A **Burning of Moscow:** Sept. 15, 1812: a disaster planned and executed by the Russians to make the place uninhabitable for Napoleon's advancing army. Napoleon offered Alexander a truce which he rejected. After waiting five weeks in Moscow, Napoleon frustrated in his hope of bringing the Russians to terms and unable to maintain himself so far from his bases, began his retreat from Moscow. (EWH)

Crossing of the Beresina: Nov. 26 - 28, 1812: one of the most horrible episodes in the retreat. Ney and Oudinot with 8500 men force the passage against 25,000 Russians. Frost, hunger and enemy attacks plagued the army. From this point onward, the army became disorganized and the retreat became a wild flight. Napoleon hastened to Paris while the remnants of his army made it th the Nieman River. It proved to be the turning point of his career. (EWH)

B **Napoleon I abdicates:** April 11, 1814: unconditionally to Louis XVIII. The Allies granted him the island of Elba as a sovereign principality with an annual income of 2,000,000 francs from France. He arrived May 4, 1814. (EWH)

D **The Hundred Days:** March 1, 1815: News of the discontent in France with the Bourbon gov't and knowledge of the discord at the Congress of Vienna in Austria, to say nothing of the encouragement of his adherents, induced Napoleon I to make another effort to recover his throne. Landed at Cannes, France with 1500 men and marched on Paris. Entered March 20 to start his Hundred Day rule and ended June 29. (EWH)

Alliance of Austria, England, Prussia and Russia: March 25, 1815: formed to overthrow Napoleon, 1 million men marched under the Duke of Wellington (EWH)

15

Council and the Berlin and Milan decrees of the French
Emperor had begun, the destruction of our Foreign commerce
for the time at least.

It was abandoned in 1809.

The entire supremacy of France on the continent and that of
England on the ocean was now undisputed.

The Treaty of Tilsit in 1807 confirmed the first. The
latter had been assured two years before by the naval battle
of Trafalgar. Both however were destined to receive a shock
in far less time than it had taken to establish them.

Political changes

The ᴬflames of Moscow and the snows of a Russian winter drove
the conqueror of Europe from his imperial throne and ᴮexiled
him to a petty island in the Mediterranean.

ᶜA single ship with a bit of striped bunting at her masthead
destroyed the prestige of the red cross of England and made
her wooden walls tremble to their base.

The downfall of Napoleon was followed by a transient glare
that for aᴰshort hundred days illumined the world and was
then scatteredᴱon the fields of Waterloo and quenched in the
waters of the South Atlantic. Who would then have believed
that from the ashes thus deposited there would in less than
half a century have arisen a new empire that is peace, and a
ᶠnew emperor whose influence in diplomacy would be greater
than that of his predecessor in arms. Who could then have
supposed that theᶜbroadsides of a single frigate would gain
for our country and our flag the honor and respect that is
now so universally accorded to them. Yet I have lived to
see these results showing changes in the destinies of men
and nations greater probably than any other generation has
ever witnessed. I have been contemporary with four
sovereigns of Great Britain, George the third, Geo. the
fourth, William the fourth and Victoria the first - with

E Battle of Waterloo: June 18, 1815: Napoleon hurles himself against
Wellington's army, believing that he had insured the junction
of Blucher's army with an attach by Grouchy. However Grouchy
was defeated. Wellington's army held its lines all day under
terrific assaults from the French. The arrival of Blucher
towards the evening probably saved the day. The French
scattered in defeat. (EWH)

F Napoleon III declared Emperor: Nov. 2, 1852: Introduced joint
stock banks, helped create railroads, shipping companies,
public utilities, improved worker's conditions, gave donation
to charitable foundatins, set up a public works program to
rebuild Paris and contributed to rise of Catholic supervision
over education, grants and schools. Reign ended in 1870.
(EWH)

C Possibly a reference to the battle between the frigate U.S.S.
'Constitution' and the 'Guerriere' in the War of 1812. In a
becalmed sea and lasting 3 days, the Constitution 'outran'
her opponent by strategy rather than sail. (EWH)

With fine

Charles the tenth.

and with I don't know.

In my own country I have see

increases from 14 to 33, its population

and its wealth & resources in probably a great

But great as has been the changes and the progress in

the political & material world, vastly greater & more

astonishing has been the advancement in science &

the arts. Many things now of the most ordinary use &

application, were in my early days entirely unknown.

Few inventions have been found more conducive to

the comfort of every family and more generally used

than the common friction match.

How often in my school boy experience, have I on a

cold winter's morning, labored minutes, that seemed

hours, in hammering out the unwilling spark between

the flint

Progress of Arts.

and still longer lingered over it in the damp

uld become bright enough to ignite

wing. The article of phosphorus

d applying it in the humble

for the convenience

Kind.

five of Russia, Catherine, Paul Alexander the first,
Nicholas the first, and Alexander the second. - with five in
France, Napoleon the first, Louis the eighteenth, Charles
the tenth, Louis Phillippe and Napoleon the third, and with
I don't know how many in Germany, Spain, etc. In my own
country I have seen the number of States increased from 14
to 33, its population from 5 to 35 millions, and its wealth
and resources in probably a greater ratio. But great as has
been the change and the progress in the political and
material world, vastly greater and more astonishing has been
the advancement in science and the arts. Many things now of
the most ordinary use and application were in my early days
entirely unknown. Few inventions have been found more
generally used than the common friction match.

How often in my school boy experience have I on a cold
winter's morning labored minutes that seemed hours in
hammering out the unwilling spark between the flint...

Progress of Arts

...and steel and still longer lingered over it in the damp
tinder before it would become bright enough to ignite the
brimstone tipped shaving. The article of phosphorus was
known but no one had thought of applying it in the humble
but felicitous manner in which it now does so much for the
convenience and comfort of all men and especially of all
womankind. We have only to be without the lucifer match one
day to appreciate its inestimable value.

The power of steam has been brought under control since
about one hundred years ago. When the genius of Watts made
it take the place of animal power, but it is only during my
own life and even during that part of it which has been
spent in active pursuits, that it has been practically
applied to the purposes of locomotion, and created the great
revolution that has within half a century taken place in the
transportation of men and matter all over the world. It was
not until 1807 that Fulton caused the first steamboat ever
built to move triuimphantly over the waters of the Hudson

Lucifers: The year 1827 saw the first really useful friction match,
made by an Englishman John Walker, a druggist. Walker's
matches contained no phosphorous but were made of chlorate of
potash, sugar and gum arabic. The method of striking to
obtain fire was to draw the splinter of wood, tipped with
this composition, rapidly and under considerable pressure
through a piece of folded sandpaper. (Encyclopaedia
Brittanica of Canada Ltd, Toronto, 1948, Volume 15, p.45)

1770: James Watt invented the modern Steam Engine (EWH)
1776: Henry Cavendish discovers Hydrogen (EWH)
1783: First small balloon invented by the Montgolfier brothers (EWH)
1784: The Robert Brothers invent the first hydrogen filled airship,
melon shaped and silk-covered (EWH)
1794: The semaphore telegraph was developed by Claude Chappe (EWH)
1802: "Charlotte Dundas" first tug built by Wm. Sumington equipped
with a steam locomotive (EWH)
1804: Trevithick built the first steam locomotive (EWH)

1807: Robert Fulton and Robert R. Livingston steamed from New York
to Albany in 32 hours in the 'Clermont', the first successful
steamboat (EWH)

Above: The First Railway cars

Left: A later steam run railway engine

from New York to Albany. A few years only subsequent to
this I made several passages with the first steam navigator
(Capt. Bunker) through Long Island Sound and then he, bold
and capable and energetic as he was, dared venture no
farther than the Connecticut Shore. Point Judith was the
stormy cape around which it was deemed imprudent if not
impossible to pass, except by the aid, and in vessels fitted
only for the use of sails. What changes have occurred since
that time. What Burke said of the American Whaler is now
true of the Ocean Steam Ship.

But it is not upon the sea alone that steam has exhibited
its wonderful energies in bringing together (in effect)
distant points and different nations. Its applications to
railroads, first effectually accomplished in 1829 on the
Liverpool and Manchester track, has changed the character of
internal commerce, and given an impetus to travel within the
last twenty-five years greater than it had obtained in two
hundred and fifty years of previous improvements. About
twenty-five years ago I travelled with Mr. Wm. Brown (since
the member of Parliament for Liverpool and then as now
distinguished for his high position as a merchant and one of
the first advocates of free trade in England) over the
Liverpool & Manchester Railway, then, I believe, the only
passenger railway operated by steam in Great Britain though
several were in progress. The first passenger road opened
in the United States was I believe that portion of the
Baltimore & Ohio Railroad between Baltimore and Ellicott's
Mills, a distance of 13 miles. It was opened in January
1831, and was operated by horses and steam locomotives so
that in less than 30 years the number of miles of rails
operated by steam has risen from 13 to 22,000. I remember
that the first time I ever went from Boston to New York was
in 1813 and I was four days on the way. Now the passage
over nearly the same route is made regularly in about twice
that number of hours. During the war with Great Britian
1813-15 the journey from New Orleans often occupied three
months, now travelling over almost precisely the same ground
it can be made in three days.

Oliver Evans's Road Engine.

It was in 1825 that the first train of passenger cars in England was drawn by a locomotive, and then they only went six miles an hour."

"I wonder they have n't tried to run steam locomotives on the roads, without rails," said Ned.

"They have tried, and still are trying to, but with no great success. The first road engine so tried was made by Oliver Evans

21

The dull light of burning tallow or oil, assisted by the constant applications of snuffers to the conducting wick, or at best, the more expensive flame from sperm or was, until a very few years the only means by which we could do our work or find our way after sundown. Now the brilliant illumination of gas is found in every considerable town and in almost every house.

I remember with what astonishment I saw in the library rooms in Philadelphia (I think 1823) a brilliant fire, made with what I had been taught to call stone coal and had supposed it as difficult of ignition as stone itself. It had just been discovered that anthracite would burn. Until then the vast beds of this mineral remained undisturbed in the mountains of Pennsylvania. A slight alteration in the draught has brought it into general use, and the consumption of it annually is now measured by millions of tons. At that time there was not probably a furnace for heating dwelling houses (except perhaps a few clumsy Russian stoves) in the United States. Now there is scarcely a decent house without one.

People have not yet done wondering at the mysteries of the electric telegraph. I recollect perfectly the day and hour when I heard announced the death of Washington. It was just after tea on the 22nd of December in the front room of my Father's house in Washington Street when a friend of the family, Capt. Benj. West, came in with the gloomy tidings. Washington died on the 14th of that month. Probably no intelligence had ever been transmitted more rapidly, for ill news flies apace. Yet it was eight days reaching us, a distance of little over 500 miles. Now it would have been transmitted in less than that number of minutes.

There are a hundred other inventions or discoveries that serve to exemplify the vast difference that fifty years have made in the comforts, the luxuries and the knowledge of man, but they are now in such common use that I find it difficult to recall them, or if I do to realize that we were ever without them. But in contrasting the appearance and

George Washington died Dec. 14, 10 p.m. 1799

1807: Gas lights introduced in London, England By 1820, most of the city was lit this way. (EWH)
1816: Regular transatlantic service was initiated by the Black Ball Line using fast sailing ships between New York and Liverpool (EWH)
1818: Iron first used in shipbuilding (EWH)
1819: The steamer 'Savannah' crosses the Atlantic under steam to Liverpool (augmented with sail) (EWH)
1825: First railway in the world opens between Stockton and Darlington, England (EWH)
1826: First all steam Atlantic crossing by Dutch steamer 'Curacao' (EWH)
1827: Nicephore Nicepce secured the first Camera image (EWH)
1829: First railroad in the United States opens in Pennsylvania between Carbondale and Honesdale, used English locomotives (EWH)
1832: Samuel F. Morse developed the first practical electrical telegraph. (EWH)
1844: Morse transmitted the first telegraph message over a line between Baltimore and Washington. During the 1850's most American and European cities were connected. (EWH)
1851: The first successful submarine telegraph cable was laid between Dover and Calais. (EWH)
1836: Invention of the first revolver by Samuel Colt (EWH)
1839: Invention of the first real bicycle by Kirkpatrick MacMillan (EWH)
1840: The first incadescent electric light invented by Wm. R. Grove (EWH)

There are... serve to exemplify... have made in the comfort... edge of man. but they are now in... that I find it difficult to recall them. realize that we were ever with them.

But in contrasting the appearance and circumstances of places, my age and actual experiences afford me proofs of facts that young persons can hardly imagine

Local Changes

When I first visited Boston the tides nearly met on "the Neck" which they sometimes overflowed. Now gardens & squares and palatial residences, cover what was then marsh or mud.

The top of Beacon hill was then higher than the tops of the splendid buildings that now cover its site. The mill pond and the dirty ditch called ... have disappeared and given place for ... and the capacious Station of the ... ed. On the other side of the ... Street & Commercial ... bour.

circumstances of places, my age and actual experiences afford me proofs of facts that young persons can hardly imagine.

Local Changes

Boston

When I first visited Boston the tides nearly met on "the neck" which they sometimes overflowed. Now gardens and squares and palatial residences cover what was then marsh or mud.

The top of Beacon Hill was then higher than the tops of the splendid buildings that now cover its site. The mill pond and the dirty ditch called the canal have disappeared and given place for vast warehouses and the capacious station of the Boston & Maine Railroad. On the other side of the city what is now Commercial Street and Commercial wharf was then part of Boston harbour, and miserable, filthy docks occupied the space now devoted to Quincy Market and the noble ranges of granite stores on either side of it.

India Wharf had just been built.

Central Wharf was not thought of till long afterwards. East Boston was only Noddle's island and seldom visited and scarcely known. So with New York. I first saw it in 1813, stepping from the stage coach into the tavern at the corner of Broadway & Courtland Street, the same wooden shanty that was pulled down only 6 or 7 years since, to make room for the ornamental iron ediface that is yet conspicuous among the more recent stores that have since risen along that crowded thoroughfare.

New York

New York then extended northerly but a short distance down the Park, Union Square was a pasture with here and there a scattering farm house. Wealthy private families dwelt in

Neal Estate at 23 Washington St.
Deeded to Jon'a Neal by
Joshua Ward Sept. 9, 1785

Wall Street and could be seen lounging in the old dutch
stoops that protected their front door steps. A splendid
city has grown up where then were fertile corn fields, or
beaver waters, and immense warehouses cover the morass that
is yet known as "the swamp".

Chicago

In the Western States the change has been as great and has
been effected in a much shorter time. Less than a dozen
years ago I first visited Chicago, then a mere village of
some 4 or 5,000 inhabitants and heard from the lips of one
who was then and is yet one of its most prominent and valued
citizens, the narrative of his arrival only about ten years
before on the banks of its river where he could find nothing
but a log hut to shelter himself and his companions.

He was then engaged in starting the Chicago and Galena Union
Railroad, the first attempt in the State, if we except the
unsuccessful effort by the government for a central route.
Chicago now contains more than 120,000 inhabitants, is the
emporium of the traffic of upwards of 2,000 miles of railway
and is the largest grain and lumber market in the world.

Boyhood

These reminiscences are I know common to hundreds of others,
and this recapitulation of them would be in bad taste if I
were writing for any other purpose than my own satisfaction,
but while endeavoring to bring together the incidents of my
life and their several dates I have almost unconsciously
recurred to these strong points of contrast as showing the
prominence of the age in which I have lived in the history
of the world.

"Mais revenous a nos moutons". I was born in the house
built and owned by my father (now 23) in Washington Street
in Salem on the Seventh of June 1793. A day having been
left off in 1800 to correct the calender brings the
anniversary of my birth since that year in the eighth.

Mais revenous a nos moutons: But to return to our subject (Ed. note)

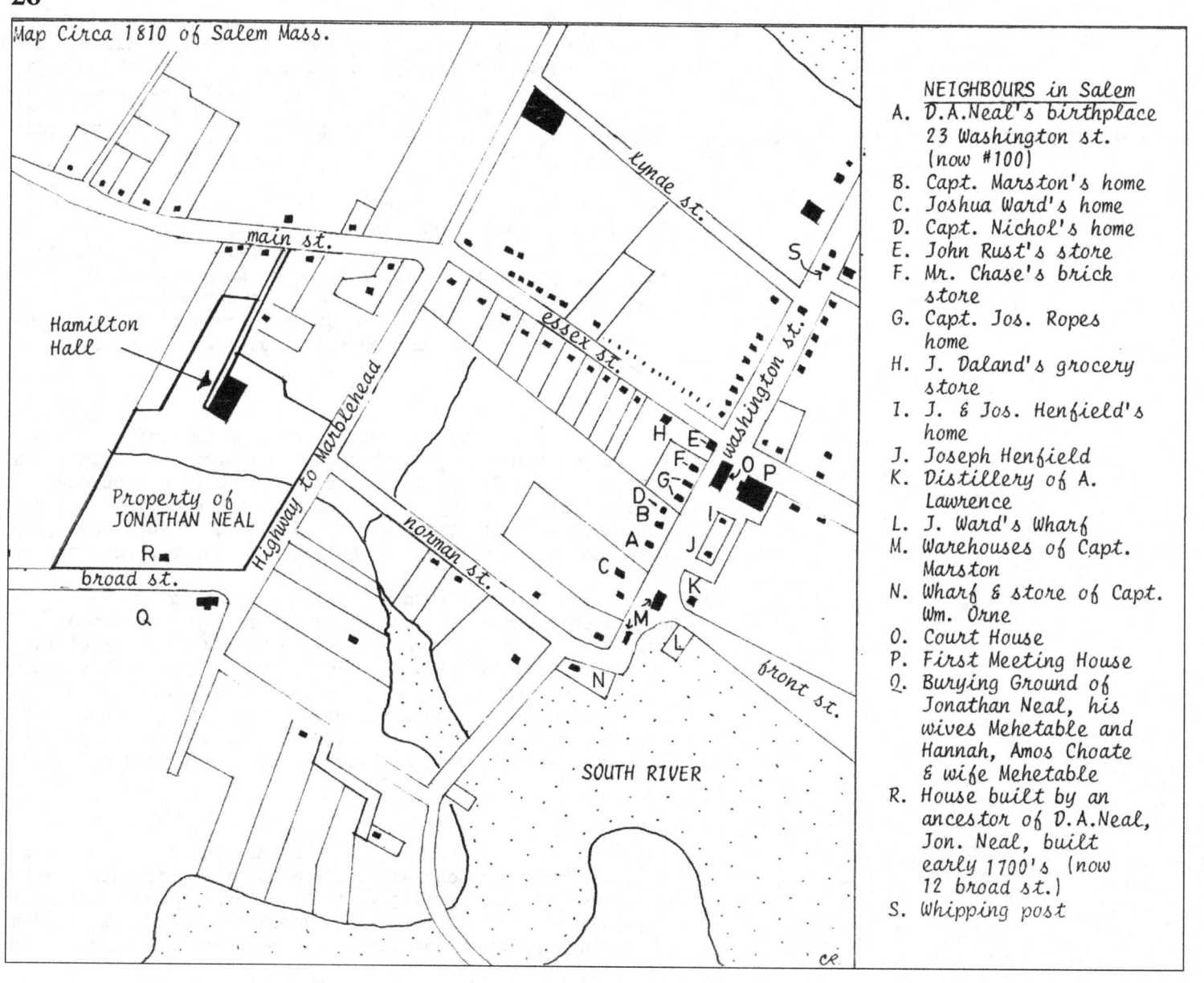

Map Circa 1810 of Salem Mass.

NEIGHBOURS in Salem

A. D.A.Neal's birthplace 23 Washington st. (now #100)
B. Capt. Marston's home
C. Joshua Ward's home
D. Capt. Nichol's home
E. John Rust's store
F. Mr. Chase's brick store
G. Capt. Jos. Ropes home
H. J. Daland's grocery store
I. J. & Jos. Henfield's home
J. Joseph Henfield
K. Distillery of A. Lawrence
L. J. Ward's Wharf
M. Warehouses of Capt. Marston
N. Wharf & store of Capt. Wm. Orne
O. Court House
P. First Meeting House
Q. Burying Ground of Jonathan Neal, his wives Mehetable and Hannah, Amos Choate & wife Mehetable
R. House built by an ancestor of D.A.Neal, Jon. Neal, built early 1700's (now 12 broad st.)
S. Whipping post

My Mother had before had twins, but they both died in
infancy so that I was her third child and for four years her
only one. The house in which I was born was built in 1790
on an old basement of stone, that had served, having had
aroof over it, in revolutionary times and probably before as
a custom house store. It was part of the estate of my
mother's uncle, Joshua Ward, from whom my Father bought it.
There was then on the opposite side of the street a lot of
ground of a heater form and on it as long as as I can
remember, there was a two story building used as a grocery
store by Capt. Wm. Marston who sometime about 1798 or 9
erected adjoining it a large three story building, the end
of which he used for crockery and hardware & the south part
for groceries, while the old store was used for bar iron &
steel and salt. Altogther he did a large country business.

Our Neighbors

Being so near a neighbor I became at one time quite intimate
with him and his two sons Wm. & Nathaniel, but he was a man
of most violent temper & inveterate in his prejudices &
owing to some trifling cause our families became estranged
and he never spoke to me afterwards. His dwelling house was
next north of ours and it is still owned by his
grandchildren and the daughters of William and occupied by
them.

Next south of us was the mansion of my mother's uncle,
Joshua Ward who was engaged both in commerce and in the
distillery business. He had made a considerable property by
his ownership in privateers during the revolutionary war.

Next north of Mr. Marsten's were two houses still standing
which belonged to Capt. Ichabod Nichols. Between these and
the corner brick building at the junction of Essex &
Washington Streets, owned by John Rust there were several
small wooden buildings where now stands the Brick stores
built by the Messrs. Chase and the brick dwelling house
built by Capt. Jos. Ropes and now owned by Mr. Gardner. On
the east side of the street there was on the corner of Essex

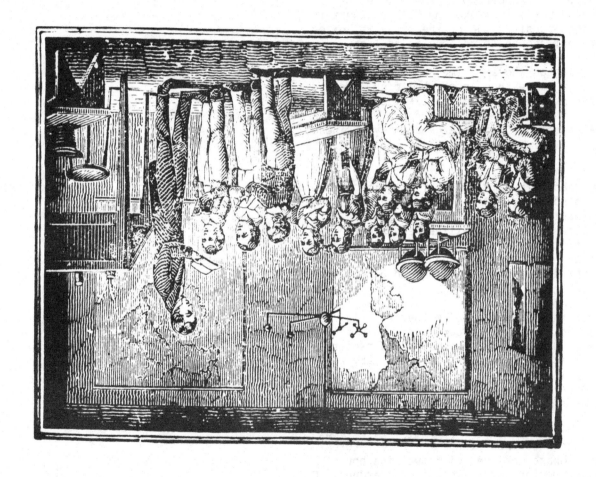

28

and Washington a store owned by the Rust family and one
adjoining by Mr. John Daland who kept a grocery store.

Next south was an old fashioned house owned by John & Jos.
Henfield and occupied by them and their sisters Mrs. John
Chapman family - the next house was owned by Jos. Henfield.
The street then bended off into Front Street on the corner
of which was the Distillery of Abel Lawrence and opposite to
it on the wharf was that of Mr. Ward.

The railroad has changed the whole aspect of this side of
the street - Marston Stores and all the rest of the
buildings have been removed or taken down to make way for
it, and to give streets on both sides of it.

Where the Depot now stands was the Wharf and store of Capt.
Wm. Orne whose vessels (of some 200, 250 tons) always loaded
and unloaded their cargoes.

At School

The days of my childhood, like those of most children offers
little or nothing on which to remark. Being for 4 or 5
years the only child I was of course petted and indulged.
The first school to which I was sent was kept by a Mrs.
Manning in the house that is now numbered 11 Norman Street,
and rotated between that and one kept by Mrs. Porter in
Market, now Central Street - very much as I pleased until I
think it must have been in 1798 I was sent to a Master's
school kept in the Stearns building by Mr. Wm. Bigelow.
Here I was the very youngest scholar for some time. Mr.
Bigelow kept the only private school of much reputation in
Salem and had a large number of scholars both male and
female.

In 1798 I was sent to a Master's school: He was six years of age
(Ed. note)

At first they were stationed on different sides of the same
room, but Bigelow was fond of changes & before long had a
board partition put up between them, a doorway being left
behind his desk, so that he could overlook both departments
at the same time, and there he would stand until the mark of

Excerpts from the diary of Robert Rantoul, Jr. 1814 Age, 9 years,
Beverly, Massachusetts

January 1, 1814, (Saturday)

Got twenty definitions, did eight sums, got to the bottom of
my class in definitions having by mistake studied the wrong
lesson; got to above W. Foster in answering question on the
last Chapter of Acts; got to the head of the class in
answering questions on the same Chapter and got a ticket.
Afternoon played at sliding and shelled a little corn and
read three chapters in the bible.

Tuesday

Past the day at house, my instructoress being gone to
Billerica to an ordination. Amused myself by making snow
cannons and balls.

Saturday

Was at school in the forenoon, the past week I have committed
to memory 190 answers from the Geography and Maps and two
columns in the spelling book. I have passed twelve lines in
the preface of Cummings...P M passed the aftrnoon at Uncle
Jonathan's wrestled with John Gee he threw me 30 times, I
threw him 5 times. One thing I forgot to mention on Thursday
last viz that I imprudently took a large pinch of snuff which
operated as an emetic (causing nausea) I therefore think that
I shall be more cautious in the use of Tobacco in any form
for smoking, chewing or snuffing.

Wed. February I

...I rode to school this morning on the stage that was to
convey Papa to Boston.

Thursday Feb. 2

... Was confined at home on account of the very wet walking
.. part of the time spent in studying. P M spent in various
employments

his nose against the edge of the board was distinctly
visible. I believe this separation annoyed the older
scholars. At any rate from this cause and the natural love
of mischief in boys they determined to have his profile cut
in this board, which was easy as he had a very large nose.
I was the youngest and it was thought I should not be
suspected, so I was boosted up and made to cut out the form
that had been previously marked out with a pencil and the
first time the master took his usual position he found a
niche for his proboscis, exactly fitted to it. There was a
flurry, but all denied doing it and I was too small to be
suspected.

I am not sure, but believe there is not a single person now
living, certainly not a single male, who were pupils of Mr.
Bigelow when he kept at this place. I cannot however
recollect the names of but two or three among them. I
recall only the names of N. Ingersoll, a son of Johnathan
Ingersoll-Orne oldest son of Jediah Orne, - Henry Whittredge,
Henry (son Rev. Doct. Prince), Benj. Nichols. Some year or
two after the death of Washington an event that is more
indelibly fixed on my memory than any other that occurred
about these years,...

School Mates 1803

...Mr. Bigelow removed his school to a new building erected
for the purpose on the rear of a lot on Marlboro (now
Federal) Street and near where the first Baptist Church now
stands.

He had then a very full school and employed an assistant,
mainly in the writing department. I continued at this
school until I should think about the year 1803 when my
Father made an arrangement with Mr. Ichabod Nichols Jr. who
was then just out of college to take me with a few of his
own family connections under his tuition. From the time of
the removal to Marlboro Street to this time there were of
course a great number of pupils and it is singular how few
names I can recall. Those I do remember are Henry Orne,

The vessel was crowded with seamen,
 Young, old, stout and slim, short and tall,
But in climbing, swinging, and jumping,
 Tom Twist was ahead of them all.

He could scamper all through the rigging,
 As spry and as still as a cat,
While as for a leap from the maintop
 To deck, he thought nothing of that;

He danced at the end of the yard-arm,
 Slept sound in the bend of a sail,
And hung by his legs from the bowsprit,
 When the wind was blowing a gale.

G is the Gas lamp that lights up the street, And which near all the gates of great hou-ses we meet.

H is the Hawk, whom the hunt-ers let fly, To seize on the He-ron, who soars through the sky.

Benj. Osgood, Saml., Richd. & Charles Derby, Pierce & David
Nichols, Francis Gray, Jessie Smith, Wm. H. Prescott, Geo.
Gerrick, Geo. Carpenter, John Foster, Haley Forrester, Wm.
Bott, Geo. Henslee, Francis Clarke, Geo. A. Ward, Geo.
Derby, John Dodge, Theodore Fisher, Edward Orne, Eben
Hathorne, Chas. Norris, and some few whom I knew at this
time but am uncertain if it was at this school. All the
above are dead. Those who are now living of Bigelow's
pupils prior to my leaving his school, are Edward Lander,
John & Horace Gray, & Henry Nichols. I know no others. I
continued with Mr. Nichols perhaps a year. The other pupils
were his brothers Henry, Pierce & David, Henry Ropes, Jos.
B. Felt and possibly two or three more that I do not
recollect. Mr. Ropes and Mr. Felt are both living. Mr.
Nichols, intending to prepare himself for the ministry, gave
up the school when several gentlemen, my Father among
others, associated for the purpose of establishing a school
and hiring a master to superintend it. The number of pupils
was limited to twenty-five. It was first opened in a hall
in a building on the estate of Nathan Pierce (since burnt
down) in Vine Street and the first instructor was Mr. Rob.
Rogers. A similar school had just before been got up by
some other gentlemen and put under charge of Mr. Abul Knapp
and was kept in the store house next south of Joshua Ward's
house in Washington St. To these two schools nearly all the
boys in town of a suitable age and whose...

School Mates 1807

...parents could afford it were sent. I remember among
those at our school were Andrew Dunlap, Wm. Rogers, George
Prince, Tucker Darland Pliny, Pierce & David Nichols, Thos.
C. Whittredge, my brothers Nathan & William, John Babbidge,
Geo. Archer, who are all dead and those now living that I
can recall to mind are Geo. C. Hodges, Wm. Waters, Geo.
Hodges, Jos. Hodges, Rich. M. Hodges, Saml. Hodges. On
reflection I recollect among the dead Andrew Sleuman, John
Winn and Benj. Howard.

After some time I think in 1807 the school was removed to a
new building erected by the proprietors in Howard Street and
next the Branch meeting house. Mr. Rogers was succeeded by
Mr. Tappan, a young collegian who did not remain long and
he, by Mr. Adams.

I had now given up the idea of going to College and had
therefore left off the study of latin over which I had been
poring for some years and devoted my time to mathematics,
bookkeeping, history, etc. in which studies my masters could
give me very little assistance and they left our class
consisting of Geo. Prince, Geo. Hodges & myself to manage
very much as we chose. I also took French lessons of Mons.
Louvrier.

Hodges & Prince left school I think in 1807. Hodges went
into the Custom House as clerk, his father being naval
officer. Prince went out as clerk in the Brig. 'Romp' to
Naples, where she was seized & condemned. He was lost in
the ship 'Margaret', Capt. Fairfield, on his passage home
with a large number of others who were left on a raft and
never heard of afterwards. Cap. F. and some others were
saved, being picked up from the boat.

Leaving School 1808

After these two left school I was the oldest pupil and was
left very much to my own discretion, the studies that I
pursued not being those in which the master, Mr. Adams, was
most conversant. He was however a man whom I greatly
respected for his kind disposition and acknowledged
ability. One day however I had a quarrel with one of the
boys (Benj. Howard) the origin of which I do not recollect,
but which eventuated in a fight, the consequence of which
was that Howard had to carry a pair of black eyes and a
somewhat ghastly countenance to school the next day, but
made no complaint until compelled by the master to state who
did it. The master taking it for granted that I was in the
wrong because I inflicted the injury and shew none myself
insisted that I should beg the boy's pardon, submit to

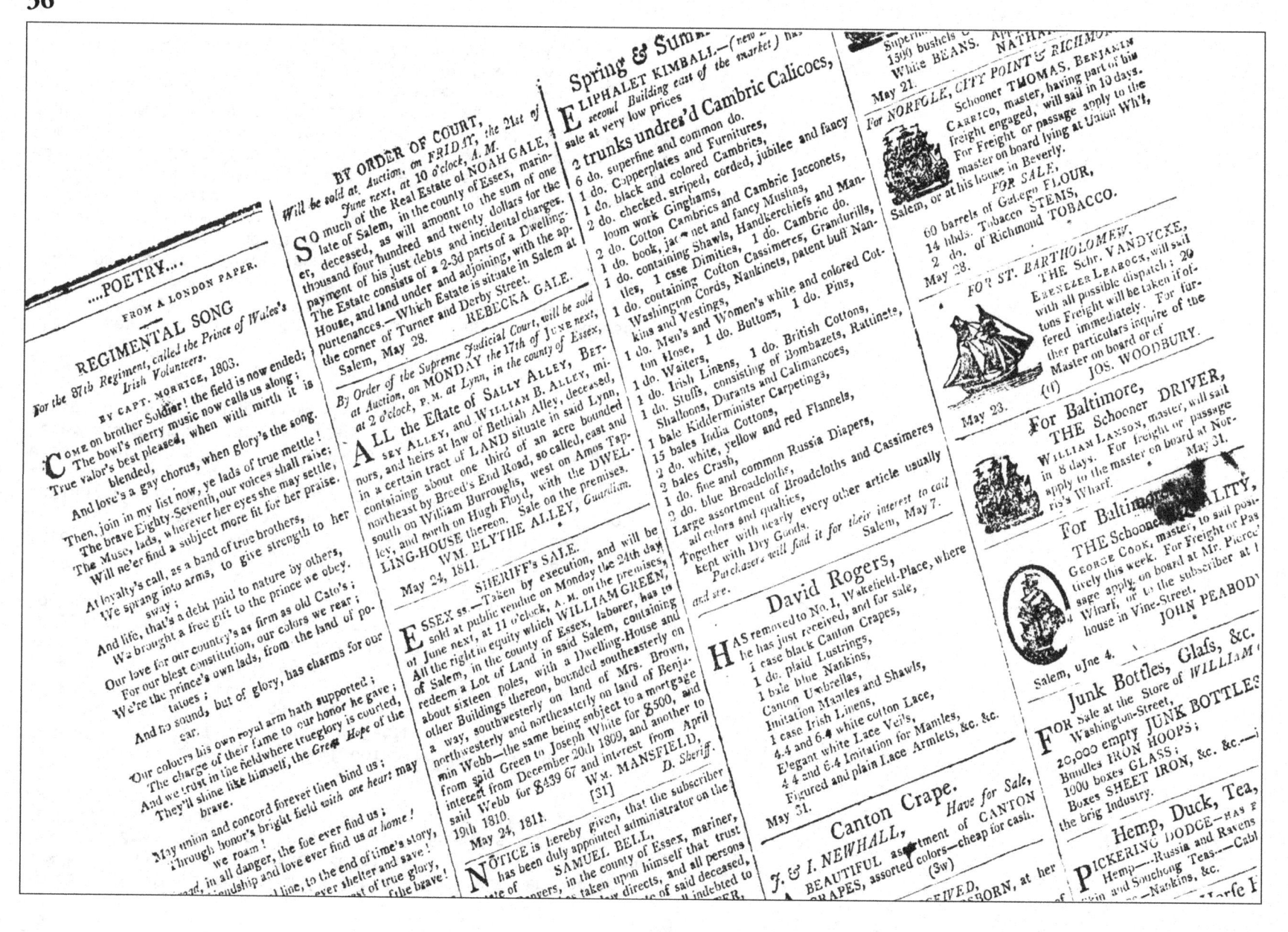

BY ORDER OF COURT,

Will be sold at Auction, on FRIDAY, the 21st of
June next, at 10 o'clock, A. M.

SO much of the Real Estate of NOAH GALE,
late of Salem, in the county of Essex, mariner, deceased, as will amount to the sum of one
thousand four hundred and twenty dollars for the
payment of his just debts and incidental charges.
The Estate consists of a 2-3d parts of a Dwelling-
House, and land under and adjoining, with the ap-
purtenances.—Which Estate is situate in Salem at
the corner of Turner and Derby Street.
Salem, May 28.   REBECKA GALE.

By Order of the Supreme Judicial Court, will be sold
at Auction, on MONDAY the 17th of JUNE next,
at 2 o'clock, P. M. at Lynn, in the county of Essex,

ALL the Estate of SALLY ALLEY, BET-
SEY ALLEY, and WILLIAM B. ALLEY, mi-
nors, and heirs at law of Bethiah Alley, deceased,
in a certain tract of LAND situate in said Lynn,
containing about one third of an acre bounded
northeast by Breed's End Road, so called, east and
south on William Burroughs, west on Amos Tap-
ley, and north on Hugh Floyd, with the DWEL-
LING-HOUSE thereon. Sale on the premises.
WM. ELYTHE ALLEY, Guardian.
May 24, 1811.

SHERIFF's SALE.

ESSEX ss.—Taken by execution, and will be
sold at public vendue on Monday the 24th day
of June next, at 11 o'clock, A. M. on the premises,
All the right in equity which WILLIAM GREEN,
of Salem, in the county of Essex, laborer, has to
redeem a Lot of Land in said Salem, containing
about sixteen poles, with a Dwelling-House and
other Buildings thereon, bounded southeasterly on
a way, southwesterly and northeasterly on land of Mrs. Brown,
northwesterly and northeasterly on land of Benja-
min Webb—the same being subject to a mortgage
from said Green to Joseph White for $500, and
interest from December 20th 1809, and another to
said Webb for $439 67 and interest from April
19th 1810.   WM. MANSFIELD,
                                D. Sheriff.
May 24, 1811.   [31]

NOTICE is hereby given, that the subscriber
has been duly appointed administrator on the
... of   SAMUEL BELL,
... , in the county of Essex, mariner,
... taken upon himself that trust
... directs, and all persons
... of said deceased,
... ... indebted to
... ...

Spring & Summ...

ELIPHALET KIMBALL.—(new ...
second Building east of the market) ha...
sale at very low prices

2 trunks undres'd Cambric Calicoes,

6 do. superfine and common do.
1 do. Copperplates and Furnitures,
1 do. black and colored Cambrics,
2 do. checked, striped, corded, jubilee and fancy
loom work Ginghams,
1 do. Cotton Cambrics and Cambric Jaconets,
1 do. book, jaconet and fancy Muslins,
1 do. containing Shawls, Handkerchiefs and Mantles, 1 csse Dimities, 1 do. Cambric do.
1 do. containing Cotton Cassimeres, Grandurills,
Washington Cords, Nankinets, patent buff Nankins and Vestings,
1 do. Men's and Women's white and colored Cotton Hose, 1 do. Buttons, 1 do. Pins,
1 do. Waiters, 1 do. British Cottons,
1 do. Irish Linens, 1 do. Ratinets,
1 do. Stuffs, consisting of Bombazets, Rattinets,
Shalloons, Durants and Calimancoes,
1 bale Kidderminister Carpetings,
15 bales India Cottons,
2 do. white, yellow and red Flannels,
2 bales Crash,
1 do. blue Broadcloths,
1 do. fine and common Russia Diapers,
Large assortment of Broadcloths and Cassimeres
all colors and qualities,
Together with nearly every other article usually
kept with Dry Goods.
Purchasers will find it for their interest to call
and see.   Salem, May 7.

David Rogers,

HAS removed to No. 1, Wakefield-Place, where
he has just received, and for sale,
1 case black Canton Crapes,
1 do. plaid Lustrings,
1 bale blue Nankins,
Canton Umbrellas,
Imitation Mantles and Shawls,
1 case Irish Linens,
4-4 and 6-4 white cotton Lace,
Elegant white Lace Veils,
4-4 and 6-4 Imitation for Mantles,
Figured and plain Lace Armlets, &c. &c.
May 31.

Canton Crape.

J. & I. NEWHALL,   Have for Sale,
BEAUTIFUL assortment of CANTON
CRAPES, assorted colors—cheap for cash.
(3w)

punishment, or leave the school. I decided on the last and
was sustained by my Father and though requested by the
trustees and indeed invited by the master after he had
learnt more of the matter, to return. I declined and my
brother Theodore took my place in the school. This must
have happened in the fall of 1808 when the "long embargo"
was in operation, and there was of course no commercial
employment to which I could turn my attention. I therefore
devoted myself to those studies that would best qualify me
for the life and occupation I had marked out for myself.

Leaving School 1808

This could have been done more effectually in a counting
room & in the pursuit of actual business operations. But
these were all stopped, and I had to do the best I could in
my own chamber. I was however of an age and temperament
that required something more exciting than continual study
and from that cause perhaps, rather than from any well
grounded conviction of its merits I had engaged on what was
then termed the republican, in opposition to the federal
party politics then raging with great force. I was at this
time quite intimate with some of the proprietors of the
"Salem Register", the organ of the republican party in Essex
county. It was published by Poole & Palfray.

Reminiscences of Elder Persons

For the fun of the thing, and to try my hand at composition,
I used to write political diatribes under the name of
"Timoleon" and so managed that the publishers of the
Register (to whom they were sent as communications) never
knew where they came from. It is probably no compliment to
their taste or judgement to say that they were received and
published, and no only so, for I was in the office every day
and heard their remarks and surmises, were attributed
sometimes to one and then another writer of established
reputation. It served however to employ and amuse me and
did nobody any harm or good.

Crowninshield Wharf
Salem, Mass.
1805

This may be the proper place to introduce some reminiscences of the elderly persons whom I had known, some of them familiarly from my childhood up to this time, for I had always been about very much with my Father and became quite intimate with all his acquaintances.

Among the persons out of my own family that I recollect as a child was that celbrated merchant Elias Hasket Derby and his wife. They had just completed the splendid mansion that stood where the market house has since been built when I was about four years old, and every day as I passed from school I was called in and always got a nice luncheon. I was also much petted by Cap. Jon. Ingersoll who lived on a farm (now owned by the Peabody family) in Danvers, and where he frequently took me on visits of two or three days at a time. Capt. Ingersoll's first wife was a cousin of my Mother's being a daughter of Mrs. Wm. Poole, by whom he had one daughter who married Nathaniel Bowditch and I think had three sons.

Lately I fell in with an old newspaper which contained a copy of the subscription got up in Salem in 1798 for the purpose of building a frigate to be tendered to the Government as a loan of so much money at a time when the credit of the country was at rather a low ebb. A meeting was held on the 25 Oct. 1798 and the necessary arrangements made. It happens that I was personally acquainted with all the subscribers, but three or four, as they were all in the habit of noticing and talking with me whenever I met them and the following recollections of them occur to me.

The Frigate, named the 'Essex', built by the above subscriptions was launched in 1799 or 1800. I recollect visiting her with my Father while she was building and was in a pleasure boat called the 'Lugger' belonging to Mr. Josh. Ward in the harbour and witnessed her launch. I remember that Mr. Ward, Mr. Wm. Clearland, Mr. Zach. Burchmore, Cap. Jon. Ingersoll were among the passengers in the 'Lugger'. This is the Frigate so distinguished in the War of 1812 by Porter's gallant defence of Valparaiso.

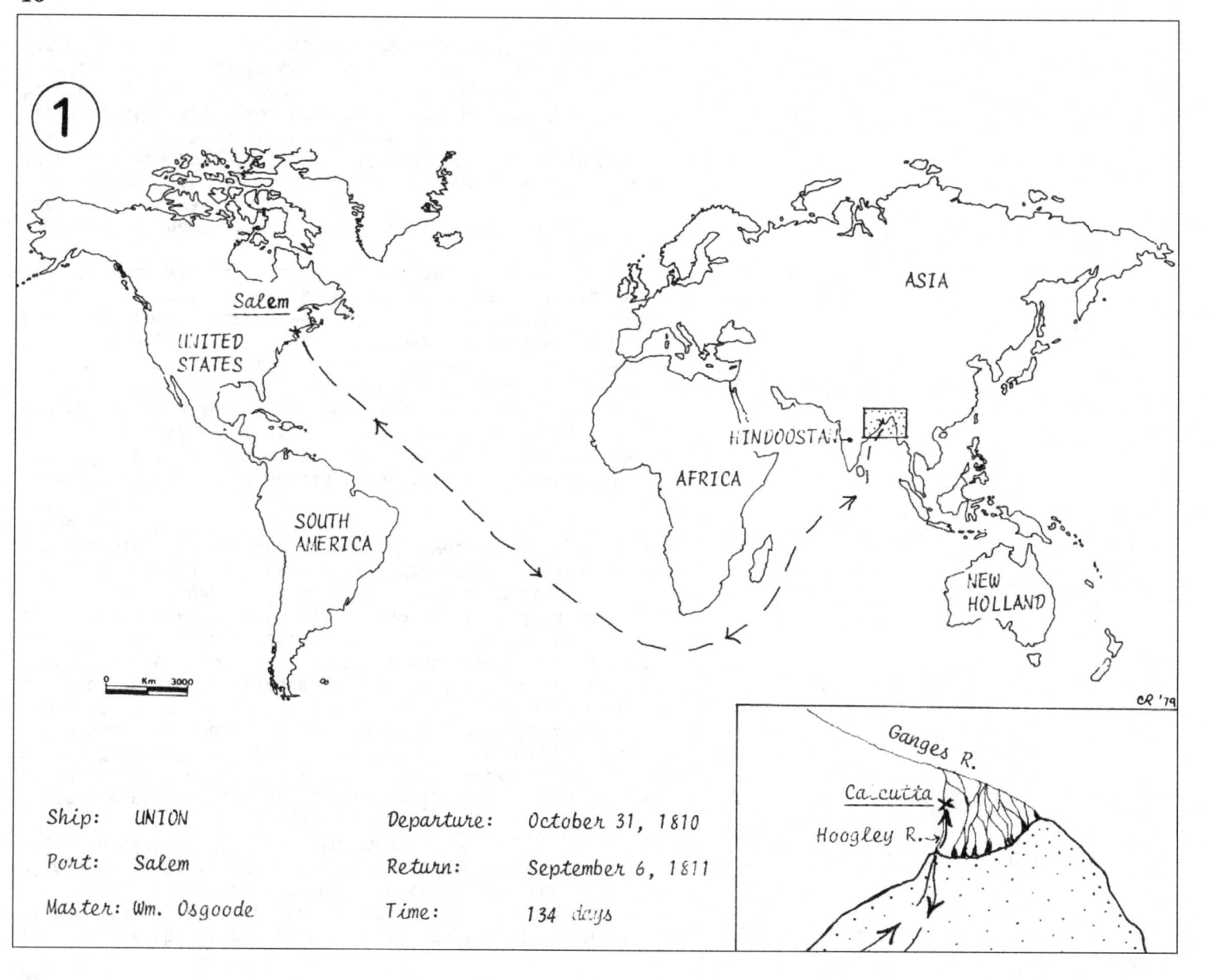

①

Salem

UNITED STATES

SOUTH AMERICA

ASIA

AFRICA

HINDOOSTAN

NEW HOLLAND

0   Km   3000

CR '79

Ship:	UNION	Departure:	October 31, 1810
Port:	Salem	Return:	September 6, 1811
Master:	Wm. Osgoode	Time:	134 days

Ganges R.

Calcutta

Hoogley R.

In the preceding list of those whom I have known I have
given the names of those only who were living and men in
business before I started on my first voyage. They have all
passed away, and in but comparatively few cases do even
their children survive.

Some of these names recall many interesting incidents of my
life - interesting to me in those days of boyhood, but of no
special importance now. Altogether they show how little
there is of life to anyone being if this is all if it, how
out of proportion to the reality are both our hopes and our
fears, our expectations and results. This feeling is
strengthened when I look around me and find how few who
started on the race with me are now upon the course.

As I proceed in my narrative I shall endeavor to refer to
those with whom I have had business or friendly relations
both at home and abroad, and where I know the fact shall
state if they are still enjoying the breath of life or if
the shadow of death has passed over them, consigning them to
the silence and the peace of the tomb.

The "long embargo" was at length lifted, but without
accomplishing any one of the objects for which it was
probably imposed except perhaps that of lessening the number
of piratical attacks on our commerce by the two great
belligerents and that for the simple reason that we had no
commerce to attack. But the times were dubious, and the
prospect of a war that would sweep whatever we might have
afloat from the ocean, held enterprize in check, and limited
distant operations. But war did not come, and confidence
that it would not, after a time led to an expansion of our
commerce that had just gained its limit when the blow came
and its destruction followed. But not to anticipate. The
"Embargo Act" was repealed in May 1809.

First Voyage 1810 Ship 'Union'

I was anxious to be in motion, but it was not until the fall
of 1810 that anything very eligible seemed to present

SHIP

The term ship is properly restricted to the full-rigged ship, that is, a large square-rigged vessel, carrying three masts, each of these being composed of a lower-mast, top-mast and topgallant-mast, and each being provided with yards and carrying a full complement of square sails. The above silhouette shows a vessel of about 1850; after that date the topsails were generally divided into upper and lower, for convenience in handling.

Supercargo: an abbreviatiion of Cargo Superintendent, a representative of the ship's owner on board a merchant ship who looked after all commercial business in connection with the ship and her cargo during a voyage. (OCSS p. 847)

Ship: The term ship is properly restricted to the full rigged ship, that is, a large square rigged vessel, carrying three masts, each of these being composed of a lower-mast, top-mast and top gallant-mast, and each being provided with yards and carrying a full compelement of square sails. (Davis, Charles G., "Rigs of the Nine Principal Types of American Sailing Vessels" Peabody Museum, Salem, 1974)

Spanish Dolls: The spanish currency of the time, solid gold and the most marketable specie in foreign markets. Most other currencies, including the American dollar were very unstable; Spanish Dollars (Ed. note)

Bills of Exchange on London: In order to conduct international trade at a time when currencies fluctuated greatly, the system of bills of exchange was incorporated. In simple terms, a man would have debts outstanding in London. Another man, also in the States owed money to someone in the States who had no relation to England wanted to purchase some goods available on the English market. The second fellow would then pay off the fellow American with the domestic debt so that an Englishman owes him. Thus instead of sending money or specie (gold coin) across the ocean the Englishman would pay for for the English goods in England and avoid overseas transactions in currency. The system still exists to-day when several currencies are involved. Of course here instead of the arrangement being started in the States it would originate in India which was British run through the East India Company at this time. (Ed. note)

itself. I had been on quite intimate terms with Henry Osgood, a son of Mr. Christopher Osgood, and he had just returned from a successful voyage to Calcutta. He was a young man of the best habits, possessed of a good mercantile education and was now offered the situation of supercargo in the ship 'Union' commanded by his brother William who was every inch a seaman. This ship was owned by Stephen Phillipa and George Pierce and was advertised for freight from Calcutta on the terms then usual in this trade, viz. Spanish Dolls or Bill of exchange on London to be sent out and invested, the ship taking out ten percent in Calcutta in lieu of freight. Mr. Osgood was only 3 or 4 years older than myself. I proposed to apply for the situation of clerk to him for this voyage for the sake of the information I might acquire, and my Father at once not only assented but made an arrangement which put me in the best possible position. He proposed to the owners to ship 10,000 dolls on freight on condition of my having the appointment. He then told Mr. Osgood and myself that he should divide between us all the profits that might occur from the shipment, which proposal was received by Mr. O. with as much surprise as gratitude for he would have been rejoiced to have had me with him without any inducement of this sort. Our relations therefore were of the most friendly nature, and he felt bound to give me all the information in his power. The ship was about 250 tons. We sailed from Salem on the 31st October 1810. Thos. Dean was our chief and Wm. Jefferson our second officer.

The voyage proved pleasant in every respect. Both the Capt. and Mr. Osgood played a good game at chess. I knew something of it and soon learnt more. We had our board perforated and our men plugged so that we could not only play without regard to the motion of the ship, but we could set away the board in any stage of the game, and resume it at pleasure and this after a while we had to do almost every evening, for we got so as to understand each other's games so well that it often took several hours to finish one.

Clerk: An officer in the merchant navy that was hired to help the Captain in any correspondance or journals he needed to keep, a favoured position in that the only requirement was reading and writing (something some Captains could not do) and automaticly gave officer status. On larger vessels this meant a private cabin. (Ed. note)

Dolls: Spanish dollars (Ed. note)

Tons: Tonnage determined the size and capacity of vessels. 250 tons is about average, the length being roughly one and a half railway cars or two Cadillacs, end to end. (Ed. note)

Plugged: The men were set into the board, similar to travel chess games to-day (Ed. note)

44

Arrival at Calcutta 1811.

We crossed the equator in the 31st day out and by the time I could not only keep the ship's reckoning on my journal, but work the lunar observations, and shortly after take the distances. So too I learnt not merely the ordi-nary work of a seaman, but that of working the ship, trimming the sails, and became somewhat of a judge of the weather. On the 9th of March 1811 we took a pilot on the sand heads off the mouth of the Hoogly river. Having a fair wind we soon got inside. The same evening Mr Osgood and myself took a Dugwalter or country boat and went up the river and having arrived off the city and finding the musquitoes determined to allow us no sleep, we landed at about two o'clock in the morning ... from Salem. ... forget my sensations at that time. ... and advancing a few rods, we found ... of (I should say) several ... ts of torches, paper lan-... marriage. ... children.

Arrival at Calcutta 1811

We crossed the equator on the 31st day out and by this time
I could not only keep the ship's reckoning in my journal,
but work the lunar observations, and shortly after take the
distances. So too I learnt not merely the ordinary work of
a seaman, but that of working the ship, trimming the sails,
and became somewhat of a judge of the weather. On the 9th
of March, 1811 we took a pilot on the sand heads off the
mouth of the Hoogly river. Having a fair wind we soon got
inside. The same evening Mr. Osgood and myself took a
Dugwaller or county boat and went up the river and having
arrived off the city and finding the mosquitoes determined
to allow us no sleep, we landed at about two o'clock in the
morning 132 days from Salem.

I shall never forget my sensations at that time. On
stepping on shore and advancing a few rods we found
ourselves in the midst of a crowd of (I should say) several
thousands of the natives bearing all sorts of torches, paper
lanterns, etc. It was the celebration of a native
marriage. The boy and girl who were thus espoused were mere
children. Their parents were no doubt rich, and this was
the usual mode of proceedings on such occasions.

The habits of the Hindoos are so simple and the only
articles they are allowed to use as substinance are so
cheap, that money cannot be spent in mere living, yet their
anxiety to amass wealth is not less than those who have so
many more calls for it. When it is obtained it is only on
the occasion of a marriage or a death in their families that
they can display it and then it is displayed with great
ostentation and profession. A loc of rupees ($50,000) is
often spent in celebrating the betrothal (for it cannot be
termed marriage) between two infants who probably have never
seen each other before, and may not again until they have
attained the proper age (which however is very early in
India) for living together. This night or rather morning
the sky was clear and the air delicious, at least to us who
had been on the ocean for the preceding 4 or 5 months. So

Ship's Reckoning: Dead reckoning: a position which is obtained by
applying courses and distances made through the water from
the last known observed position, or the ability to determine
position of the vessel mid ocean, taking into consideration
wind, currents and the time taken since last point of land or
solid marker was seen. (OCSS p.234) CR

Lunar Observations: the observation of a lunar distance for finding
longtitude at sea before chronometers were perfected. The
moon has a relatively rapid motion across the heavens in
relation to the fixed stars, so that the angular distance
between the moon and any fixed star which lies in the moon's
path changes comparitively rapidly. (OCSS p.503)

Taking a Pilot: A qualified coastal navigator taken on board a ship
at a particular place for the purpose of conducting it into
and from a port or through a channel, river or approaches to
a port. In all maritime nations the jurisdiction over pilots
is invested in national authorities who specify the
conditions under which pilots must be taken on board and the
pilotage fees to be charged. In many ports and navigable
water ways local regulations make it compulsory for ships
over a certain size to embark a pilot. (OCSS p.647)

Rod: A linear measurement of 5½ yards or 16 feet (AMD)

A Palanquin or Palaquin

47

we amused ourselves by following the procession. Crowded as
were the streets we found no difficulty in making our way.

Everywhere the natives made the path clear before us. We
were white men and as such were treated with the greatest
deference and respect, indeed with a humility and
submission...

Living in Calcutta, 1811

...too great to be altogether agreeable to me who had never
witnessed such a manifestation of it before. As soon as it
was daylight we repaired to the house of the Banian whom Mr.
Osgood had determined to employ Dock Bassoner Ghasee of the
firm of Callisumker and Dock Bassoner Ghasee. We were each
soon fitted out with a palangium with a kittasae (or
conductor) and four bearers who were engaged to attend us
night and day and carry us wherever we chose to go during
our stay in Calcutta. I don't remember the cost but think
it was at the rate of about 15 rupees per month for each.
We then proceeded to select a house, suitable both to live
and do our business in, and this together with the
engagement of servants, to with, the campredor (or steward)
the porter (to keep the gate) the cook, sculleon, sweepers,
barbers, boys to wait and tend, in fact one for each thing
there was to be done for here one person can do but one
thing, and thus by dinner time we found ourselves at
housekeeping in a fine building with a large court yard,
spacious verandas and on the lower floor extensive go-downs
or warehouse rooms for the deposit of the goods we were to
purchase. One of the rooms on the second floor was
appropriated for dining, and three or four for sleeping -
all the rest, including a large hall for the selection and
examination of the piece cotton and silk goods that we
expected to purchase for our homeward cargo, for at this
time these articles composed the bulk of our investments for
the United States. Some sugar for ballast was usually
taken. Shellac was an article of limited use in this
country then, and of course not a great deal was taken.
Goatskins were sought for, but only a limited quantity

Palangium: A structure containing a bench or seat, roofed equipped
    on both sides with rods through loops so four bearers could
    carry it, allowed complete privacy if windows covered;
    palaquin. (Ed. note)

Ballast: additional weight carried in a ship to give her stability
    and or to provide a satisfactory trim for and aft (to balance
    both ends evenly). In the merchant navy, cargo was brought
    back as ballast whenever possible taking water casks or grain
    for the outgoing trip that could be easily left behind.
    (OCSS p.55)

Captain Shreve of Salem buying
textiles in India about 1820

49

could generally be obtained. Some few buffalo hides were
taken, but not at this time to any great extent. The export
of saltpeter was prohibited. Indigo was the most valuable
article and the quantity taken generally depended on the
funds that could be spared for it, after providing the
balance of the cargo of cheaper goods. Some ginger and
tumeric root was generally taken for loose storage and also
gunny bags, but gunny cloth was not known as an article of
importation into the United States till years after.
Linseed was then entirely unknown as an article of East
India export, at least to the United States.

The process pursued in making these investments was curious
and satisfactory. All piece goods whether of cotton or silk
that were offered for sale and which were likely to be
wanted, were brought to us and deposited in the go-downs.
When wanted they were brought up into the large hall and
opened - negotiations as to the price then took place
between the owners or their agents and our banian, but these
were so conducted that we could know nothing of ...

Business in Calcutta 1811

...their progress, all offers and counter offers being made
by the two parties touching each others hands under their
robes. All we could do was occasionally to reject their
conclusions and send the goods away. The price being agreed
upon, the goods were first measured by persons who did
nothing else, and this was done by taking the width and
counting the folds of each piece. Then they were to be (as
it was termed) washed, and this was done by opening every
fold and then ascertaining if there were any defect.

The next operation was to classify those that were found to
be of the right dimensions & perfect, into three kinds of
qualities and marked. They were then packed, sent to the
screw-house to be compressed and marked and then through the
custom house, to the ship, being if cotton goods done up in
neat bales and if silks in boxes. Indigo was also generally
brought to the house and taken out of the boxes and examined

Ship
Hazard
of Salem
Built 1799

cake by cake. This however was not usually done with <u>Indigo</u> from the plantations of Europeans whose marks were well known, as the quality could be depended on as uniform with the musters (or samples).

All gruff goods, as Sugar, <u>Ginger, Tumeric</u> etc. were purchased in the bazaars and there weighed, marked and sampled and sent directly on board ship.

These reminiscences may be amusing now that this trade has so completely changed its character. Now instead of bringing cotton cloths from Calcutta, American ships frequently take large quantities of them manufactured in New England to that port for the consumption of the natives of India.

The bandannas and <u>Chuppas</u> that then formed part of importation from Calcutta by every ship have now been entirely superceded by the <u>foulards</u> that come from Germany or are made by <u>stamping Chinese pongees</u> in this country. Sugar is now seldom imported it ...

Indigo: a blue dye obtained from plants (ACD)

Ginger and Tumeric root: food spices (OCSS)

Chuppas: Indian type of clothing, possibly the baggy pants that are still common (Ed. note)

Foulards: a soft lightweight silk with printed design (ACD)

Stamping Chinese pongees: silk of a plain weave made from filaments of wild silk woven in natural tan colour, presumably then stamped with colours (ACD)

Character of Benjalees

...being obtained more advantageously from other places. Indigo is brought still but what is used in the United States is supplied to a very considerable extent from London, where a better selection can be made than from direct importations. Ginger continues to be brought in considerable quantitites and the consumption of Shellac and gunny bags has clearly increased, so that these articles are now quite important parts of every cargo. The entirely new descriptions of goods, that were formerly unobtainable, and not then suitable to our market are salt petre, Gunny Cloth (now used for Cotton baling) & Linseed and these now constitute the bulk of every cargo. Before the War of 1812 a dozen or 15 ships, generally from 250 to 400 tons did all the business between British India and the United States. Now they amount to seven or eight times that number and are at least twice as large. The value of their investments are

Dej.
250 to 400 ton
the United States. Now
that number and are at lea
of their investments are however very
Thexe ach registator of ship. Brot. an investment
$500 to 1000, Now they do not average $700. It is doubtful
the whole annual import at this time by 100 ships, efceed
that of the 12 or 15 of those days, in the first cost.
The present traffic is however for more beneficial in as
much as it employs so large a tonnage.

The character or rather the conduct of the Native Bengalese seemed
to me to be the extreme of docility & submission to their white masters.
I saw but one instance of spirit among them and that was manifested by a noted Banian (Ram- chunder metee) in a dispute with
Mr Osgood, but it was at length amicably settled. I heard however
of some instances of determined resistance, when their religious
prejudices were attacked. For instance on the occasion of one of
the Bulls of the country getting wild or mad in the streets of
Calcutta, the authorities had him seized & confined. This animal
ong the Hindoos and they will allow him to walk
bles and eat or destroy whatever comes
he arrest above mentioned.
ative was closed,
native

however much reduced. Then each registror of ships brought
an investment costing from $500 to 1000. Now they do not
average $100. It is doubtful if the whole annual import at
this time by 100 ships exceeds that of the 12 or 15 of those
days in the first cost. The present traffic is however far
more beneficial in as much as it employs so large a tonnage.

The character or rather the conduct of the Native Benjalese
seemed to me to be the extreme of docility and submission to
their white masters. I saw but one instance of spirit among
them and that was manifested by a noted Banian (Ram-chunder
meter) in a dispute with Mr. Osgood, but it was at length
amicably settled. I heard however of some instances of
determined resistance, when their religious prejudices were
attacked. For instance on the occasion of one of the Bulls
of the country getting wild or mad in the streets of
Calcutta, the authorities had him seized and confined. This
animal is sacred among the Hindoos and they will allow him
to walk into their shops or shambles and eat or destroy
whatever comes in their way. As soon as the arrest above
mentioned was known, every shop kept by a native was closed,
every sircac (clerk) deserted his desk, every native
official his duties, and nothing would induce them to
return, but the release of the enraged brute.

It was finally arranged that he should be carefully conveyed
to the Sulkee side (across the river) and there be set at
liberty. It is well known that the recent rebellion
throughout British India was from quite as trivial a cause,
the use of Beef Suet for greasing the cartridges of the
<u>sepoys</u>.

Sepoys: A native soldier (in India) in the military service of
Europeans, especially the British (ACD)

But though the submission of the natives seemed perfect and
would no doubt continue so under ordinary circumstances as
it was evident that their government fully understood the
terms on which it would be continued, and the greatest care
was taken to do nothing to alarm their prejudices, or to
give reason for any rebellious movement. Their customs were
respected; their religious rites protected, and in any case

54

Ward, Rev. W. " A View of the History, Literature and Religion of the Hindoos", J. Higginbotham, Madras 1863

P. 223: Gifts – 3 ways of presenting gifts; persons who worship the receiver, an act of benevolence, giver prays for a blessing on giving the gift.

P. 235 Burning of a Widow alive:
- bodies anointed with clarified butter, eyes coloured with stibium
- believes a woman expiring on the funeral pire purifies her family and also purifies her husbands sins, her sins,
- of wife away on death of husband and wished to burn with him, will wait, also will wait till end of menstral discharges, if husband dies in a far off country, wife can tie a garment or slipper to herself and light a separate fire, a woman with a young child, pregnant or possibly so cannot burn
- few wives tell husband while alive if they intend to burn or not – dying in the sight of Ganges sometimes done in the case of eventual death, wife can declare her intention then and treated with great respect – brought delicacies by friends and when he dies, breaks small piece of a mango tree, clutches it, sits down beside corpse – barber then paints the side of her feet red, she bathes and puts on new clothes, a constant drum beat accompanys this.

- **Preparations:** head man or son prepare, hole dug in the ground, stakes driven into the earth, thick green stakes laid across to form a bed – laid on top – dry faggots, hemp, clarified butter, pitch etc. – official bramin prays with her that as many as there are hairs on the human body, she may abide in heaven with her husband and all her ancestors may ascend to heaven
- she presents her ornaments to a friend, ties red cotton on both wrists, puts 2 new combs in her hair, paints her forehead and takes into the cloth she wears parched rice and kourees

- meanwhile dead body is annointed with clarified butter and bathed
- prayers said over it, dressed in new clothes – son takes a handful of boiled rice and offers it in the name of his deceased father
- ropes and another piece of cloth are spread upon the wood and the corpse is laid out upon it
- the widow walks around 7 times strewing parched rice and kourees as she goes – spectators trying to catch them in the belief they will later help cure diseases
- widow throws herself down beside the corpse – a few female ornaments are placed beside her – ropes drawn and bodies tied to-gether and faggots placed upon them – son with head averted lights fire by the face of his father and other men at various places put a torch to – cries go up, more faggots thrown on, 2 bamboo levers brought down to hold the bodies down, more clarified butter, pitch and faggots thrown so bodies quickly consumed.
- takes about 2 hours but woman probably died in several minutes
- bones etc. that are left are thrown into the Ganges
- place where bodies were burnt is thoroughly washed
- later son of deceased makes 2 balls of boiled rice and in the name of his father and mother, lays them on the spot they were burnt
- persons engaged in the process, bathe, each one taking up water in his hands 3 times repeating incantations and pours out drink offering to the deceased

- son binds his loins in new cloth which he wears if a bramin for 10 days – when family return home they light a hot iron and fire to protect against evil spirits
Moral Problems: many wives have not been so resolute about this ceremony and have often been forced into it by their friends and family since it purifies so many sins
- as many as 43 wives have been burned with one husband leaving 30, 40 children, some wives as young as eight, as old as ninety

of litigation between a European and a native it was well
understood that if any favor was shown by the judges it was
to the latter.

Hindoo Suttee

Up to this time they had not ever dared to do away with the
horrid practice of the Suttee or the immolation of the widow
on the funeral pile of her husband. They had thrown around
it some restrictions. It could not be performed within the
limits of the City of Calcutta or elsewhere, not without the
written permission of the local authorities. I witnessed
one while on this visit. We were advised before hand when
and where it would take place in the evening and about four
miles above Calcutta. Capt. Osgood, Mr. Henry Osgood and
myself proceeded in our paloquins to the spot where we
arrived about sundown. We were able to get on board an old
dinga walla (county boat) that was lying on the muddy bank
of the Hoogly river, perhaps 80 feet from the water. The
pile on which lay the dead body of the husband was about
fifty feet from us and towards the edge of the stream, the
bank being slightly shelving. The pile was about three feet
high, made of logs and sticks. The man appeared to have
been of middle age, and it was said a person of some
importance among his country men. We were the only white
persons present, but there was a large collection of the
Benjalese, but of course all men. After waiting perhaps an
hour the widow appeared, coming from a building in the
immediate neighborhood. She was dressed in the fashion of
the country (I hardly remember how) with her face
uncovered. She was good looking and I should judge about 25
years of age. Accompanied by two men said to have been her
nearest relations, she walked firmly from the house or hut
through the mud to the river, stooped downward and bathed
her head with its sacred (muddy) waters, then turned back to
the pile, walked around three times after which with some
assistance got upon it and lay down by the side of her
husband, placing her right arm under his neck. Immediately
the natives, with loud shouts, piled on them faggots (or
light sticks of wood) to the depth of 3 or 4 feet and

The burning of a widow was a very influential religious act
in that she succeeded in purifying the sins of her husband,
family and children besides herself. It was a noble act to
die for their sins and originally the widow had no choice.
However by the early 1800's they were allowed to refuse,
technically speaking. Families were not unknown to create
heavy pressure and more than one case was cited of sons or
brothers throwing a screaming widow into the pyre for
salvation of the family.

The British tried very hard to outlaw this procedure but at
the date of my reference, 1863, they still had a significant
way to go. (Ed. note)

56

O Fire, let these women, with bodies
annointed with clarified dyes with stibium, and void of tears, enter thee,
the parent of water, that they may not
be separated from their husbands, but
may be in union with excellent husbands,
be sinless, and jewels among women.

Rg Vedas

There are 35,000,000 hairs on the human
body. The woman who ascends the pile
with her husband, will remain so many
years in heaven. As the snake-catcher
draws the serpent from its hole, so she,
rescuing her husband from hell, rejoices
with him. The woman who expires on the
funeral pile with her husband purges
the family of her mother, her father,
and her husband. If the husband be a
bramhuncide, and ungrateful, or a
murderer of his friend, the wife by
burning with him purges away his sins.
There is no virute greater than a
virtuous woman's burning herself with
her husband. No other effectual duty is
known for virtuous women, at any time
after the death of their lords, except
casting themselves into the same fire.
As long as a woman, in her successive
transmigrations, shall decline burning
herself, like a faithful wife, on the
same fire with her deceased lord, so
long shall she not be ex empted from
springing again to life in the body of
some female animal.

Ungiras

The future of the women who chose
Not to burn is made equally clear
in the texts of Hinduism:

The widow who practises self-
control and austerities after the
death of her husband, goes to heaven.
A widow shall never feel any inclination to dwell in the house of a stranger
nor should she be querulous in her disposition. A widow as well as the wife
of a man who is absent in a distant
country, should never decorate their
persons, and live in a temple and worship the gods for their husband's good.
A wife in the latter case shall wear
a few ornaments for the good or her
husband.

Agni 222.19,
19-23

A widow should not anoint her body
with oil. She should not see her face
in the looking-glass or behold the face
of any other man. She should not witness
an opera, dance, a grand festival or see
the face of a dancer, a singer or a
well-dressed man. She should always
listen to pious narratives.

Brahma-Vauvarta Krisna Janma Khanda
83.101-24

secured them down with some kind of cords or bands. They
then threw upon quantities of inflammable matter, as ghee
(butter) resin etc. and immediately applied the torch to
that part of the pile where the head of the woman rested.
It was said this was done by a son of the deceased, but of
course we had only the word of our Killesalls (or head
bearer) for this. The object of applying it in this way was
no doubt the merciful one of producing suffocation and
insensibility before the flames should reach the living
flesh and they were probably successful. If there was any
cry from the victim it was drowned in the vociferations of
the people about the pile, which burnt with great rapidity
and in a few minutes all was over, leaving nothing but a
mass of cinders in which nothing human could be
distinguished from the point where we stood.

I have been the more particular as this was probably among
the last of the suttees allowed to take place publicly in
the vicinity of Calcutta and possibly the very last
witnessed by an American. Probably there are very few white
men now living who ever saw one, it having been totally
prohibited for a great many years all over India. That it
was permitted so long under the English rule must have been
owing to the cause I have indicated.

Regaining Caste

While in Calcutta I witnessed also what seemed more
revolting, because the pain inflicted was more apparent and
more protracted. It is well known that the lower castes of
the Hindoos permit those who have by any violation of the
rules of their religion lost their social position to regain
it by the self infliction of certain kinds of punishment.

It is also known that the state of such criminals who thus
become parias and being considered the vilest of the vile
are excluded from all the ordinary intercourse of life with
any other human beings, is so dreadful that there is no
punishment they will not endure to regain their Caste. It
is only the very inferior orders as coolies (or labourer)

Instrument Described by D.A. Neat
For Regaining Caste.

and those engaged in the meanest trades, or most menial
offices that can do this. To all of the higher classes the
caste once lost is lost forever. For the purpose of
enabling those who can do it to have the opportunity,
certain days are set apart and certain facilities are
provided for the infliction of self torture. These consist
of strong poles perhaps sixty feet high, set in or secured
to the ground. A platform say 20 feet from the ground is
erected around them and a swingle tree in their tops over
which is placed horizontally another pole or yard, the whole
very much resembling the old fashioned apparatus for drawing
water from wells. At one end of this horizontal pole or
yard descends a long, stout rope which reaches to the ground
- at the other are fixed several small lines like cod lines
about 20 feet long or long enough when that end of the yard
is drawn down to reach the platform on which the victim and
those who assist in the operation are standing, the former
with strong iron hooks inserted through the sinews of the
back, generally one on each side. These hooks have an eye
at the end of the handle through which the lines are rove.
A tight bandage is put around the body to sustain him in
case the hooks tear out - he is then launched off the
platform and the mob below taking hold of the rope at the
other end run round with great rapidity, whirling the man at
the other end so fast as to throw his body out almost in a
line with the yard itself and render it scarcely visible.

This operation continues from 10 to 20 minutes, when he is
taken down and another put in his place to undergo the same
process. It must have been a very painful one, yet it
seemed to be bourne not only with composure, but with
pleasure. It was curious to see the eagerness it was sought
not once only, but several times. When I witnessed it there
were three machines in operation within about 500 feet of
each other. The moment the sufferer was taken down and this
was done generally against his earnest protestations, he
would rush through the dense crowd and claim the chance to
swing in the ...

60

"Harper's Family Library, "History of British India" Series XLVIII J. and J. Harper, New York, 1832

Manners: Vol. 2 p. 238: Village - each ploughs a separate area and some common area left, assignments to various functionaries principal man: POTAIL, judge and magistrate, registrar, watchman, distributor of water, astrologer, smith, carpenter, potter, barber, washerwoman and silversmith- villages units unto themselves, unchanged by revolution

Four Castes: Bramins, Cshatryas, Vaisyas and Sundras sacred books say Bramins at the moment of Creation from the mouth of Bramin, the Cshatryas from his arm, Vaisyas from his thigh, Sudras from his foot - extremes from divine privilege to denial of basic human rights.

Bramins: Demand alms from his parents or company after being invested with his "poita" or cotton thread of his order, no taxes levied against him or for his benefit, exist solely on alms from lower castes - cherish in the people all those debasing superstitions to which the mind of man is prone while they exalt in an extravant degree the dignity of their own place and office as well as the merit of those who confer donations on them - sacred books tell of extraordinary powers of them - a murder of a Bramin is a deeper atrocity then that of any other individual but punishes crimes of the most trivial slights offered to that sacred class: i.e. if a Sudra sits on the carpet of a Bramin, the part that is thus sacreligiously deposited is either burnt with a hot iron or entirely cut off, if he spits at a hollowed person, he is deprived of lips if he listens to reproaches against him, melted lead is poured into his ears, if he plucks him by the beard, hands are forfeited - to treat Bramins with honour and confer gifts atones for every sin - at great festivals when the opulent make a great display of wealth, object is to collect great numbers of Bramins and send them away with gifts, entertainments - given by kings this could amount to thousands - the rank is so far above, even the poorest Bramin's daughter considers a king as no equal match.

Cshatryas: military class, second in dignity - originally kings and generals taken from this class during Hindoo independence but with foreign powers limited use - they often enter British service though rank is of a limited nature - Only body of this level having power are the Rajpoots who occupy wild tracts of country on the Western Desert, a strong but peculiar tribe who have complete domination of this area.

Vasisyas: industritous past, third in rank, some believe them to be traders, other shepherds or cultivators, any business requiring the investment of capital, manual labour performed by inferiors

Sudras: lowest, suffer a degree of degradation greater than befalls any other class of persons not actually bondmen - severe toil - debarred from improving their circumstances, illegal to accumulate property and gives pain to Bramins to do so, can't hope to reach heaven, are not permitted to perform any religious ceremony - only hope is by profound homage, lavish gifts and do menial services to the sacred caste which may only raise himself above his fellows though may never even in future lives raise up his caste level - originally agricultural

Loss of Caste: Reasons: tasting of food or holding communion with persons of an inferior caste, dealing in certain commodities, eating certain types of food, the chief deadliest sin is to swallow beef, even if involuntarily makes a Bramin an outcaste - He can no longer face his father, mother, brother, sister, wife or children, they will flee as if he was infectious
- so great are the punishment of the total outcast, some commit suicide, others flee to wander about the earth, hidden from those who know them in purity - in the South, there is a tribe called Pariahs who are entailed from birth with this form of degradation, employed as scavangers, meanest labour, must avoid touching anyone as it is considered polluting by this action, eat every description of food and other excesses equally shunned
- no regard for truth, selfishness though occasionally loyal to superiors   (cont.)

61

Devotees - Chundrakona

...next machine, apparently as a great privilege. We had a
good place to see the whole performance, having been
conducted to the veranda of the house belonging to some
native nabobs directly in front of which was the centre
pole. The street was not less than 100 feet wide and it was
densely packed with natives for more than half a mile.
Beside this many of these poor pariahs to be more sure of
recovering their position would torture themselves in the
most excruciating manner such as running rods of iron
through their flesh, tongues, etc. and all this to get into
a condition which at the best was far below that of the
Slaves in the United States in dignity and still more so in
comfort.

In every street in Calcutta was to be met by the roadside
the devotees who have been so often described in all sorts
of horrid shapes and forms, brought about by their
perseverence in keeping in one particular position so long
that the sinews had become stiffened, and their only
enjoyment was the admiration they excited and their only
subsistance the alms they received from those who believed
in their piety or were struck with compassion for their
helplessness. I had no opportunity of visiting any of the
environs or country about Calcutta. Our drives were
confined to the esplanade and the roads around and within
Fort William a fortress of 1,000 mounted guns and garrisoned
by several thousand sepoys under English officers. It
stands south of the city and on the left bank of the Hoogly
River, and here might every evening be seen the very splendid
equipages of the English residents. On one occasion Capt.
Osgood and myself took a boat and went up to Churndunogne, a
French settlement about 20 miles above Calcutta and on the
opposite and Western bank of the river, but at this time
under English rule, but since ceded back to the French. We
spent a day or two with an Indigo planter with whom Capt.
Osgood had some acquaintance, having on a former voyage
taken his son-in-law and his daugher as passengers to the
United States. He had a wife and a young daughter and

Gang Robbery: a system of plunder as basic a habit as any,
sanctioned by the law, rob outside their neighbourhoods,
regular chiefs, watched over by their villagers - press into
service on pain of death whoever they want - apply tortures
to find hidden treasures: lighted straw and torches to the
body, or having twisted round it hemp with clarified butter,
set on fire and applied and utter threats (menaces) to deter
people from calling injustice i.e. suggest cutting them to
pieces, drown them with earthen pots tied around their necks,
- they could disappear into jungles and with no witnesses
baffled government officials - have had numbers of them
reduced of late

Domestic: Hindoos stay very much to themselves, and mingle little,
marriage the basis of family ties, girl of 15 or youth of 25
and unmarried, a very pitiful state, an example: a party of
old maids uniting to an old Bramin as he was carried to the
Ganges to die rather than be an old maid forever

Women: unlawful to open a book, cannot join in public services at
temples and any man, even husbands would be disgraced by
conversation with them - new bride subject to almost slavery
by her mother in law, often causing them to run home until
mothers in law makes the first advances to reconciliation -
wear long flowing robes, heavily adorned with trinkets and
jewels, a recluse life in their homes and is a breach of
decorum for a man to look at them - on the death of their
husbands either they can sacrifice their lives on the funeral
pyre or live forever in a state of widowhood - veils often
restrict any breaches of conduct by men

- scandals occasionally do happen but marital vows do induce
fidelity in women

Home: they accumulate wealth but don't spend it on themselves - low
mud-houses - eat off ground, no table or furniture,
regardless of being rich or poor - a shed, naked walls, mud
floor sprinkled with water and cow dung each morning for
coolness - spread food among the indigent but never
entertains friends at dinner - rich often entertain in large
numbers, thousands, money going mostly to fireworks and

processions - marriages cost 500 pounds to 1200 Pounds
Sterling - savings of years going into this single occasion
often putting families in debt.

Vol. III Chapt. XVI P. 326

Navigation: East India ship contains: 1 captain, 6 officers, 6
midshipmen, 1 clerk, 1 surgeon, 1 assistant surgeon, 1
purser, 1 ships steward, 1 copper, 1 boatswain and 4 mates, 1
gunner and 2 mates, 1 carpenter, and his 3 mates, 1 armourer,
1 sailmaker, 1 claker, plus servant and seamen totalling 130
men - carries 20 x 18 pounders, on the main deck and 6 of 32
pound carrona des on the upper deck - wartime: 32 guns plus
100 muskets, 50 pistols, 50 cutlasses and 100 pikes (Oxford
def: similar to a spear or lance)

Misc. flying fish often land on deck can be attracted by putting a
fish head over the side which attracts flocks, making good
eating
- Trinidad to the Cape: strong winds, fine weather
- Trista d'Acunha: 3 barren islands, a watering place
- Cape to India trhough the Mozambique channel - strong
southward current on east coast of Africa

63

seemed to be in prosperous circumstances. He showed us the
mode of cultivating, steeping and preparing the plant and
the process used in the manufacture of indigo.

Departure From Calcutta

Our trip was a very pleasant one, principally on the river,
but diversified by occasional rambles through the thick
groves or through the scattered native villages along its
banks. The Hoogly, being one of the branches or rather
outlets of the Ganges, partakes in the ideas of the Hindoos
of the sacred character which they ascribe to the main
stream, and they believe that who ever is drowned in it is
sure of heaven. It is to this superstitious notion, no
doubt, is owing the practice of some of the castes bringing
those whose lives are despaired of to its banks and allowing
its swelling waters to sweep them off, and it is the bodies
of such that are or were daily seen floating by the
anchorage at Calcutta.

In the investment of the cargo for the 'Union' the selection
of the cotton and silk goods, and of the Indigo, was of
course made by the Supercargo, but he devolved on me the
purchasing, weighing and shipping of all the gruff goods.
This was done in the bassars and not in the house, but as it
occupied comparatively little time I had full opportunity of
informing myself of the business. This was completed and
our ship left the chain moorings at Calcutta on the 18th of
April, 1811. Mr. Osgood and myself joined her at Diamond
Harbour on the 21st and on the 26th having had a tolerable
chance down the river for the S.W. Monsoon, we dishcarged
the pilot on the 26th bound to Salem.

It is now just half a century since I commenced this my
first voyage and my first effort in the active duties of
life. It is my purpose in the following pages to recall the
most prominent events that have occurred during that period,
aided by occasional but not continuous journals, but mainly
from recollection. There must be in the course of fifty
years within every man's experience who has passed that

Pleasures of Old Age.

recollection. If enemies have been made, they have th...
If friendships have been formed, they have probably been
dissolved as far as death could dissolve them, but they have not
escaped from the memory. It is thus that we secure to ourselves
the best solace of old age. The animosities of competing interest are allayed—
the strong passions of youth are stilled, the thoughts of the past dwell on the happy hours of
social intercourse & calm reflection takes the place of sanguine expectation. With these
views I am inclined to believe that under equally favorable circumstances old age is not
the most unhappy if it be not the happiest period of our existence. If it has more
pains, it has some compensations, in decrease and sensibility. If it has fewer enjoyments,
it has more content. If its aspirations are more moderate, its disappointments are less
frequent. To secure the greatest possible enjoyment in our later years.
I do not believe the possession of a large fortune is necessary, or even
desirable. An extensive property presents too many points to be secured,
...ny cares for anxiety and too much temptation to annoying af-
...ot to swindling operations to be consistent with the quiet
the pathway to the grave. A moderate com-
the partner of his bosom prolonged
...e character have been
...in need be enter-
serenity

65

length of time in the ordinary pursuits of life many
occurances that he can recall with interest, many
misfortunes, the bitterness of which has passed away, and
many circumstances that yet leave an aroma of pleasure in
their recollection.

Pleasures Of Old Age

If enemies have been made they have been forgotten, if
friendships have been formed they have probably been
dissolved as far as death could dissolve them, but they have
not escaped from the memory. It is thus that we secure to
ourselves the best solace of old age. The animosities of
competing interests are allayed - the strong passions of
youth are exhaled, the thoughts of the past dwell on the
happy hours of social intercourse and calm reflection takes
the place of saguine expectation. With these views I am
inclined to believe that under equally favorable
circumstances old age is not the most unhappy if it be not
the happiest period of our existence. If it has more pains,
it has some compensations in decreased sensibility. If it
has fewer enjoyments it has more content. If its
aspirations are more moderate, its disappointments are less
frequent. To secure the greatest possible enjoyment in our
later years I do not believe the possession of a large
fortune is necessary or even desirable. An extensive
property presents too many points to be secured, too many
causes for anxiety and too much temptation to annoying
applications if not swindling operations to be consistent
with the quiet that should surround the pathway to the
grave. A moderate competency well secured, the life of the
partner of his bosom prolonged with his own, the presence of
children whose characters have been formed, and of whose
well being, no apprehension need be entertained, ought to
give and usually will give a degree of serenity to him who
has attained what is called a good old age, that the near
approach of dissolution will not be able to disturb,
especially if he can bring himself to believe that death is
but the passage to a new youth and another life.

Letters from Harriet Charlotte Price (later to become the wife of
David Augustus Neal) to her sister Margaret. She would have
been seventeen years of age, D. Augustus a year older.

Salem, 9, September, 1811

Dear sister,

Good news, Goodnews. This morning when Uncle came in to
breakfast, he sail the ship, that August, Neill is in, was seen off,
about three leagues and that she would be in by twelve o'clock.
Aunt then enquired of mr. Neill if it was assertain'd, he said oh
yes they had seen the signal, and he was as sure, that it was her, ·
as he was sure that Augustus, had been gone, I was sitting in the
parlour alone in come Mrs. Neill who caught hold of me and said Oh
Harriot I am distress'd to death, I dont know where to go she walk'd
across the room two or three times. and says I sit down Mrs. Neill
what is the matter, Why Harriot I know as well that my Augustus is
dead or sick and this ship is a going to bring the news, as can be.
I burst out a laughing, if I had been to die I could not have helped
it, why says I Mrs. Neill, I should be so overjoyed I should not
think of such things as that Why Harriot how can you laugh so, our
Children are all the time a whispering and I know as well that
something has happened to that dear boy and I dont want any body to
tell, me, says she if margaret Gibbs was here she would jump and fly
about the house and call me old grunter and every thing, she could
think off. but I dont care. So we have been expecting Augustus
every moment since, after dinner I was hearing Eliza read and who
should come up Mrs. Neill's steps but Augustus he stop to see his
mother a moment and then hopp'd over our fence and came to see Aunt
Ward he apeared to be very glad to see her came and shook hands with
me enquired after the margarets said he wanted to see them very
much, but supposed Margaret Gibbs was married he took a chair and
talked about matters and things told a thousand little anecdotes
about the customs and manners of the people in Calcutta Aunt gave
him peaches and wine, she said she would not ask me to drink any as
she was sure of a refusal, Augustus said Miss Price you are just
like your sister Margaret she never would drink any wine, I must
tell you he is a going to take supper with us to night, Augustus is
very much burnt and tanned, his teeth are as white as snow and he is

a perfect beauty with exceptions, not without I did not say, now I
believe I have given you every particular Concerning the Gentleman,
which I suppose will tire your patience O. by the way Aunt Ward
ask'd Mrs. Neill if Augustus gave her a good kissing, no she said
but the dear boy squeezed her hand as if he would kill her, he
appears to be in perfect health, I received your kind Epistle with
lively sensation of pleasure which you know your favours always
afford and thank you for your Good advice and hope I shall profit
from it, give my love to Margaret Gibbs and tell nothing would give
me more pleasure than to write her but I have not an opportunity
please to give my filial love to my mother I shall write her soon,
and I hope her health is better than it has been, give my regards to
Henry respect to my Grand parents and Aunt and Uncle Ward join me in
love to you and all the family,

Dear sister I remain yours
affectionately
H.C. Price

tell Mrs. Nash I am sorry I offended her in calling her Mrs. Upham
but in future I shall remember, and tell her I dont believe about a
certain person being in prison for stealing oxen it is all a .....
and I dont believe it at any rate she has not sent me the charcoal
she promised for .....

I want to write relief (Foster) but I have not time please to give
my love to the girls

Dear Sister Do answer this the first conveyance

H.C.P.

****

Arrival Home - Second Voyage, - Schooner 'Columbia'

From this my first voyage I reached home on the 6th of Sept. 1811 after a passage of 134 days. Our voyage resulted very well, giving the shippers about 50 percent net profit.

At this time my Father had at home a high decked Schooner called the 'Columbia'. The Messrs. Silsbees, Pickman & Stone offered to load her in part with pepper for Gilbraltar, or the Mediterranean, and consign it to me, if I would go out in her as Supercargo. I was but 18 years old, and the offer from such old and well established merchants to a boy was flattering, and I agreed to accept it. The vessel was filled up with various articles and we sailed on the 9th of Nov., 1811, the schooner being under the command of Capt. Josiah Dewing who is still living. My cousin, David Preston was our mate. We cleared for Tangiers to avoid, if boarded by a French cruiser, detention for being bound to a British port, the English Orders in Council and the French, Berlin & Milan decrees being then if force. At this time the war was being carried on between the French and English in Spain. Our vessel was very deep and dull and we had a very rough passage of 39 days, arriving in Gibraltar Bay on the 19th of December.

On our passage out when some 90 or 100 miles west of Cape Trafalgar and of course 120 or 130 from Tarifa we plainly heard cannonading which we subsequently ascertained must have been at the latter place, which was held by the French and bombarded from the English fleet. At the time the sea was smooth and the wind light from the N.E. proving how far sound, under favorable circumstances may be heard over water. At Gibraltar we were subjected to a quarantine of ten days, which made it necessary to select a consignee, and I made choice of an English House to whom I had letters. They made sales of some of my goods, and among others, of the pepper, but which the purchasers declined to take. After getting out of quarantine I found my consignees gave themselves very little trouble about my business and I took it from them,

Schooner: The schooner is a vessel of two or more masts, fore-and-aft rigged. The fore-and mainsails are suspended from gaffs and laced to booms on the foot of the wails. (Davis, Charles G. "Rigs")

Letters: Business was best conducted amongst merchants who could recommend a service. Letters of introduction verified the reputation of the ship and the business in the foreign ports. CR (See Bills of Exchange)

the came... Aunt had candle... Augustus and I had coffee &... a walk and went to mr. Samuel...

a great deal about you, Augustus wants m... is about ten or twelve miles from here I have no... I shall go, or not. Yesterday we went to Andover to... we had a very pleasant ride there, we saw mr. Griffins house wh... is a very handsome building indeed, mrs. Sam, Ward was with us

and sadly we found mr. Ward very much deranged much more so than we expected, and you may judge it was a very affecting scene jack was with him the one I danced with, he carried me to the cider mill and was very polite and attentive to me, showed me every thing that was to be seen just after we got their Gamaliel Ward and mrs. Briggs drove up, we dined their, and about half past three set out for Salem, and reached home at seven, Aunt Ward has had one of her headache's a day or two ago, but I am in hopes her ride to andover will make her feel better, give my love to aunt jarvis and tell her Eliza makes great improvements, give my best love to my mother fitz Henry and accept a share for yourself I suppose you have not heard from papa remember me to Grandpapa and Grandmama and all enquiring friends

I remain dear Sister yours affectionately

G H H C Price

October, 11, 1811

Dear sister,

it is now half past ten friday evening, Augustus has just bid us good night, as Aunt Ward is going to Boston tomorrow and is uncertain of her reaching Dorchester. I thought I would inform you of my good health and my late excursions day before yesterday, Augustus and myself went to Marlbehead with Aunt's roses, from then we went a round about way to the Springs we found Mrs. Neill and Mrs. Osborn, their. Augustus gave me some Lemonade made of the spring water, we were there three quarters of an hour when Mrs. Neill ask'd Augustus to bring her chaise to the door, he told her he would not for he did not belong to her party, and that she might go as she came and so brought our chaise to the door and welcome the new way Aunt had candle when we got home, and had drank coffee of course August and I had coffee by ourselves, when we had Aunt proposed taking a walk and went to Mr. Samuel Wards he was at andover Mary enquired a great deal about you, August want me to go to topsfield with him which is about ten or twelve miles from here I have no concluded whether I shall go, or not. Yesterday we went to Andover to see Mr. Ward we had a very plesant ride their. we saw Mr. Griffins house which is a very handsome building indeed, Mrs. Sam. Ward was with us and sally we found Mr. Ward very much deranged much more so than we expected, and you may judge it was a very affecting scene jack was with him the one I danced with he carried me to the cider mill and was very polite and attentive to me showed me everything that was to be seen just after we got their Gammaliel Ward and Mrs. Briggs drove up, we dined there and about half past three set out for Salem, and reached hom at seven. Aung Ward has had one of her headaches a day or two ago, but I am in hopes her ride to andover will make her feel better, give my best love to Aunt Jarvis and tell her Eliza makes great improvements, give my best love to my mother, Fitz henry (her brother) and accept a share for yourself, I supposed you have not heard from papa remember me to Grandpapa and Grandmama and all enquiring friends

I remain dear Sister yours affectionately

G H   H C Price

H. C. Price

1809

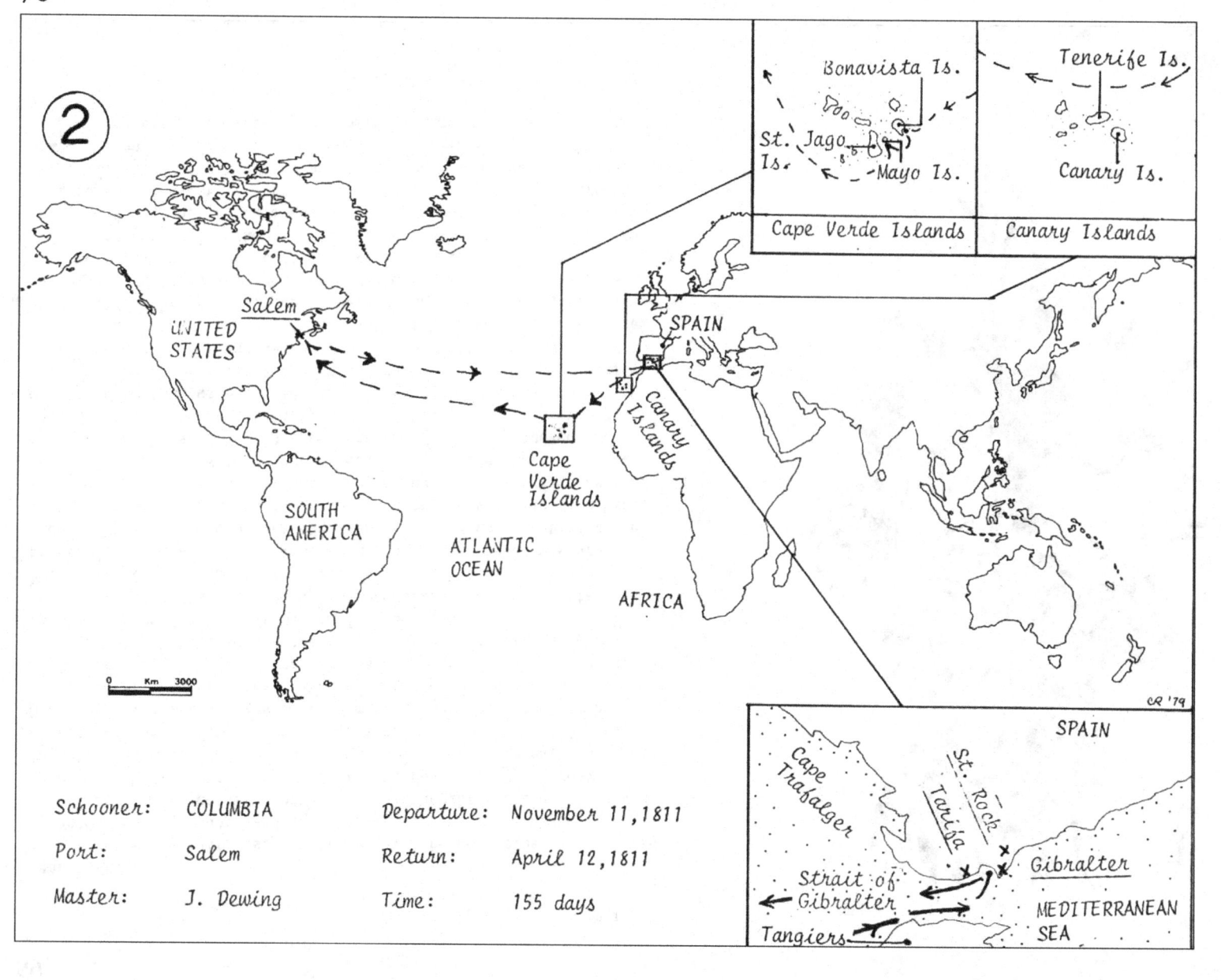

② Cape Verde Islands

Bonavista Is.

St. Jago Is.

Mayo Is.

Canary Islands

Tenerife Is.

Canary Is.

SALEM

UNITED STATES

SOUTH AMERICA

ATLANTIC OCEAN

Cape Verde Islands

Canary Islands

SPAIN

AFRICA

CR '79

SPAIN

Cape Trafalger

St. Roch

Tarifa

Gibralter

Strait of Gibralter

Tangiers

MEDITERRANEAN SEA

Schooner:	COLUMBIA	Departure:	November 11, 1811
Port:	Salem	Return:	April 12, 1811
Master:	J. Dewing	Time:	155 days

selling a considerable part of the cargo myself and the
balance through Mr. Horatio Sprague who had just arrived and
opened an American Commission House.

Horatio Sprague, Gibraltar, Departure for Cape De Verds Islands

I gave him the first consignment he had, except what he
brought with him. The high position which Mr. Sprague
afterwards held as a merchant and a gentleman makes me proud
of this fact. I closed the sales of all my cargo here,
finding the markets in the Mediterranean were all glutted.
I had an order to purchase a fine Brig, the 'Romp', that had
been owned in Salem and condemned under the French decrees
at Naples on her first voyage, but I could get no
satisfactory information of her whereabouts. After a little
fracas with my English friends who wanted to charge me
commission on what they did not and could not sell, which
claim I defeated, I sailed in the 'Columbia' in ballast for
the Cape de Verds Islands on the 12th Feb., 1812. At the
time of this visit to Gibraltar, the neighboring country
bore evidence of the recent invasion of the French troops,
but it was now abandoned by them. The village of St. Rock,
just north of the neutral ground which is the strip of sand
lying between the Mediterranean and the bay of Gibraltar and
connecting the fortress with the mainland, had been left by
them only a few weeks before I went to see its condition.
The fronts of many of the houses had been knocked in to make
way for the French Cavalry. Great numbers of women and but
few men were to be seen at St. Rock. The French still held
Tarifa, and every week numbers of the British soldiers and
sailors who were wounded in the attacks upon it were brought
to Gibraltar.

I think it was surrendered shortly after I left, or was
abandoned by the French.

At this time there was a large business carried on at
Gibraltar (which was then as now a free port) and the point
of supply for all the Spanish smugglers. The condition of

In ballast: when there is no cargo on board ship that is
        marketable, the vessel is considered empty fo valued goods,
        but something must always be in the hold so the ship will be
        stable, called
        ballast. Could be water casks, grain, pig iron etc. (OCSS)

③

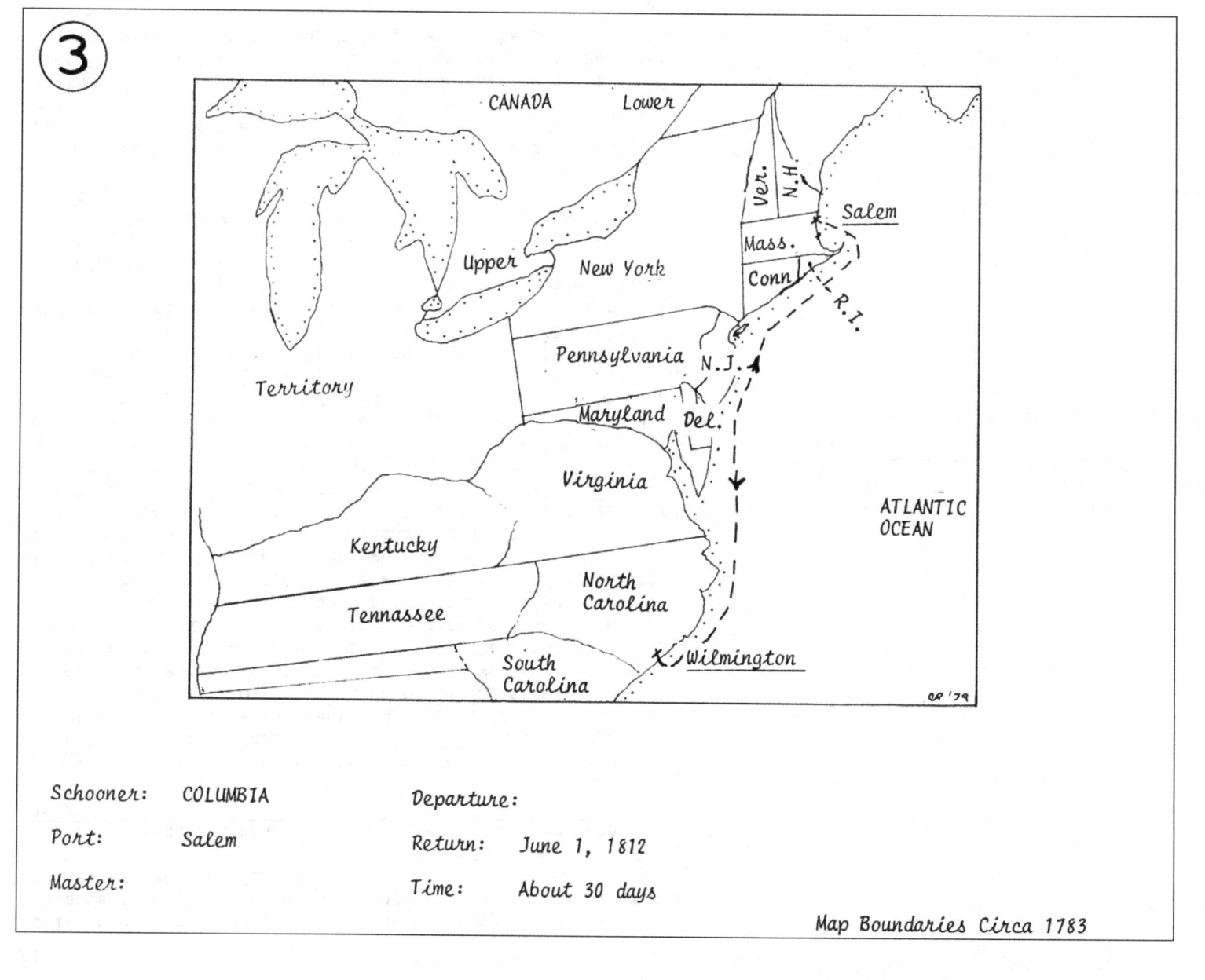

CANADA　　Lower

Ver.　N.H.

Salem

Mass.

Upper　New York　Conn.

R.I.

Territory

Pennsylvania　N.J.

Maryland　Del.

Virginia

ATLANTIC
OCEAN

Kentucky

North
Carolina

Tennassee

Wilmington

South
Carolina

Schooner:　COLUMBIA　　　Departure:

Port:　　Salem　　　　　　Return:　June 1, 1812

Master:　　　　　　　　　Time:　About 30 days

Map Boundaries Circa 1783

Spain threw nearly all its import business into their hands. Independently of this, the French Imperial decrees had as effectually barred all the continental ports in the Mediterranean against any legitimate commerce as the whole British navy acting as a blockading squadron could have done.

Third Voyage-Peak of Teneriffe, Cape De Verde Islands, Isle Mayo

It seemed as if the two great contending powers had united in one objective no other, to wit, to drive all commerce from the ocean or to make it so hazardous as not to be worth pursuing. On the 20th of February we passed close to the Canary Islands, having fine views of the Peak of Teneriff. On the 25th, being in lat. 17 and long 21, the air was full of a fine yellow dust which covered our decks and sails and obscured the sun like a thick haze. It was brought from the African coast by the strong Easterly wind. On the 27th we anchored at Bonavista, (one of the Cape de Verd Islands) and finding nothing here but a miserable looking Portuguese who was called governor, we got under way the next morning and run over to the Isle Mayo and anchored in English roads. We found here three ships waiting for salt. The process of getting it off is a slow one, being sent off on guys from the shore anchored off and dropped in to boats, and thence taken on board ship. The salt is made entirely by sun evaporation. Occasionally the sea breaks over the rocks into a natural basin where it evaporates and the salt when thus made is raked up and shipped. Finding it would be two months before we could get a cargo, concluded not to wait, but filled up our water and sailed on the 1st. of March for the United States (Salem) where we arrived on the 9th of April.

Coastal Trip

At this time an embargo was in force against all foreign voyages so with the view of employing the vessel and myself, my Father concluded to let the schooner run out to Wilmington S.C. where I purchased a cargo of naval stores and rice and returned to Salem about the 1st of June.

English Roads: Popular routes used by or ports occupied by the English (Ed. note)

Guys: ropes used to control the lifting mechanism of a derrick. (OCSS)

Ninety-Day Embargo: April, 1812: (United States) to insure that American ships would be safely in port when war with England began. By this time England, fighting the Peninsular War (Gibralter) in Spain, needed American supplies. She therefore would have gladly revoked the Orders in Council if she could have been certain that Napoleon would absolutely withdraw his decrees against American shipping. (EWH)

Naval Stores: tar, pitch and turpentine
Tar: used on ships to prevent the hemp ropes from rotting
Pitch: used over oakem to caulk seams in vessels (oakem is rotten hemp that is pulled apart for just this purpose)
Turpentine: a varnish for decks, masts, etc.
(Ed. Note.)

Salem, 9, Feb. 1812

Dear Sister,

Uncle inform'd us that he asaw Fitz on Monday and you were all well, Aunt Ward and Mama expects to visit you next week, if the roads are good, the travelling has been very dangerous, we have had no assemblys this winter, but their has been a number of large partys, and balls, the miss Stearnes gave a ball not long since William Stearnes had business with Uncle, and call here to see him, he made a very handsome apology for his sister's not inviting me to their ball, he told me that it had been such extreme bad walking, they intended calling upon me as they had hopt, they thought it would be an impropriety in asking me, However week before last William Stearnes his sister and miss Eliza White called upon me and George Hodges waited upon them as far as our gate, last Wednesday William Stearnes came and invited me to his sisters party, which was on Thursday evening I went their was about twenty young ladies twelve or fourteen gentlemen among the rest was George Hodges, I played cards with him and asked me if I ever played backgammon, I told he yes he then called for a board and we played a number of games, we then played 'stir the pudding', I told George I did not understand the game, he said it was very simple, their must be one chair less than their was person's that played, one to be in the center, with a stick, then point hands and form a circle, round this one in the middle run round as fast as you could race, till the one in the middle knocked this stick on the floor, then run to your seat as quick as you could the one, that was up must be in the middle, we played it a long time then took our seats, talk and laughed and William Stearnes came home with me, judge how muchI enjoyed myself every one in the room were utter strangers to me, give my love to Relief and joanna tell them I really ashamed of myself for not writing to them but my intention in good, I have never answer Susan Cunninghams letter yet, I expected Fitz or Henry would have wrote by Uncle I received your letter and am glad to hear you had such a delightful time at Mrs. Briggens, I am sorry to hear Fitz thinks of going into the army and am in hopes he has give up the idea of it, Aunt Ward and mama join, me in love to you all,

I remain dear sister yours affectionately

Harriot C. Price

Salem, 12, 1812

Dear Sister

I received your letter of the 27th of February, and thank you for inquiring after my Health, which I perfectly enjoy at present, as I wish and hope you do yours. Mrs. and Mrs. Miles, and little Mary, arrived here yesterday about half past one, and expect to return this afternoon, and I shall intrude upon their Goodness to forward this scrawl. Mary sweet little Creature she takes up all my attention she is so cunning, and so still, and behaves so pretty, that she diverts us all. Augustus Neill arrived fast day. he looks much better than he did before he went away, he made particular enquiries after your health and Fitzs. he says he has not made so fortunate a Voyage as he expected. I began with my school first of April as Aunt Ward informed you I should, she wishes me to send mama a specimen off my first painting, for her to look at, not as a present. I hope the progress I make in my learning will in some measure make returns for Aunts goodness, Gratitude, and duty, make me fully sensible how much I ought to labour, for my improvement Mr. Codmans sermons has a wonderfull effect upon the minds of some of our Salem young ladies a miss Lawrence a neighbour of ours from hearing mr. Codman was converted and is taken into mr. Worcester church I suppose this part of my letter is more interesting to you than all the rest, give my love to Mamma, Fitz and Henry, I have not time to write them. Aunt Ward joins me in love to Granpapa, and Grandmama, and the rest of the family, I expect to make you a visit before I receive an answer to this

Adieu
I remain your affectionate Sister

Harriet Charlotte Price

N.B. Dear sister you sent me the constitution of the United States instead of my Arithmetic which I wish you would be kind enough to get as Uncle will be up next week

H C P

In Wilmington I visited a lady who had for her first husband
a brother of my mother, Mrs. Nathan Ward, and after his
death had married his partner, Mr. Langdon who was now
living. Mrs. Langdon had visited us in Salem some time
previous so that she was an old acquaintance. Found there
also Mr. John Ward, a cousin of my mother. He was, I think,
in the Custom house. Capt. Chas. Treadwell was also there
in a ship from Boston.

War With England Blundering Policy 1812

A few days after my return to Salem, say on the 12th of
June, 1812, war was declared by congress against Great
Britain. Never probably was a measure of so much importance
adopted with so little deliberation and at so impolitic a
moment. That there was cause enough for war and had been
for five years before there can be no doubt. That the
character of the country was suffering because it had been
avoided so long is certainly true. But we had missed the
proper time, which was when the long embargo had been in
operation some twelve or fourteen months. The country was
then prepared for it. All our ships were snug at home. All
our resources were in hand. Our seamen were panting for the
opportunity to spread themselves over the ocean in ships of
war or as privateers. The enemies of England were in full
tide of success, and Europe was in arms against her. But
instead of seizing that propitious moment when we could do
her vast damage and receive none, Congress after
perservering two or three years in their ------- policy of
non-intercourse or entire cessation of all commerce,
abandoned it without attaining one object for which it had
been undertaken, and without any relaxation of the hostile
acts of the European belligerents against our commerce or
any reliquishment of the British claim to impress our seamen
on the high seas took off all restrictions, suffered our
ships to spread themselves to the farthest ends of the
earth, and our wealth to be scattered over the wide world
and then, without preparation, without notice, without any
new cause, in the middle of summer, when our coasts were
envisioned by the superior fleets of our enemy, war is

War declared on England by the United States: June 18, 1812 on the
ground of impressement (taking men to sea against their
will), violation of the three mile limit, paper blockade and
orders in council

Impress: The name give in Britain for the state authority to
require the service of a subject for the defence or the
country. Later it meant prisoners of war being put into
naval service on the level of seamen, usually against their
will instead of filling up the prisons with war criminals
(OCSS p. 415)

Constitution and Guerriere
29 August 1812

declared, and the whole mercantile navy and capitol of the country thrown into their clutches, from which only a very small proportion actually escaped. But notwithstanding all this blundering legislation, the inefficiency of our armies on land, the weakness of our seaboard defences, and the capture and conflagration of the capitol at Washington the ...

Good Results in Spite of Bad Management, Privateering

...gallantry of our little navy, redeemed our national character, and the activity of our fleet of private armed cruisers inflicted so severe an injury on the commerce of Great Britain, that we had at least some offset for the capture of our undefended merchantmen. The bit of striped bunting at our mast heads became and has continued to be respected. Our seamen have ever since travelled the ocean without fear of being torn from their ships and walked the streets of England without the risk of imprisonment. Great Britain, victorious over all her foe but us, having conquered the capitol of her great European enemy and driven its chief from his throne, nevertheless sought the first opportunity to put an end to the unprofitable contest of seeing which could do the other the most harm. In the meantime, however, two years and a half intervened, and they were not the least interesting of my life.

Privateering

There was now nothing for me to do but enter the Army or the Navy, or engage in the more independent and not less exciting employment of privateering. I declined the offer of a lieutenancy in the Engineer Corps (equal to a captaincy in the regular army) being conscious of my want of knowledge in that department, as well as of a strong disinclination for military service of any kind. The Navy even if I could have got a desirable position did not offer much inducement to me. There were some bright chances, on which one might possibly stumble, but they were few and far between. A long period of inferior service, not far removed from slavery,

Privateering: a privately owned vessel armed with guns which operated in time of war against the trade of an enemy. The name has come to embrace both the ships and the men who sailed in them. In the War of 1812, the United States had a handful of legitimate naval vessels and the private ones, partly run for the sake of a quick wartime profit, augmented the numbers substantially. (OCSS 670)

Salem, 24, August, 1813

Dear Sister,

I wrote you these few lines by Mrs. Saunders and Miss Beach. Augustus says Mehitable mentions in her letter that she was to see you last week, you must give my love to her when you see her and apologize for my not going in to see her the day she was so unwell not observing the direction on the billet I did not open it till we rode away from the door and concluded she was too sick to see me. Please to give my love to mama tell her I want two knitting needles a large size and a small size if she will lend them to me as I wish to knit me a bag I believe Mamma has give some of the needles I mean if you will send them to me with a skein of Cotton I will knit you a bag also. Since you was here we have not done any thing but go to parties and receive company week before last Aunt Ward had a very large party Mr. Stackpole and Mr. Frazier were here and we danced till one o'clock and the company said they never enjoyed themselves better. Mr. Ingersoll, Mr. Frazier came down last week and spent a night here, Margaret I was in hopes Fitz would bring you down to see the funeral of Capt. Lawrence it is believed their never was so many persons assembled in Salem, before upon any occasion whatever. The Rev. Mr. Spalding's meeting house, was very handsomely decorated by the young ladies. The Gallery's and Pulpit, were hung in Black, with wreath of Cypress and evergreen. Margaret, Blagge Susan and myself, went one afternoon with Aunt Ward to assist in dressing the meeting, the Names of Lawrence, and Ludlow in gold letters executived by Miss Hannah, Crowninshield were encircled in festoons of evergreen on the front of the desk. Capt. George Crowinshield with sight of ten Master's of vessles voluntarily went to Halifax to obtain the bodies of Capt. Lawrence and Lieut. Ludlow their remains were entombed in this town, on Monday last, the sides of the streets were --- the procession Pass'd were crowded, and the windows were filled with spectators, all the vessels in the harbor wore their colours half mast. at 12 o'clock the bodies were conveyed from the Cartel, Brig, 'Henry' (which lay at anchor in the harbor) in barges and preceded by a long procession of Boats filled with seamen, in uniform of blue jackets, and trousers, with a blue ribbans on their hats bearing the motto of 'Free trade and Sailors Rights' Minute guns were fireing during their passage, from the Brig to the Wharves. The ceremonies were very solemn and impressive, and the multitude was so great that a small part only could be accomadated, to hear the Euology delibered by the Hon. Judge Story. The procession consisted of the officers, of the United States Navy and Army, the Clergy of all denomination, the several Marines and Masonic Societies together with citizens and strangers from Boston and its vicinity moved under the excort of the elegant company of light infantry commanded by Capt. James King, of this town. The Remains are to be re-embarked in the Cartel 'Henry' and carried to New York, preparations are making their for his funeral. Aunt Ward joins me in love to all she expects to go to Dorchester soon but it is uncertain what time you mention'd in your letter Grandmama seems to be relieved from the medicine she has taken I am very glad to hear it and I hope Grandpapa's health is better give my love to them both and to papa Mamma, and Brother tell them they must not forget me tell Papa if he will condescend to write a few lines to me the first opportunity I shall feel highly obligated to him perhaps it will be a satisfaction for him and mama to read this letter as I have not time to write them, Dear sister I am exerting my power to make my letter as long as yours, Aunt Ward is very much obligied to Grandpa for those pears he sent by Mr. Bently My love to the Foster girls.

I remain your ever
effectionate Sister

H.C. Price

N.B.   Give my love to Molly and tell her I always think of her

A Receipt to make ginger bread

2 tb. flour, 1½ tb. sugar, 1 tb. butter, 4 eggs, 2/3 of a small cup of ginger -- this is Mrs. Hobrooks and Madame Wells

must intervene before a rank could be obtained that would
give an independent command, and even when attained, it gave
no control over one's own movements or left for hardly a
single day at his own disposal. In privateering there was
something attractive in its adventurousness, its liberty of
place and action, and its comparative freedom from the rigid
discipline of national ships. But it was not in every
private armed ship, nor under every commander, that I was
disposed to enlist. I was urged to take the berth of
Master's Mate in the 'America', the best privateer that was
fitted out of Salem, but it was one with the duties of which
I was not conversant and I declined it. My friend Jas. W.
Chever took it and by his energy and courage, after 2 or 3
cruises, was raised to the command over a large number of
his then superior officers and much older men. I therefore
remained at home, taking some little interest in one or two
small privateers from which no great results were obtained.
What little money I had, I invested in Treasury Notes, at a
heavy discount and still held them til peace when they were
worth par.

It was during this period that I formed the engagement which
eventuated in my marriage some years afterwards. An
engagement that after half a century's experience I can say
has resulted in all and more than all the happieness I then
anticipated from it. My great uncle, Mr. Joshua Ward, was
our next door neighbor. He had married for his second wife
Mrs. Susan Magee, the daughter of Mr. Stephen Hall of
Dorchester. Mrs. Ward had several sisters, as well as her
Father and Mother then living. These last were Mrs. Blagge,
the wife of Saml. Blagge, Mrs. Gibbs, the wife of Caleb
Gibbs, Mrs. Jarvis, the widow of Mr. Benj. Jarvis, and Mrs.
Price, the wife of Mr. James Price.

Engaged To Whom

Previous to my departure on my voyage in the 'Union' Mrs.
Ward had two of her neices visiting her - Miss Margaret
Price and Miss Margaret Gibbs. The latter was then engaged
to Mr. Saml. Adams Wells, a grandson of Saml. Adams of

with the duties of which I was not conversant: Master's Mate is a
seamen's post rank and until this date, D. Augustus Neal had
only been involved with the merchant end of things (Ed. note)

Salem Feb. 8, 1814

Dear Sister

Aunt Ward had sent you all the gingham she has, she thought
she had two or three yards if a part of what she has sent you will
answer your purpose you can have it for she has not a scrap left for
Eliza gown which she has almost outgrown already. I received a
letter from Augustus last week with his miniature which is esteemed
a good likeness and handsome painting it is a locket set in gold
with a gold stone on the back part it has a very handsome gold
chain. Mehetable left us on Sunday to go to take charge of her
fathers family she sends her love to you all --

Do write me Margaret the first opportunity for I long to hear
from you, give my love to Papa and Mama and Brother Fitz tell him he
must not expect me to write now for this is all the paper I have,
give my love to Henry when you see him and all inquiring friends, I
am rejoiced to hear of Grandpapas being well enough to ride into
town Aunt Ward joine me in love to him and Grandmama and all her
friends I must conclude for my pen is so bad I cannot write any
more, Believe me

Your ever affectionate Sister

H.C.P.

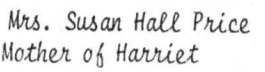

Mrs. Susan Hall Price
Mother of Harriet

Fitz James Price
Brother of Harriet

(Uniform of War of 1812)

Revolutionary memory. With these young ladies who were
older than myself, I formed a very pleasant acquaintance and
occasionally met with other members of their families. On
my return home from that voyage I found in the place of
those ladies a younger sister of the former of these, Miss
Harriet Charlotte Price who had come to Salem for a short
visit to the Aunt Ward, a visit however that was prolonged
til we were married, some 6 or 7 years. She was about one
year younger than myself, having been born Sept. 3rd, 1794.
She had no other sister than Margaret, but had two brothers,
Fitz James & Henry, both older than herself. Her Mother,
born May 17, 1770 and died Nov. 27, 1848, aged 78½, was the
fourth daughter of Mr. Hall & of Margaret (nee Cunningham)
Hall. Her grandfather, James Price, who died Aug. 20, 1802,
aged 62 yrs., was I believe born in New Jersey and died in
Montreal. He married a French lady, and in the breaking out
of hostilities between Great Britain and the Colonies he
espoused the cause of the latter and was in consequence
eventually obliged to fly from the Canadas to this country.
He acted as Commissary of the American Armies, giving
gratuitously his services, and spending besides a
considerable part of his large fortune, for which as all his
documents were lost in the fire that destroyed the war
office, he never recovered a dollar. A large part of what
remained he afterwards lost by the failure of a merchant
(Mr. Tracy) of Newburyport. He had but one child (James)
who married Mary Hale and was the Father of the children
before named and of whom Harriet who was the youngest was
born in Boston and shortly after removed with her parents
and grandparents to Concord, Mass. and resided there till
she was nine years old, when they returned to Boston. Our
engagement was made in the summer of 1813. It did not make
me less solicitous of active employment. I had some
experience of life upon the Ocean, and had not found it
unpleasant. On the contrary I loved its changes, if not its
dangers, and looked upon it as the theatre where I was to
peform at least the first few acts in the drama of life.
The Sea, The Sea, The Open Sea, was the burden of my song.
As to fighting my way upon it, I certainly had no particular
penchant for gunpowder, but I was too young and too sanguine
to fear very much its consequences.

news as late ...
ning: at which time the...
the enemy's veffels of war off the
nds. A fmall veffel, loaded with clams,
ad been taken by them, and liberated, after
aking out her cargo—While the Captain of
the clam boat was on board of the enemy's
veffels, he heard fome converfation among
the officers about an intended attack upon
New-London.

BOSTON, Sept. 26.

The Enemy in the Delaware.

We received by laſt night's Expedition
Stage, the Philadelphia papers of yesterday.
They ſtate that two 74's and ſix frigates were
at anchor at the bottom of the Brown in the
D———, and that Com. Rodgers had
left Baltimore for Philadelphia.

A Wilmington (Del.) article fays,
"the enemy's ſhips in our bay have difap-
peared."

*Extract of a letter from a gentleman in Balti-
more to his friend in New-York, dated*

"BALTIMORE, 21ſt SEPT. 1814.

"The flag that went down to the enemy
on Sunday, has returned, and reports that
two of the Admirals had gone to fea, one to
Bermuda, and one to Halifax, the other remained with the fleet off the Patuxent. It
is fuppofed they will all leave our bay.
unfortunate men made priſoners will be carried off."

FROM THE EASTWARD.

Extract of a letter from Wiſcaſſet, Sept. 21.

"I left my family at Caſtine on Sunday
noon. The enemy's force at that time was
the Bulwark 74, one frigate, and one armed
brig, 14 tranſports, of which 6 are brigs, and
about 2200 troops, being the 98th, 62d and
a part of the 29th regiments. The tenders
and one large tranſport arrived as I left the
harbour, Sunday noon—the tranſport had on
board the remainder of the 29th regiment,
being the part of that regiment that was at
Machias.

"I am this moment informed by a gentleman from Caſtine, who left there on Wed-
neſday, that on that day the 98th regiment
and the French and German ridemen, in all
about 1200, were embarked, and faid to be
... up Penobſcot bay to Caſtine ...

GUARD SHIP.

We underſtand the Guard Ship mentioned in our lift, is now completely officered and
manned. Capt George Crowninſhield, commander. Capt. Henry White 1ſt, and Capt.
Joſeph Felt, 2d Lieutenants. A number of
young men of this town have volunteered
their ſervices to man her. She will probably
be on her ſtation this evening.

We underſtand a line of *Telegraphs* is nearly completed, by which intelligence may be
conveyed in fifteen minutes from Sandy Bay
(Gloucester) to Boston.

It is reported that his Excellency the Governor has been aſſured by the General Government, that no pay will be allowed by them
for the ſervices of any of our Militia, except
ſuch as are given up to U. S. officers. When
our Legiſlature meet, we ſhall doubtleſs have
full information on this intereſting ſubject;
and the part that Maſſachuſetts as a ſtate is
to take in the war, will be more diſtinctly
marked out.

KILLED & WOUNDED.

Among the killed and wounded in the late Baltl-...

IMPORTANT PRIZE.

SATURDAY, SEPT. 24.—At B. ordnance ship
... 2700 tons of ſhipping ...

POSTSCRIPT.

From Boſton, laſt evening.

A square rigged veſſel is at anchor off the Light,
wind and tide ahead.

Brig Mary and Eliza, from St. John's N B for
Havanna, with lumber, prize to the letter marque
... of Boſton ... has been chaſed aſhore

SALES AT AUCTION.

NEXT FRIDAY, at 10 o'clock,
At T. DELAND's Office, Franklin Plate,
A VARIETY of articles, Engliſh and American
Goods, Glaſs Ware, 1 ſuperb Watch, 1 ſtop
do. &c. Alſo,
... Furniture, ſwelled Bureau's, fancyChairs
... 11 o'clock.
... 170 lb. Powder

It happened about this time that Mr. John Crowninshield with whom I was quite intimate, and on very friendly terms, had commenced the building of a vessel in New York, purposely for a privateer.

Fitting Out Privateer, New York 1813

Capt. John Crowninshield had been one of the House of Geo. Crowninshield & Sons, long distinguished for their enterprise and wealth. Previous to the commencement of the war, perhaps 2 or 3 years it had been dissolved by the death of Mr. Jacob Crowninshield and the retirement of John & Richard. The House was continued under the firm of Geo. Crowninshield & Co. - the partners being Geo. Crowninshield & Son, Geo. C. Jun. & Benj. W. Mr., Richard C. went to New York, was there unfortunate and failed. Mr. John C. engaged in Commerce in Salem, and built a Brig called the 'Diomede'. She was returning home, with a valuable cargo, on his account, from the East Indies, early in the war, but was captured. Mr. C. had no insurance. In this and some other ways he lost a large portion of the property with which he had retired from the firm of G. C. & Sons. But he was enterprising and determined. He was curious in regard to vessels, and thought he could model one that would sail very fast and with the assistance of some friends had made a contract with Mr. Burrough (pronounced Brock) in New York, a celebrated ship builder for a schooner of about 160 tons. He decided to take command of her himself, and urged me to go out with him, promising if possible to land me in France and give me there the management of any <u>prizes</u> he might be able to send in there, for it was his plan to beard the lion in his den or in other words to make the coast of England his cruising ground. The whole plan as laid out exactly coincided with my wishes. It seemed to me that it would be glorious fun to make prizes in sight of the enemies towns or to run away from their channel fleet. Of course I assumed that we could do either. Then I had a great desire to visit Europe, then the scene of the most stirring events and it would be pleasant as well as profitable to have something to do while there. I therefore accepted his proposition,

prizes : Captured British ships in the War of 1812 (Ed. Note)

TOPSAIL SCHOONER

The topsail schooner is a two-masted vessel, the mainmast of which has a fore-and-aft mainsail and gaff topsail identical to those of an ordinary schooner. Both masts are made in two spars, but the lower foremast is a little shorter than the corresponding spar of the mainmast, and the topmast is a little longer. The foremast and sails carried on it are exactly like the mainmast of a brigantine, i.e., a fore-and-aft topsail, above which are yards carrying square fore-topsail and fore-topgallantsail.

Share Divisions of a Privateer, Marine Regulations, 1812

Owner of Ship: 50% of total if crew was paid on a per capture basis
100% if crew paid regular wages, regardless of captures

Other 50%:

Capt.	12 Shares	First Lieutenant	6 shares
Second Lt.	6	Third Lt.	5
Master	5	First Mate	4
Second Mate	3	Surgeon's Mate	4
Lt. of Marines	4	Gunner	3
Gunner's Mates	2	Boatswain (crew master)	3
Boatswain's mates	2	Purser	3
Cooper	2	Musician	2
Able Landmen	3/4	Land Boys	1/2
Caulker	2	Master at arms	2
Armourer	1 1/4	Midshipmen	1 1/2
Quarter Master	1 1/2	Ground Gunner	2
Corporals	1 1/2	Sail Maker	1 1/2
Yeoman of Powder Room	2	Steward	2
Capt's Steward	1 1/2	Master of Longitude	1 1/2
Capt's Clerk	2	Ship's Cook	1 1/2
Capt's Cook	1 1/2	Able Seamen	1 1/2
Sea Boys	3/4	Land Boys	1/2

Editor's Note: This list was designed, to include all the possible ranks of an active Privateer. Due to the size restriction of most of the vessels, only the most necessary posts were filled with the men doubling for the other positions when the job needed to be done.

though against the wishes of my parents, who looked more to
the dangers than the pleasures or profit of the expedition.
Finding me strenuous they withdrew their opposition and bade
me God Speed.

'Diomede', My Mother's Death 1814

I took the office of Captain's Clerk, as one of the duties
of which I understood better than any other, and which also
brought me into more confidential communication with the
Commander. Capt. Crowninshield then wished me, and Mr.
Saml. Briggs, first Lieutenant, to go on to New York and
attend to the outfit of the vessel, then on the stocks. I
went on in November. Messrs. Bailey & Willis were the agents
in New York. The hull of the schooner appeared to be well
built and her model somewhat novel, but well calculated for
speed. She was however too small to make good headway in
very rough weather. It was originally intended that she
should carry one long gun on a circle forward, and a number
of small ones on carriages. When I got there I advised
decking over the main hatch-way and putting 3 circles
mounted with 12 or 18 pounders between the masts and leaving
out all but 4 of the small guns. This plan was adopted.
She was fitted in the best manner for 75 men and a four
months cruise. She was called the 'Diomede' after the
vessel which Capt. C. had lost by capture. I returned to
Salem to spend the Christmas holidays and then returned to
New York. On the 4th of February we were ready for Sea but
just previous to this date I received the sad news of the
sudden death of my Mother on the 26th of Jan. She had been
for some years affected by dropsical complaints, and
suffered a good deal, although she was at the time of her
death only 38 years of age. She had retired as well as
usual at night - about 1 or 2 in the morning my Father
peceived some change in her breathing and endeavored to wake
her, but could not. He sent in for the neighbors, but by
the time they got in she ceased to breathe, having never
awaked after she had fallen asleep on the evening before.
It was a case of lethargy. Before even I had the news for

Outfit of the vessel: preparation for sea-going, from everything
being put on board for the sailors to recoppering the bottom
to prevent decay.

one long gun on a circle forward: For the outfitting of this
vessel, guns were placed facing outward around the entire
deck. A circle forward implies the installation of a gun on
the foredeck, thereby protecting attack from that direction.
From his further reference to three circles mounted, he
refers to the system by which a cannon is mounted on a
circular frame.   (Ed. note)

Gun carriages and mounts: Due to the size and weight of cannons
and cannonades, they were equipped with a system of ropes and
pulleys so they could turn almost half a circle in the middle
of battle with least amount of effort. The mounts were
necessary to support the cannon at the height of the port
hole for firing accurately. The backfire of these guns were
also stabilized by this system since they could rip across
the deck easily if not secured in some way. (Ed note)

Salem

Mass.

ATLANTIC
OCEAN

New York

Sandy
Hook

Brig Friend

Schooner
William

Schooner
Lord Ponsonby

Schooner Hope

Schooner Joseph

Schooner Margaret

Schooner Mary

Bermuda

CR '79

Schooner: DIOMEDE

Port: New York

Master: J. Crowninshield

Departure: February 9, 1814

Return: March 8, 1814

Time: 30 days

Map Boundaries Circa 1783

the mails were 4 or 5 days on the route at this time, her funeral had taken place, so I concluded to make no change in my plans.

Our officers were besides Capt. Crowninshield as Commander, and myself as clerk, Saml. Briggs, 1st Lieut., Rich. Downing, 2nd Lieut. John Dumpsey 3rd Lt. Joseph Preston sailing master. Parsons surgeon, Jos. Strout, Saml. Upton, Geo. Laffesty, Obed Hursey, Chas. Leach, Thos. Cloutman prize masters, and 55 men, making 67 persons all told on board. We proceeded at once to the anchorage at Sandy Hook and lay there waiting for the absence of British men of war, to give us a chance to get out, till the 9th inst. when we sailed and proceeded towards Bermuda.

On the 17th we fell in with a British wargun Brig and outsailed her easily, thus giving us confidence in the sailing qualities of the 'Diomede'. On the 21st captured Br. sch. 'Lord Ponsonby', cargo rum, sugar, coffee and cocoa. Put on board Chas. Leach as prize master and 6 men and ordered her for the U. States.

Early in the morning of the 23rd heard report of a gun and steered in the direction from which it came. At daylight saw a fleet of fine vessels. In the course of the day captured the whole of them. They proved to be Schooners 'William', 'Joseph' & 'Mary', 'Margaret', 'Hope' & Brig 'Friends' - all with cargoes of rum, sugar, etc. from St. Thomas bound to Nova Scotia - manned them out putting on board Jos. Strout, Saml. Upton Jr. - Geo. Lafferty, Obed Hussey & Thos. Clausman as prize masters, and ordered them for the U.S. These vessels had parted with their convoy H.M. Brig. 'Carybdis' the day before their capture and the gun we heard was from one of them that undertook to act as commodore.

We proceeded on our cruise, but of course quite short handed. On the 26th fell in with a "74" but lost sight of her in the night. On the 27th chased by a Frigate which having the weather gauge of us and it blowing a gale, came

Sandy Hook; located just south of Manhattan Island, now New York City. It was an ideal departure point for seagoing vessels, being a penninsula protecting the bay beside it. (Ed. note)

Prize Master: a member of an American Privateer who is an officer whose sole duties are to take charge of the captured ships (British) and sail them back to the closest American port so that the goods can be sold. According to rank, the money is divided between each crew member of the privateer for his efforts in the capture, in lieu of regular pay. (Ed. note)

Fell in with.....another ship: This term applies to a ship, in trying to overtake another one, tried to get in line with her wind and direction so that they would be sailing parallel to one another. However, if the circumstances involves a proposed capture, the ship that is upwind, having got enough speed up can cut across the ship that is downwind and demobilize her completely. Combined with gun fire, this is a very effective procedure since a ship with wind always had the advantage to one without (in irons and standing still). (OCSS)

Having the weather gauge of us: This term is in association with 'falling in with another ship' in that the second ship that is coming up from behind has managed to sail under the same wind and is the weather gauge of the first. More precisely, the ship having the weather gauge is upwind and very likely to overtake the first.

It must be taken into account that these battles were not won and lost by the toss of a coin though his brevity might infer just that. The biggest advantage that the Americans had over the British was the use of volunteer trained crewmen whereas the British used impressed (enslaved) men to man their many naval ships. Thus co-operation had a great deal to do with it. Also the British Navy, for all the size and weight of its battle ships, was extremely clumsy and could not outmanoeuver American vessles, no matter how they tried. Having a good wind, however and the right circumstances, they could outrun a privateer. (Ed. note)

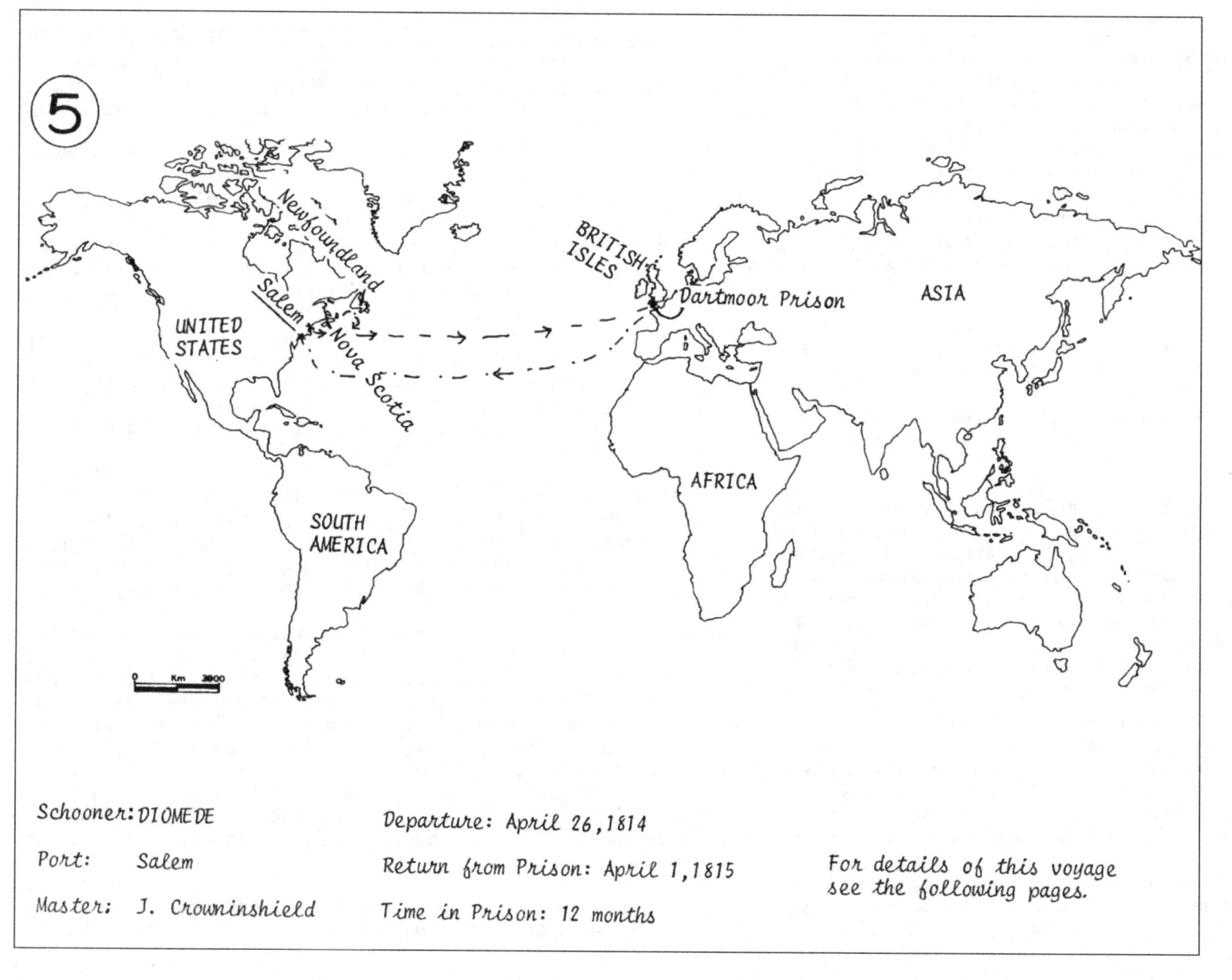

88

⑤

Newfoundland

Salem

Nova Scotia

UNITED STATES

SOUTH AMERICA

BRITISH ISLES

Dartmoor Prison

ASIA

AFRICA

0   Km   3200

Schooner: DIOMEDE

Port: Salem

Master: J. Crowninshield

Departure: April 26, 1814

Return from Prison: April 1, 1815

Time in Prison: 12 months

For details of this voyage
see the following pages.

upon us until we threw overboard our lee six pounders. Some provisions, spars boat, shot wood etc. after which we left her. At noon in a heavy squall we sprung our main mast in the partners. Next day nothing in sight - fished the mast and laid our course for the United States and on the 8th of March after just one month's cruise, arrived in Salem. It had been short and successful but I was disappointed that we had not reached Europe as originally intended, but hoped for better luck the next time. Several of our prizes arrived safe in different parts of the United States. The Schooner was refitted and we sailed on her second cruise with pretty much the same officers on the 26th of April 1814.

Second Cruise Schooner 'Diomede' 1814

This time we steered for the Nova Scotia shore. On the 29th chased a Brig into a port just east of Cape Negro, which is between Cape Sable and Shelbourne. Scuttled her. Next day recaptured a Spanish Brig detained by and Eng. Cruiser. May 3rd had an exciting chase by a Br. "74". We were near the land, the wind directly off shore and the ship outside of us. We of course could not keep our wind and must cross his bows, taking the outside of a circle, while he was steering on a straight line. After seven hours chase we brought him into our wake, and then soon left him, he was giving us 2 or 3 bow guns, but their shot fell short. We supposed it was the Victorious Line of Battle Ships. On the 5th we stood into Sydney harbour in chase of a Brig, till we saw a battery on the shore, when we about ship and stood out, Cape North and the island of St. Pauls in sight, the land covered with snow. On the 8th we run into a bay and sent a boat ashore for wood and water, which we obtained.

On the 11th off Miquelon Island & surrounded by fishing boats stood in among the islands in Placentia bay off Cape Chapeau Rouge & into Great St. Lawrence harbour, but finding the inhabitants were flying from the village and not wishing to alarm them, hove round and beat out. Cruised about in the fog, doing nothing till the 21st, when we captured, after and hour's action Ship 'Upton' of 6 guns and 15 men,

threw overboard our lee 6 pounders: This was done to lighten the ship and pick up speed. The lee 6 pounders were cannons shooting 6 pound cannonballs that were located on the lee side as opposed to the windward side during this encounter. (OCSS)

Sprung our main mast to the partners: Springing the mast is to drop the main mast to a height no greater than the other two masts, possibly to the level of the partners. Partners, means the hole that the mast comes up through the deck at. The masts were made in three parts and, considering the storm while this procedure is taking place, the logical solution seems to be the operation of taking the main mast out of its frame work and with lines, etc. intact, bringing it down and securing it on deck. (Ed. note)

Fished the Mast: Putting the mast back in place and securing it. (Ed. note)

refitted: to outfit a vessel

scuttled her: deliberately to sink a ship by opening her seacocks or scuttles (portholes), or by blowing holes in her bottom with explosive charges so that she fills with water (OCSS)

wake: the calm water that follows a vessel's path (OCSS)

Victorious Line of Battle Ships: a British vessel (OCSS)

battery: a whole armament of guns mounted on a vessel of war (ACW)

stood out: left the shore-line (OCSS)

hove round: as inconspicuously as possible left the area (OCSS)

90

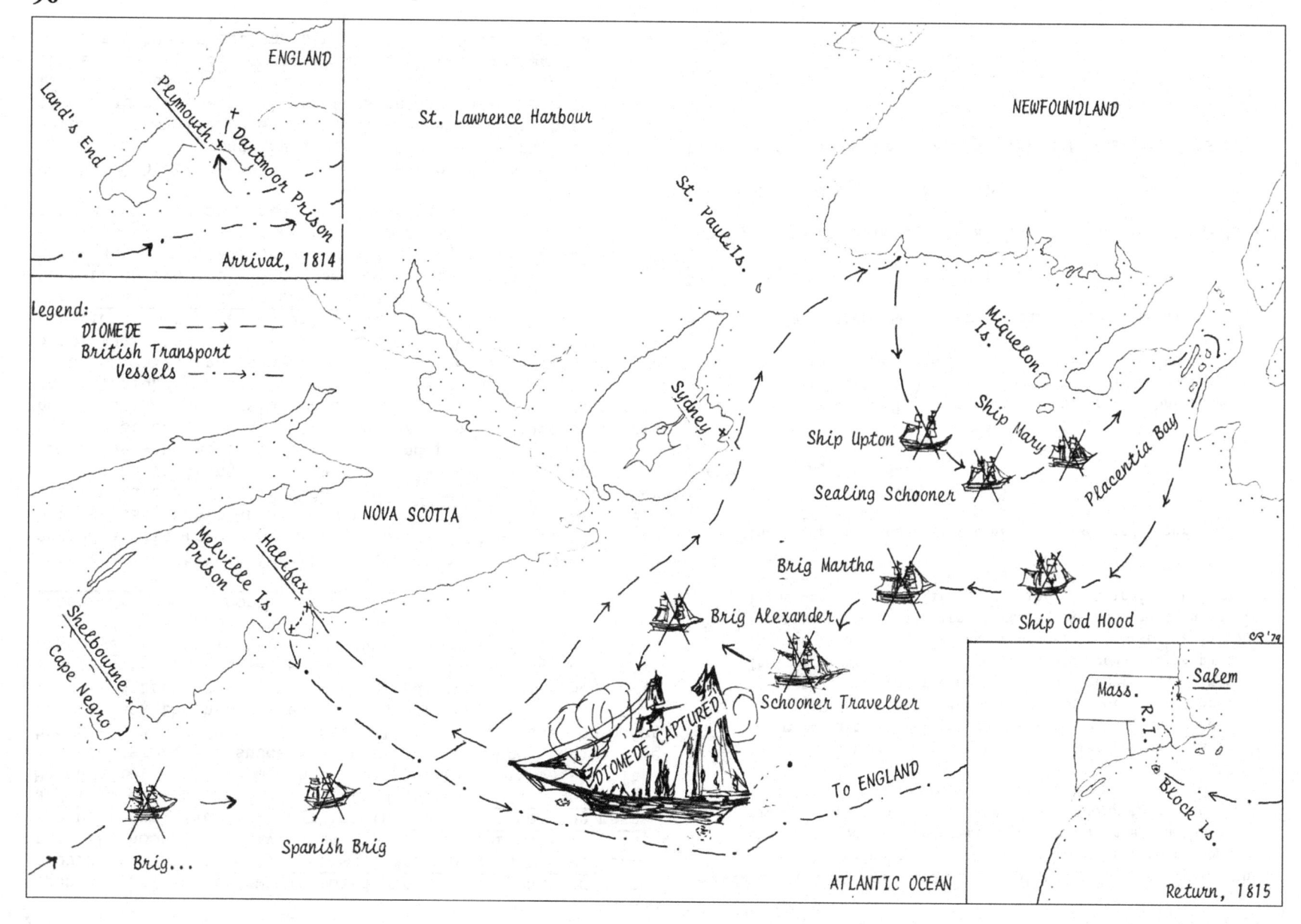

with 90 Irish passengers - one man killed and one wounded on board her. We sustained no injury. In the afternoon took a sealing schooner and put the passengers and part of the crew of the 'Upton' on board and released her. Sent the ship with Henry Jaques as prize master to U.S.

22nd captured ship 'Mary' with 3,100 bbls. flour and 20 pipes wine. Put Sam Upton on board as prize master and ordered her for the U.S. Same day was decoyed within musket shot of an English Sloop of war disguised. He threw shot over us for an hour, without doing us any injury, but we beat him and finally lost him in the fog.

24th captured ship 'Cod Hood' and sent Obed Hussey in her as prize master to U.S. Also took Brig 'Martha' in ballast which we gave up.

26th had an action with a ship but being short of ammunition and there being two other vessels in sight left her and took them, but they were in ballast and we scuttled them.

27th captured Sch. 'Traveller', cargo rum. Put on board Wm. Tucker as prize master and ordered her to the U.S. Also took Brig 'Alexander', in ballast, gave her up.

28th afternoon - chased by Brig Sloop of war - 'Smartchap of a Sea' - she gained on us, but we lost sight of her in the night-after which we lay bye. Next morning fell in with her again in a thick fog, close aboard and to windward - made sail on a wind in hopes to be able to cross her bows, but she was too near and the captain then ordered her to be put before the wind. The Brig was pouring her broadsides into us and the officers mostly and almost all the men run below. Capt. ordered and begged them to come up in vain - he had the helm himself - I went and offered to take it - he told me to bring up the signal bag ready for throwing it overboard and to try to get the officers to come up. I found them at work at their chests, and could not start them - went up with the signals, but shot in the bag when the Brig being close along side, I threw them over, and we

pipe of wine: cask containing wine, if a standard size, 126 gallons (ACW)

disguised: carried American flags though a British vessel to get within range of an American vessel to fire on her (OCSS)

gave her up: same as scuttled her, to sink her (OCSS)

lay bye: to proceed on course without tacking (taking: a zig-zagging motion used to make the most of the wind) (OCSS)

pouring her broadsides into us: firing all the guns located on her broadside (OCSS)

signal bag: this could be presumed to contain 4 signal letters assigned to a ship under the rules of the International Code of Signals so that the ship could be easily recognized for insurance purposes. Also called "making her number" Since he threw them overboard at the last minute it is possible that he meant the letters to be picked up by another American vessel to take home for the records (OCSS p. 801)

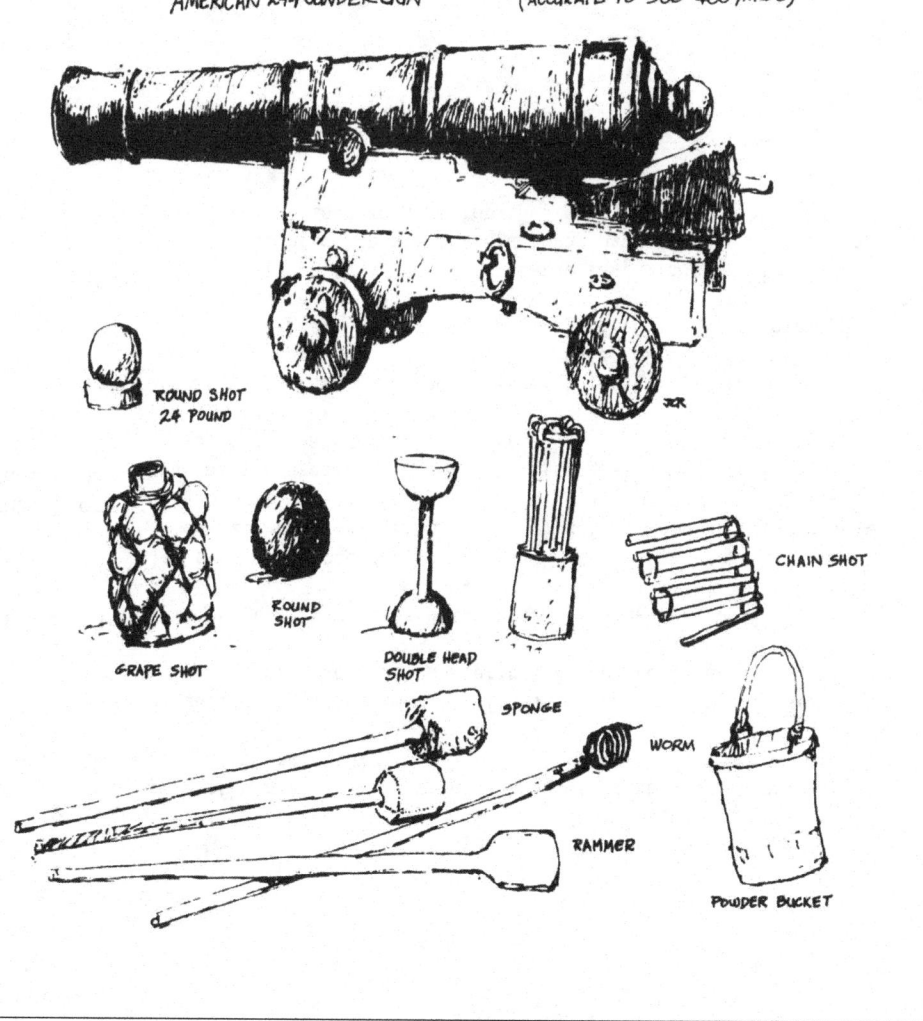

WEIGHT, ABOUT 6,500 POUNDS
POWDER CHARGE, 8 LBS.
MAXIMUM RANGE, ABOUT 1,500 YARDS
(ACCURATE TO 300-400 YARDS)

AMERICAN 24-POUNDER GUN

ROUND SHOT
24 POUND

GRAPE SHOT

ROUND SHOT

DOUBLE HEAD SHOT

CHAIN SHOT

SPONGE

WORM

RAMMER

POWDER BUCKET

93

struck to H.M. Brig 'Rifleman', Capt. Peace of 16 guns. It
is not probable that anything could have been done, after
falling in with this vessel so near aboard, to have
prevented the capture, but it would have been more
satisfactory if the officers had shown some of the pluck of
the commander, and at least have made some effort to obey
his orders. When we saw her we were laying with our ------
peak dropped and helm hard down. The Capt. said at once it
is the same vessel that beat us yesterday before the wind.
We must get the wind of her, and made the attempt, but we
could not forereach enough and was running directly into her
when he put the helm up and ordered the sheets eased off and
sail made. But there was nobody to do it. My station was
on the trunk in action or in chase to note down every
manoeuvre or order. I took it as soon as I got on deck,
after the vessel was seen, and left it only to go to offer
to take the helm, when he directed me as above and the
surrender took place immediately after.

struck to: pulled up along side (OCSS)

Prisoners Arrival At Halifax 1814

It will be only just in this place to exonerate from the
obloquy thrown on the officers of the 'Diomede' in the
preceeding relation, the 3rd Lieut. Dempsey and the sailing
master Preston, who both stood to their stations firmly,
during the whole time and did all they could to carry out
the orders of the commander. Every one of the officers, and
probably every soul then on board the vessel, but myself,
are now dead; I am I know the only surviving officer, and am
sorry to be obliged in thus giving a truthful relations to
cast what may be considered a stigma on the memory of my
shipmates. It must be considered however that courage often
depends on circumstances and that in this case the desire to
save their valuables, when there was no hope of escape, may
have been as predominant as fear of the grape shot that was
passing over, but as we were so near, did not strike on our
decks.

grape shot: A type of cannon fire; a metal cylinder full of iron
pellets or similar size weights, very deadly because the shot
goes in many different directions. A simple cannon ball
would be first used to pierce the sails and the grape shot
would follow to kill the men on board (OCSS)

Immediately after the surrender we were all, except the
surgeon and a few of the men, transferred to the 'Rifleman'.

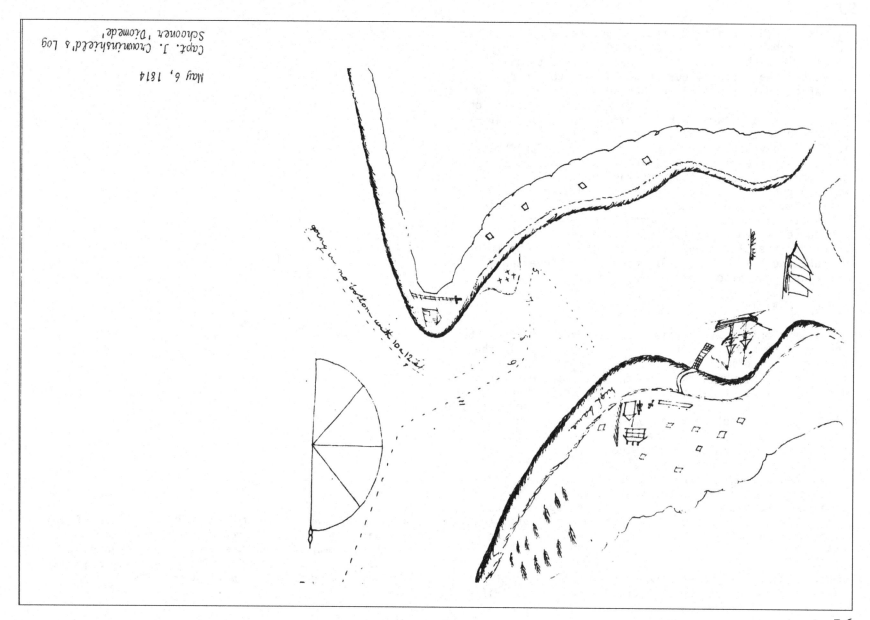

May 6, 1814
Capt. J. Crowninshield's Log
Schooner 'Diomede'

94

95

two lavit fishing houses

May 12, 1814

Capt. J. Crowninshield's Log
Schooner 'Diomede'

Crowninshield, Capt. John, "Diomede" Log Book, April 1814

- 56 men and boys, passed by Cape Ann
- recaptured 2 Spanish brigs, destroyed 3 brigs, gave up 2 brigs and 1 schooner, captured and manned 3 ships and 1 schooner: 12 total
- 33 prisoners on board when captured
- April 29, 1814: chased the Brig. "Recovery", North Perry, into Cape Negro Harbour (Nova Scotia), he run on shore, sent the boat being empty, dismasted and destroyed her, laid clos't along side her with the 'Diomede,' came out and laid to off the cape and caught fish till the dark then bore up easterly Shelbourne light house, north East
- May 6, 1814 we were running down the shore from Cape Breton NW by N and this was the first opening we had perceived and lufted up into and saw a large light brig and laying there lost under a fort, went in as far as prudence could justify then hove about for the other side as far from the guns as possible then bore out and run out and passed the shore a long N by E for Cape North and made it at sun down and also St. Pauls at N by E .. Port Sidney or Spanish Harbour

- May 12, Thurs. stood into the Great St. Lawrence quite up to the village above where the Man of War generally anchored and we soon perceived that the inhabitants were running from the place in all directions men and women with their bags on their backs then instantly hove about then running with only the main sail and had to hoist the Jibbs (sails) while luffing at the risk of missing stays and going on shore - not wishing to hurt them or their prperty in the least beat out - it is very narrow perticularly up at the head of the harbour we made 9 or 10 tacks before we were clear out from Chapeau Rouge - my intentions were to get water but thinking from what was perceived that the inhabitants might threw fear be induced, turned immediately and came out - we want the rich man's property, we are not to make poverty still poorer - discharged the fishing boat and gave him some small stores and to tell the people on shore the reason we came out and boat went in, there were only a few small boats in the place and it looks very poor indeed

Privateer General Armstrong
Being Boarded Sept. 26, 1814

Capt. Crowninshield was invited to mess with the Lieutenants in the ward room, and to take with him any one of his officers that he chose, and he chose me. The other officers were accommodated with the midshipmen and the men allowed to go free among the crew of the Brig. All our personal effects were delivered to us without search and we were treated both by the captain and the officers with great kindness. After the capture of the 'Diomede' the Sea became smoother and we found she would beat the 'Rifleman', either before or in the wind. The two vessels proceeded in company to Halifax where we arrived on the 31st May 1814. Our privateer was too small to allow, under the rules, the officers to remain on parole, but an exception was made in favor of Capt. Crowninshield in consideration of the kindness he had shown to the prisoners taken by himself. All the rest of us were sent to Melville Island prison on the 2nd of June. Some of us hired a carriage and drove to it passing through the town - the men were marched there in a body. On the 8th I was 21 years of age and of course passed the day I became legally free within the walls of a British prison.

Melville Island Prison, Transport Ship 'Benson' Sent To England

Having some money with me I was not altogether dependent on the prison fare, but it was not always easy to obtain what we required even by paying for it. At this time all exchange of prisoners between the two countries had been stopped, at least in relation to persons taken in Ships of War and privateers and the policy of Great Britain seemed to be to concentrate all such in one depot in England. Accordingly on the 11th of July I was included in a draft of about 200 and sent from Melville Island on board a transport ship called the 'Benson', and ordered for England under convoy of H.M. 'Razie Goliath' of 60 guns. Capt. F.F. Maitland. We sailed on the 13th. The ships company of the 'Benson' consisted of about 30 men. There was also on board, to secure the prisoners, a detachment of some 25 or 30 Marines, under charge of two lieutenants. About a dozen

Boarding and Taking of the
American Ship Chesapeake
by the Officers and Crew
of the Shannon June 1, 1813

British Navy officers going home on furlough were passengers. The prisoners were all confined together in the Between decks. The main hatch was strongly secured by gratings with room for one only to come up at a time. Not more than two were allowed to be on deck at once. The ship's crew lived in the middle steerage the marines in the fore castle, the passengers of course with the captain and officers in the Great Cabin. We knew that we largely outnumbered the British and that we should at this season have thick fogs when we got to the Banks of Newfoundland. If we could get out of the way of the convoy, there would be a fair chance of getting possession of the ship, even without any arms, but those that nature had given us, if we could depend on only one half of the prisoners. It was therefore determined to make the attempt and if we succeeded to proceed either to the western islands or the United States as the winds might favor..

On the afternoon and night of the 18th of July we were on the Banks and enveloped with thick fog. The convoy kept ahead but indicated her position by firing signal guns.

We watched the sound all night, the wind strong from the west. At daylight on the 19th the report of the guns gradually died away in the distance, indicating that the 'Goliath' had ranged ahead out of our immediate vicinity. The fog was of intense thickness. Two of the prisoners were on deck. A preconcerted signal was given by them and almost at the same instant and while 3 or 4 of us were getting up through the opening in the hatchway, a volley of musketry came from a party of· marines who had been concealed under a sail on the quarter deck. It was evident we had been betrayed and this at once cooled the courage of some and afforded an excuse to themselves of others who had none, but who had been foremost in talk at least, in promoting the attempt. Out of the 200 I think only about 9 persevered in gaining the deck. Of these some 5 or 6 rushed aft, as had been arranged, to close over the companion way and the after hatch by which last access was had to the steerage. My place was to be (with others who did not come up) on the

Between Decks: the space contained between any two whole decks of a ship. The term has become widely associated with the streerage of passenger vessels, the space below decks in which passengers, and particularly emigrants, who could not afford cabins, travelled, often in conditions of gross overcrowding and discomfort. (OCSS p. 81)

middle steerage: a large space below deck. The sides were lined with wooden bunks, and often with one or more tiers of bunks running longitudinally in the space between the sides (OCSS p. 831)

Forecastle: Indicates the living space of the crew, for many years in the forward end of the ship below the forecastle deck (OCSS p. 320)

Great Cabin: place where the captain would have his quarters, often an office as well as a sleeping area (OCSS p. 125)

The following is a newspaper account of this same incident, possibly from the Salem Gazette. It was glued into the 'Neal Record' that had followed all the family doings i.e. marriages, deaths, births beyond the dates it was printed.
Reprinted at the time of Neal's Death, 1861

An Incident In the Life of David A. Neal

During the imprisonment of the writer at Darmoor, in part of the years 1814 and 15, he had his mess contiguous to that of the late Mr. Neal, who was then suffering much from the effects of his wound. Mr. N. said but little himself of the affair, but from other participants in it, the facts were learned which are embodied in the following narrative. A series of papers, written by me, was published in the Democratic Review in 1846, which contained the narrative, but perhaps its republication at this time may be interesting in this community in which Mr. N. lived and was so well known. B.F.B.

In the midsummer of 1814, two hundred and fifty prisoners were removed from the prison at Melville Island near Halifax and were sent on board of four transport vessels for England, under convoy of the 'Goliath', a razed seventy-four carrying 56 guns and commanded by Captain Frederick L. Maitland, who afterwards commanded the Bellerophon 74, and to whom Napoleon surrendered himself after his final abdication. Among these prisoners were most of the officers and crew of the privateer 'Diomeded', late of Salem, including Mr. Neal.

After being at sea two or three days, the prisoners on board one of the transport vessels perceived, when they were on deck-which they were permitted to be one at a time-that the weather was almost continually foggy, they being on the banks of Newfoundland, and that the 'Goliath' was out of sight; as were also the other vessels, for five or six hours at a time. Some of the more daring, who had reconnoitred the crew and marines closely while on deck, and saw that they felt under no appehensions of a revolt, and were consequently on their guard, conceived a project of regaining their freedom by capturing the vessel. When below, they proposed to their fellow prisoners to rush up and take possession of the ship at once.

Now there is very little doubt that, had they done so, they would have succeeded and most of them agreed to the proposition, and sprang on their feet for immediate action; but one or two who had been officers of privateers and who as the event proved, considered 'discretion to be the better part of valor', dissuaded those who were for immediate action and proposed to lay some plan and then go to work systematically on some future day.

Then then consulted together, and agreed that the first day when the fog was dense enough to obscure them from the view of the other ships, they would make the attempt. The plan was, for one man to go on deck and reconnoitre, and if the prospect was good, to seize the sentinel at the hatchway and cry "Keno", as a watchword for the others to rush up. It was three or four days before the attempts was made, and in the meanwhile they had divided themselves into parties, to each of which some specific duty had been assigned. One party was to guard the quarter-deck, and secure the companion-way and helmsman; another was to secure the fore-hatchway, where the marines were berthed; and another was to take charge of the forecastle and secure the scuttle, to keep the watch below from gaining the deck.

But during all this discussion and hatching of plots the courage of some, who, from their position, should have been leaders, being of the Bob Acres kind, oozed out and worse than all there was treason in the camp. A foreigner, who had been a carpenter of a privateer, gave information to the captain of the ship of what was going on among the prisoners; and in consequence he adopted every precautionary measure to prevent the success of the attempt.

On the morning assigned for it, the British officers and passengers armed themselves and kept below in the cabin so as to have no unusual bustle or appearance on deck. The sailors also were privately armed, and the armed marines were concealed on the quarter-deck, being covered with an old sail.

CONTINUED ....

forecastle; in getting up through the scuttle from between decks, being just forward the main-mast on the larboard waist, I found the man who had been one of the two men who were on deck and had given the signal, struggling with a marine who had a musket in his hand and who had probably been the sentry over the hatchway. I was fortunate enough to find laying on the spars a cook's axe, and the marine finding I was about to try its force on his cranium, dropt his musket and run forward. We picked it up, I taking the bayonet and my companion the gun, and we separated, he going aft and I forward. Just then the marines from the quarter deck, or some of them, rushed by us going forward. I pursued them and hit the last one as he was jumping over the windlass. They succeeded in getting into the forecastle, when I closed over the lid, and having no other means of securing it, used the bayonet for a toggle. The forecastle was now all clear. I was there alone, from the foremast all round to the beams I was lord of the sheets and the tacks. As the ship was going before the wind all I had to do was to tend them, whenever the party aft should be ready to brace up and bring the ship to the wind, which of course was our first object, so as to increase our distance from the convoy. I had no time however to reflect much about it, for I almost instantly heard the sharp crackling report of fire arms aft, and found there was nobody coming...

Unsuccessful Wounded 1814

...forward to support me, supposing that the ship's company had succeeded in closing the scuttle and so prevented the prisoners from coming. I stepped to the larboard side, where I had left the axe, and was proceeding round the bows of the long boat to the other side in hopes to be able to break in the grating and let them up, when I saw a number of persons on the quarter deck firing carbines and pistoles in every direction, and met a man whom I presumed to be one of the Prisoners (as he really was) in shirt and trousers, struggling along with a shot hole in his left breast. I mechanically caught him as he was tottering, dropping my axe, and had just placed my right hand over the wound from

scuttle: a circular port cut in the side of a ship to admit light and air, consisting of a circular metal frame with a thick disc of glass which is hinged on one side and which can be tightly secured to the ship's side by butterfly nuts (OCSS p. 763)

larboard waist: larboard is the left side or ports waist: that part of the upper deck between the fore and mainmasts (OCSS p. 466, 922)

windlass: a type of rotary hauling device used for heavy lifting such as an anchor, similar to a capstan with handles for manual rotation but on a horizontal shaft. (OCSS p. 942)

toggle: a wooden pin through a loop, the type commonly used as buttons on duffle coats to-day. (OCSS p. 874)

brace up and bring the ship to the wind: bring the yards of the sails around to catch the best advantage of the wind. (OCSS p. 104)

'INCIDENT' Part 2

The prisoners were ignorant of the discovery of their plot and of the measures taken to frustruate its execution. The spy from on deck reported no unusual appearance and that the weather was favorable, and they resolved to make their attempt for freedom.

Accordingly an active, daring young man, named Obed Hussey of Maine, who had been Captain of the fore-top on board the 'Diomede', went on deck and proceeded to the head, and while there, observing that the convoy was not in sight, returned to the hatch-way as if to descend into the hold as usual, but timing his movements in such a manner as to arrive at the hatch just as the sentinel turned his back toward him to walk aft, Hussey grasped him, calling out, "Keno"; and had his musket from him in an instant. This was executed with so much daring rapidity, that from ten to a dozen of the prisoners, - among whom was Mr. Neal, - gained the deck before the British had time to recover from the surprise; and if those who assumed to be leaders, and who had talked most valorously during the plotting, had shown the same spirit as those daring fellows who gained the deck, the issure might have been different from what it was. But those men of brave words but small deeds showed the white feather and the others, seeing that those they relied upon to head them, hung back, immediately retreated into the hold, and left those on deck to the tender mercies of the British.

Meanwhile the party on deck proceeded forward and secured the fore-scuttle, and were proceeding to secure the fore-hatchway, when they found the officers and passengers rushing on dek from the cabin, with arms in their hands, and at the same time they received a volley from the marines who had formed on the quarter deck and were marching forward on both sides of the deck with charged bayonets, while the officers and passengers kept up a galling fire with their pistols, etc., from behind the marines; and to their utter astonishment, they found themselves unsupported by their fellow captives. A young man belonging to Baltimore named John Nantz, received a shot through both arms at the first fire; Mr. Neal caught him in his arms, and while holding his wounded comrade, received the wound which deprived him of three fingers. He then got below through the fore-hatchway, with four or five others, while such of the remainder as were not too badly wounded got out of the way in the best manner they could, by getting under the fore-channels, etc., etc. The marines, after they had cleared the deck, fined down the fore and main hatch-ways, but as the captives had got well into the wings, they hurt no one. After the British saw that all was quiet, they took those who were wounded into the cabin, where a brute in human form, who called himself a surgeon, operated on the, cutting off one of the arms of Nantz and three fingers of Mr. Neal, with a dull knife, and during the whole time he was abusing and insulting them, and appeared to do his best to give as much pain as possible.

The fog cleared off the same day in the afternoon, when the wounded were sent on board the 'Goliath'. Her surgeon was Barry O'Meara, who was afterwards surgeon to Napoleon at St. Helena. From him they received every care and attention, and were indebted to his skill and kindness for the proper treatment of their wounds - Mr. Neal had not recovered his health when the vessel arrived in England, and he was sent to the naval hospital, near Portsmouth, till his wound was progressing favourably, when he was sent to Dartmoore.

His subsequent career, in which he displayed as much energy and activity, in his extensive business operations, as he did of valor and determination on board the transport ship where he was a poor captive, is familiar to most of your readers.

· · · · · · · · · END · · · · · · · ·

which the blood was flowing profusely, having my left behind
him, when a volley was fired at us, and a ball struck him in
the forehead and as I suppose killed him at once, as he
dropped instantly. Finding myself the only prisoner in
sight, and several persons advancing on me, and firing at
the same time I made for the fore hatch which was open and
led into the fore hold, being bulkheaded all round to
prevent communication with the between decks; and succeeded
in landing on the water casks stowed there, when I was
followed by a discharge of small arms. One shot I suppose a
slug from a carbine, took effect, shattering three fingers
of my left hand. I got out of the way, when they stopped
firing, and called out for all in the forehold to surrender
themselves. There was one other person there, but who he
was or how he got there I never knew. I got on deck, and
was taken aft with many imprecations and there of course
well guarded. By this time the 'Goliath', alarmed by some
reports from the carriage guns on board the 'Benson' and
which as we were to windward, were heard at once, lay by for
us, and was soon alongside, the first seen of her, so thick
was the fog, being her jib boom over our quarter. After the
surgeon who was attached to the marine corps. on board had
taken his time to dress the wound of the only person who was
hurt on the British side (an officer of the Navy, a captain
I believe, who was going home of furlough)...

bulkheaded: watertight divisions to separate compartments, in this
case to separate prisoners from the main areas. (OCSS p. 117)

Transfer To H.M. Ship 'Goliath', Black Hole, Doct. O'Meara

...he proceeded to dress the wounds of the prisoners. Two
if not more of our side had been killed and their bodies
thrown overboard. Another was badly wounded in the side and
he afterwards died on board the 'Goliath'. Another, John
Nants of Baltimore, a Lieutenant of a Baltimore privateer,
had both arms shattered. One the surgeon cut off and the
other splintered and bandaged. My turn came next - my
fingers were hanging by the flesh and skin, but badly
shattered. He very roughly cut them off and bound them up
in a rag, but leaving the bone ragged and projecting. All
the time cursing and swearing at me for having been the
means of one of H.M. Navy officers being made a cripple for

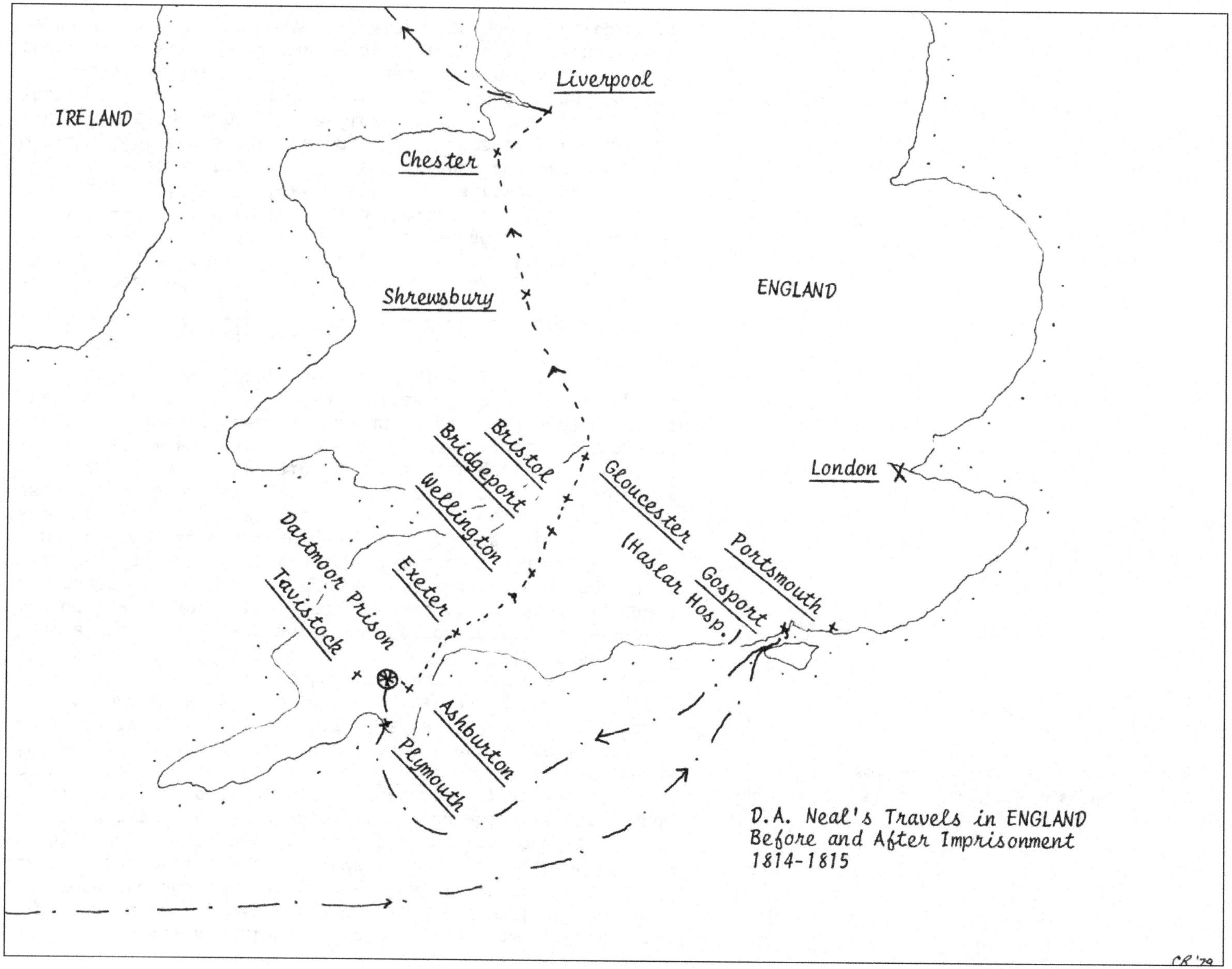

IRELAND

Liverpool

Chester

Shrewsbury

ENGLAND

Bristol
Bridgeport
Wellington

London

Gloucester

Portsmouth
Gosport
(Haslar Hosp.)

Dartmoor Prison
Exeter
Tavistock

Ashburton

Plymouth

D.A. Neal's Travels in ENGLAND
Before and After Imprisonment
1814-1815

CR '79

life. It appeared that the only shot fired, or which we had
the means of firing was from the musket which I had got from
the marine in the waist and given to the American who had
been struggling for it. This he fired and hit the above
officer in the right wrist, so that his hand had to be
amputated. From some cause or other it was evident the
officers of the marines had got the impression that the
result, as they called it, had originated with me, and when
it was decided to send some of the prisoners on board the
Goliath I was designated as the ring leader, for the other
two who were wounded were put in charge of the surgeon and
placed in the sick bay, while I with about 25 others, who
were taken, I believe, promiscuously from the prisoners in
the between decks, was put in irons and stowed away
altogether in a black hole in the lowest part of the ship,
where there was scarcely a breath of air, and the heat
excessive. From the bad state of the atmosphere I fully
expected mortification would ensue, and no doubt it would
had I not been relieved by the interposition of the surgeon
who, hearing in some way that one of the prisoners thus
incarcerated was wounded insisted that he should be sent to
the sick bay and placed under his charge. This was acceded
to with a very bad grace, by the Captain who directed that
two men with cutlasses should be constantly stationed at the
door with orders to cut me down at once, if they saw me
speak to anyone...

Treatment of the Killed & Wounded

...of the crew, or attempt to leave it for any other part of
the ship. In addition they served me out no allowance of
provision, so I was likely to be starved, if not otherwise
murdered. The Doctor however as soon as he found it out,
remedied all this. He sent me all my meals from the
wardroom so that I fared as well as the officers
themselves. He examined my wounds and pronounced the
treatment of it, as well as that of Nants' arms, to have
been disgraceful to the service and such as ought to be
reported to the Transport Board. In fact the whole conduct
of the surgeon of the 'Goliath' towards the Americans was of

NAPOLEON IN EXILE;

OR,

A Voice from St. Helena.

THE

OPINIONS AND REFLECTIONS OF

NAPOLEON

ON THE

MOST IMPORTANT EVENTS OF HIS LIFE AND GOVERNMENT,

IN HIS OWN WORDS.

By BARRY E. O'MEARA, Esq.

HIS LATE SURGEON.

ἐγὼ δὲ ταῦθ' ἅπαντ' ἠπιστάμην,
Ἑκὼν ἑκὼν ἥμαρτον, ἐκ ἀρνήσομαι·
Θνητοῖς δ' ἀρήγων, αὐτὸς εὑρόμην πόνους.
Ου μήν τι ποιναῖς γ' ᾠόμην τοιαῖσί με
Κατισχνανεῖσθαι πρὸς πέτραις πεδαρσίαις
Τυχόντ' ἐρήμου τοῦδ' ἀγείτονος πάγου.

Æsch. Prom

IN TWO VOLUMES.

VOL. I.

FOURTH EDITION.

London:

PRINTED FOR W. SIMPKIN AND R. MARSHALL,

STATIONERS'-HALL-COURT, LUDGATE-STREET.

1822.

Drawn by Mr Heffernan. from a Statue presented by the

EMPEROR NAPOLEON

to Mr O'Meara July 25 1818. Etched by T Woolnoth

the most noble character, and this will be readily accounted
for when I state that he was the Barry O'Moera who
afterwards became so distinguished as the physician and
defender of Napoleon at St. Helena. Doct. O'Moera had been
a surgeon in the army of Wellington in Spain and ranked high
in his profession, but being of a chivalrous temperament he
became in behalf of a friend involved in an affair of honor,
and was consequently obliged under the rules to quit that
service, but only to receive an appointment in the Navy, and
he was now the surgeon of the 'Goliath'. On his arrival in
England Capt. Maitland was transferred to the 'Bellerophon
74' line of battle ship and took Doct. O'Moera with him. It
is well known that the next year, 1815, Napoleon surrendered
himself a prisoner to this ship and when it was decided by
the British Government that he should be sent to St. Helena,
his own surgeon declined to accompany him. When Doct.
O'Moera promptly volunteered to take his place and he was
accepted. He remained with him until sent off by that
savage Sir Hudson Lowe, whose tool he refused to become in
annoying his illustrious patient and then he published the
work that was so much read and applauded, his journal at St.
Helena. A few days after we were transferred to the
'Goliath' the American who was wounded in the side died.
Nants, who had lost one arm, and had the other very badly
shattered was of course helpless and I having the use of my
right hand...

Affairs of Honour: This I believe to mean an armed duel. It was
illegal since it ended in some one's murder. (Ed. note)

Arrived England, Robbing, Haslar Hospital 1814

...was able to assist him materially.

We arrived at Spithead about the 4th of August and orders
were given the next day that Nants and myself should be
removed to Haslar Hospital at Gosport. My trunk had been
sent with me from the 'Benson' to the 'Goliath', but I was
not allowed to have it till it was announced that I was to
be sent on shore. It had been kept in the officers' baggage
room where it was said to be under charge of the ship's
cooper. The lock was as I left it, but on overhauling the
contents I found that all the money, consisting of about

Court Martial – at Portsmouth. – John Nants, continued

to be tried for my life, and would hardly believe me when I stated the simple facts. Whether the Lieutenants got promoted or not in consequence I never knew. My hand soon healed, but owing to the helplessness of Mr. Nants, I was allowed to remain with him until, I should think some time in October when I was sent on board the Orpheus frigate then

Dartmoor Prison – 1814.

lying at Spithead. There were on board of her a considerable number of American prisoners, who had I believe been taken the prison ships at Woolwich The ship took us to Ply-e were there marched to Dartmoor prison a dis-It is situated on a barren tract of and quite elevated. This had l and was now for s on liberated of the

twenty guineas in gold and some small articles of jewelry
had been taken out. I made complaint to Capt. Maitland who
called up the cooper to him and laid the robbery to him, or
to his neglect, assuming of course that no one of H.M.
officers of higher grade could have been guilty of the theft
and threatened if he did not account for it in 24 hours to
have him tied up and flogged. This was all a farce. Why he
did not pretend to disbelieve me I don't know, but it was
evident that he and everybody else on board knew that the
property had been stolen by some of the officers who had
free access to that room and to whom the sight of a golden
guinea at that time was a greater temptation that was likely
to be resisted by much better men than they probably were.
Accordingly before the 24 hours were expired I was
dispatched to the Hospital and learnt from persons who
afterwards left the ship that no punishment was heard of on
board.

Doct. O'Moera accompanied Nants and myself to the hospital,
and saw that we had good quarters in the same ward and left
us deeply impressed by his kindness. He called at the
hospital some months afterwards to see us, but it was after
I had been sent away. I have never met him since.

Years afterwards when I was in England I enquired for him
but could not learn his whereabouts. I have since learned
that after his return from St. Helena he married and
afterwards died in England. He was born in Ireland had been
highly educated and had all the accomplishments of a
gentleman and the principles of a man of honor.

Court Martial At Portsmouth - John Nants

The royal hospital at Gosport called Haslar is one of the
largest institutions of that kind in England and is devoted
to the sick and wounded of the Army & Navy of all ranks. It
is located in full view of the ships lying at the mother
bank Spithead, and it is said at one time during the
Peninsular War it had 5 or 6,000 patients, but then every
spare room and even the chapel was crowded. It can

Ship's Cooper: one who makes or repairs vessels, casks, wooden
constructions and thus similar to a carpenter. (ACD)

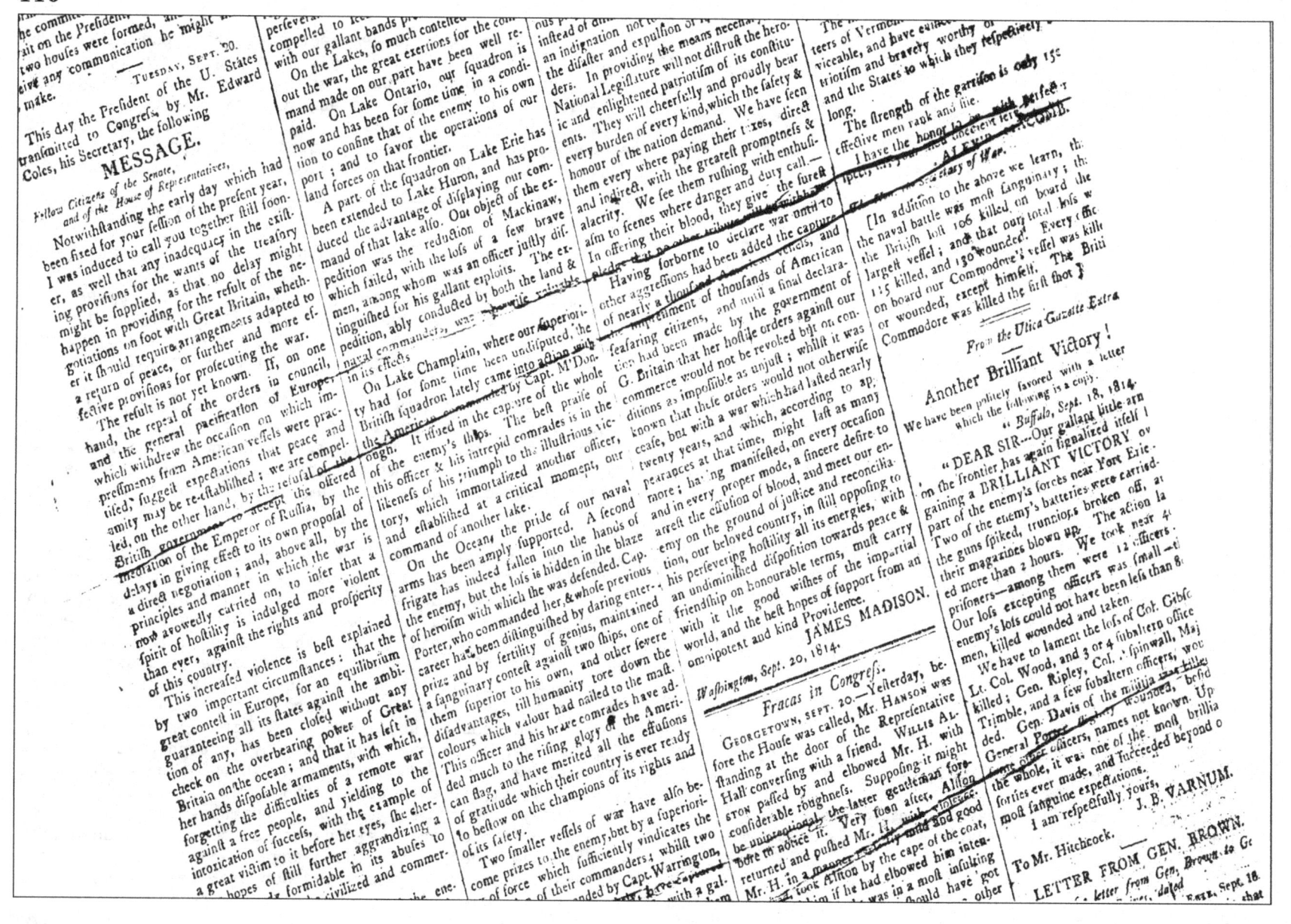

TUESDAY, SEPT. 20.

This day the President of the U. States transmitted to Congress, by Mr. Edward Coles, his Secretary, the following

MESSAGE.

Fellow Citizens of the Senate, and of the House of Representatives,

Notwithstanding the early day which had been fixed for your session of the present year, I was induced to call you together still sooner, as well that any inadequacy in the existing provisions for the wants of the treasury might be supplied, as that no delay might happen in providing for the result of the negotiations on foot with Great Britain, whether it should require arrangements adapted to a return of peace, or further and more effective provisions for prosecuting the war.

The result is not yet known. If, on one hand, the repeal of the orders in council, and the general pacification of Europe, which withdrew the occasion on which the orders were founded, had led to a corresponding pacification of American vessels were practised; suggest expectations; we are compelled, on the other hand, by the refusal of the British government to accept the offered mediation of the Emperor of Russia, by the delays in giving effect to its own proposal of a direct negotiation; and, above all, by the principles and manner in which the war is now avowedly carried on, to infer that a spirit of hostility is indulged more violent than ever, against the rights and prosperity of this country.

This increased violence is best explained by two important circumstances: that the great contest in Europe, for an equilibrium guaranteeing all its states against the ambition of any, has been closed without any check on the overbearing power of Great Britain on the ocean; and that it has left in her hands disposable armaments, with which, forgetting the difficulties of a remote war against a free people, and yielding to the intoxication of success, with the example of a great victim to it before her eyes, she cherishes hopes of still further aggrandizing a power already formidable in its abuses to the ...... civilized and commer-

perseverance ... with our gallant bands ...

On the Lakes, so much contested ... out the war, the great exertions for the command made on our part have been well repaid. On Lake Ontario, our squadron is now and has been for some time in a condition to confine that of the enemy to his own port; and to favor the operations of our land forces on that frontier.

A part of the squadron on Lake Erie has been extended to Lake Huron, and has produced the advantage of displaying our command of that lake also. One object of the expedition was the reduction of Mackinaw, which failed, with the loss of a few brave men, among whom was an officer justly distinguished for his gallant exploits. The expedition, ably conducted by ... naval commanders, was ... ... in its effects.

On Lake Champlain, where our superiority had for some time been undisputed, the British squadron lately came into action with the American ... commanded by Capt. M'Donough. It issued in the capture of the whole of the enemy's ships. The best praise of this officer & his intrepid comrades is in the likeness of his triumph to the illustrious victory, which immortalized another officer, and established at a critical moment, our command of another lake.

On the Ocean, the pride of our naval arms has been amply supported. A second frigate has indeed fallen into the hands of the enemy, but the loss is hidden in the blaze of heroism with which she was defended. Capt. Porter, who commanded her, & whose previous career had been distinguished by daring enterprize and by fertility of genius, maintained a sanguinary contest against two ships, one of them superior to his own, and other severe disadvantages, till humanity tore down the colours which valour had nailed to the mast. This officer and his brave comrades have added much to the rising glory of the American flag, and have merited all the effusions of gratitude which their country is ever ready to bestow on the champions of its rights and of its safety.

Two smaller vessels of war have also become prizes to the enemy, but by a superiority which sufficiently vindicates the ... of force ... of their commanders; whilst two ... commanded by Capt. Warrington ... with a gal-

instead of ... an indignation not to ... the disaster and expulsion of ... ders. In providing the means necessary the National Legislature will not distrust the heroic and enlightened patriotism of its constituents. They will cheerfully and proudly bear every burden of every kind, which the safety & honour of the nation demand. We have seen them every where paying their taxes, direct and indirect, with the greatest promptness & alacrity. We see them rushing with enthusiasm to scenes where danger and duty call. In offering their blood, they give the surest ... pledge ...

Having forborne to declare war until to other aggressions had been added the capture of nearly a thousand ... vessels, and the impressment of thousands of American seafaring citizens, and until a final declaration had been made by the government of G. Britain that her hostile orders against our commerce would not be revoked but on conditions as impossible as unjust; whilst it was known that these orders would not otherwise cease, but with a war which had lasted nearly twenty years, and which, according to appearances at that time, might last as many more; having manifested, on every occasion and in every proper mode, a sincere desire to arrest the effusion of blood, and meet our enemy on the ground of justice and reconciliation, our beloved country, in still opposing to his persevering hostility all its energies, with an undiminished disposition towards peace & friendship on honourable terms, must carry with it the good wishes of the impartial world, and the best hopes of support from an omnipotent and kind Providence.

JAMES MADISON.

Washington, Sept. 20, 1814.

Fracas in Congress.

GEORGETOWN, SEPT. 20.—Yesterday, before the House was called, Mr. HANSON was standing at the door of the Representative Hall conversing with a friend. WILLIS ALSTON passed by and elbowed Mr. H. with considerable roughness. Supposing it might be unintentional, the latter gentleman forbore to notice it. Very soon after, Alston returned and pushed Mr. H. in a ... Mr. H. in a manner ... and good Alston by the cape of the coat, ... him if he had elbowed him intentionally ... was in a most insulting ... should have got ... other

teers of Vermont ... viceable, and have evinced ... triotism and bravery worthy of ... and the States to which they respectively ... long.

The strength of the garrison is only 15 effective men rank and file ... ... I have the honor to be ...

ALEX ... ...

Secretary of War.

[In addition to the above we learn, the naval battle was most sanguinary; the British lost 106 killed on board the largest vessel, and that our total loss was 1 ; 5 killed, and 130 wounded. Every officer on board our Commodore's vessel was killed or wounded, except himself. The British Commodore was killed the first shot]

From the Utica Gazette Extra

Another Brilliant Victory!

We have been politely favored with a letter which the following is a copy.

"*Buffalo, Sept. 18, 1814.*

"DEAR SIR—Our gallant little army on the frontier has again signalized itself in gaining a BRILLIANT VICTORY over part of the enemy's forces near Fort Erie. Two of the enemy's batteries were carried, the guns spiked, trunnions broken off, and their magazines blown up. The action lasted more than 2 hours. We took near 400 prisoners—among them were 12 officers. Our loss excepting officers was small—the enemy's loss could not have been less than 800 men, killed wounded and taken.

We have to lament the loss of Col. Gibson. Lt. Col. Wood, and 3 or 4 subaltern officers killed; Gen. Ripley, Col. Aspinwall, Maj. Trimble, and a few subaltern officers, wounded. Gen. Davis of the militia was killed. General Porter slightly wounded. Up ... some other officers, names not known. Upon the whole, it was one of the most brilliant sorties ever made, and succeeded beyond our most sanguine expectations.

I am respectfully, yours,

J. B. VARNUM.

To Mr. Hitchcock.

LETTER FROM GEN. BROWN.

... letter from Gen. Brown to Ge ... ... dated ... Sept. 18 ... that

comfortably accommodate 2 or perhaps 3,000. It had a
Governor, Steward, clerk and several surgeons and surgeon's
mates, with any quantity of nurses both male and female and
the other subordinates. The walls which enclose the
buildings and spacious grounds for exercise are guarded by
soldiers to prevent desertion or escape. The fare was good,
but being wounded I was kept on a low diet, but having a
credit on Saml. Williams, Esq. my Father's banker, I was
enabled to get what pocket money I wanted, though it had all
to be obtained through the officers or with their
knowledge. In this way however I had the means and could
obtain from the nurses what I wanted as meats, beer, wine,
etc.

Soon after I entered Haslar a court martial was held at
Portsmouth on the two marine officers who were in charge of
the detachment on board the Benson. It was got up of course
for the glorification, not the justification of those
gentlemen and judging from the reports of the evidence
published, one would infer that they had been engaged in a
most perilous conflict with the whole 200 Americans on board
the transport instead of some half a dozen unarmed men. The
British officers who were in the hospital and with whom I
frequently conversed asked me if I did not expect to be
tried for my life, and would hardly believe me when I stated
the simple facts. Whether the Lieutenants got promoted or
not in consequence I never knew. My hand soon healed, but
owing to the helplessness of Mr. Nants, I was allowed to
remain with him until I should think some time in October
when I was sent on board the 'Orpheus' frigate then...

Dartmoor Prison - 1814

...lying at Spithead. There were on board of her a
considerable number of American prisoners who had I believe
been taken from the prison ships at Woolwich. The ship took
us to Plymouth and we were there marched to Dartmoor prison,
a distance of 15 or 20 miles. It is situated on a barren
tract of country as its name implies and quite elevated.
This had been the general depot for the French and was now

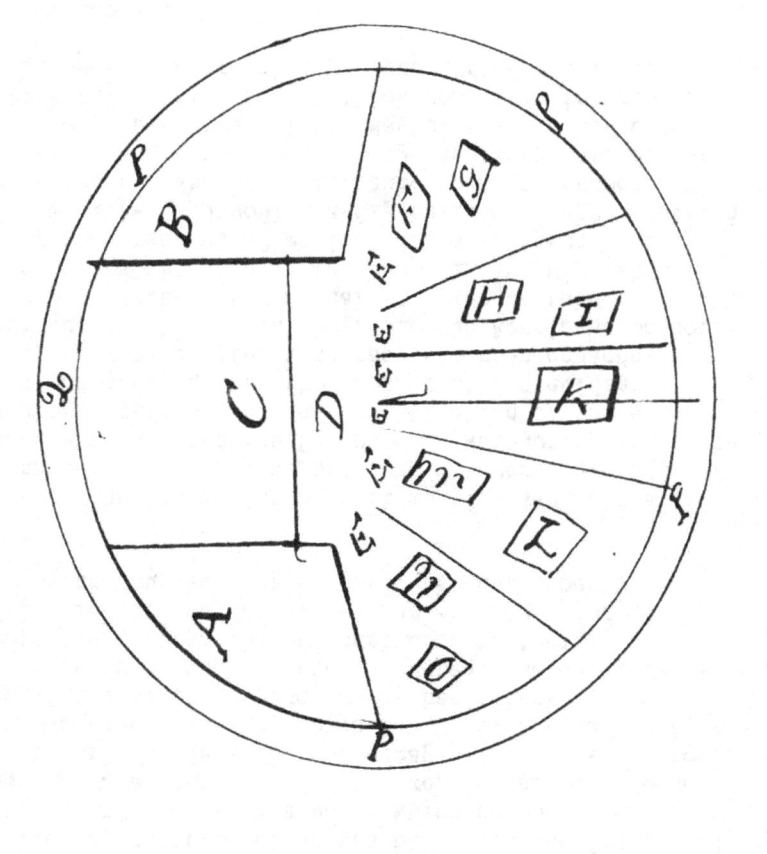

David A. Neal's Sketch of Dartmoor Prison

A	Squad Houses
B	Officer's Quarters
C	Parade Ground
D	Market Area and Main Entrance
E	Gates
F	Prison #1
G	" #2
H	" #3
I	" #4
K	" #5 (J omitted)
L	" #6
M	" #7
N	" #8
O	" #9
P	Military Walk

for the American prisoners. The former had been liberated a short time before my arrival there, in consequence of the conquest of Paris by the Allies in March, and the subsequent restoration of the Bourbons in April of this year 1814.

There were now nearly 6,000 Americans confined here, among them some 1,500 or 2,000 who had been discharged from the British Navy, having been impressed from under the American flag, or having other evidence of their nationality. There were nine prisons all enclosed by two circular walls, having a space of some 50 feet between them. There were six guards separated by high walls, in each of which were two prisons, except the two centre ones which had been made by dividing one yard and one prison by a wall to separate the American from the French prisoners. One part of it was now used for the blacks. All these yards converged to a common point where the gates opened into an area or court where was held the market and in which also was situated the officers and guard houses etc. The following is nearly the form and plan of this celebrated depot. (See facing page.)

Under ordinary circumstances the prisoners were allowed during the day to go freely from one yard to another and to purchase anything in the market except intoxicating liquors, but these were clandestinely introduced in any required quantities, and apparently not objected to by the officers who on their tours of inspection could not help seeing them spread out for sale. The market was well supplied with provisions by the people from...

Prison Fare & Treatment Quarrels

...the neighboring country, and anything could be ordered from the towns of Tavistock and Ashburton in the vicinity. The Am. Government paid to each prisoner monthly 6/8 sterling and as there were 6,000 prisoners, 2,000 British pounds sterling monthly was obtained from this source alone. Then many of the men discharged from the British men of war received considerable sums for wages and prize money. Some did work, such as braiding straw etc. which

1A Prison.
2A   ,,
3A   ,,
4A   ,,
5A   ,,
6A   ,,   (New Building).
7A   ,,   ,,
B   Cookeries.
C   Cachot or Dungeon.
D   Watch-houses.
E   Basins.
F   Petty Officers' Prison.
G   Market-place.
H   Hospital.
I   Receiving-house.
J   Pharmacy.
K   Bathing-place.
L   Matron's House.
M   Washing-house.
N   Storage.
N   Store-houses.
O   Storage.
P   Jailor's Lodgings
Q   ,,   Lodge.
R1 Mr. Holmden's (Clerk) House.
R2 Mr. Bennet's House.
R3 Mr. Winkworth's House.

S   Captain Cotgrave's House.
T   Agent's Office.
U   ,,   Garden.
V   Doctor's House.
W   ,,   Garden.
X   Stables.
Y   Reservoir.
Z   Barracks.
1   Mr. Carpenter's House.
2   Bakehouse.
3   Bell.
4   Miller's House.
5   Burial-ground.
6   Dead-house.
7   Military Walk.
8   Ramparts.
9   Iron Rails, inside of which prisoners are confined.
10 Streams of water running from the reservoir.
11 Tavistock Road.
12 Princetown Road.
13 Morton Road.
14 Prison where Mr. V. made his first entry on December 12, 1811, with the track.
15 Prison where Mr. V. lives now, and track of walk allowed.
16 Mr. V. has liberty to go as far as 5th *Gate*.
17 New latter wall, is a mile in circumference.

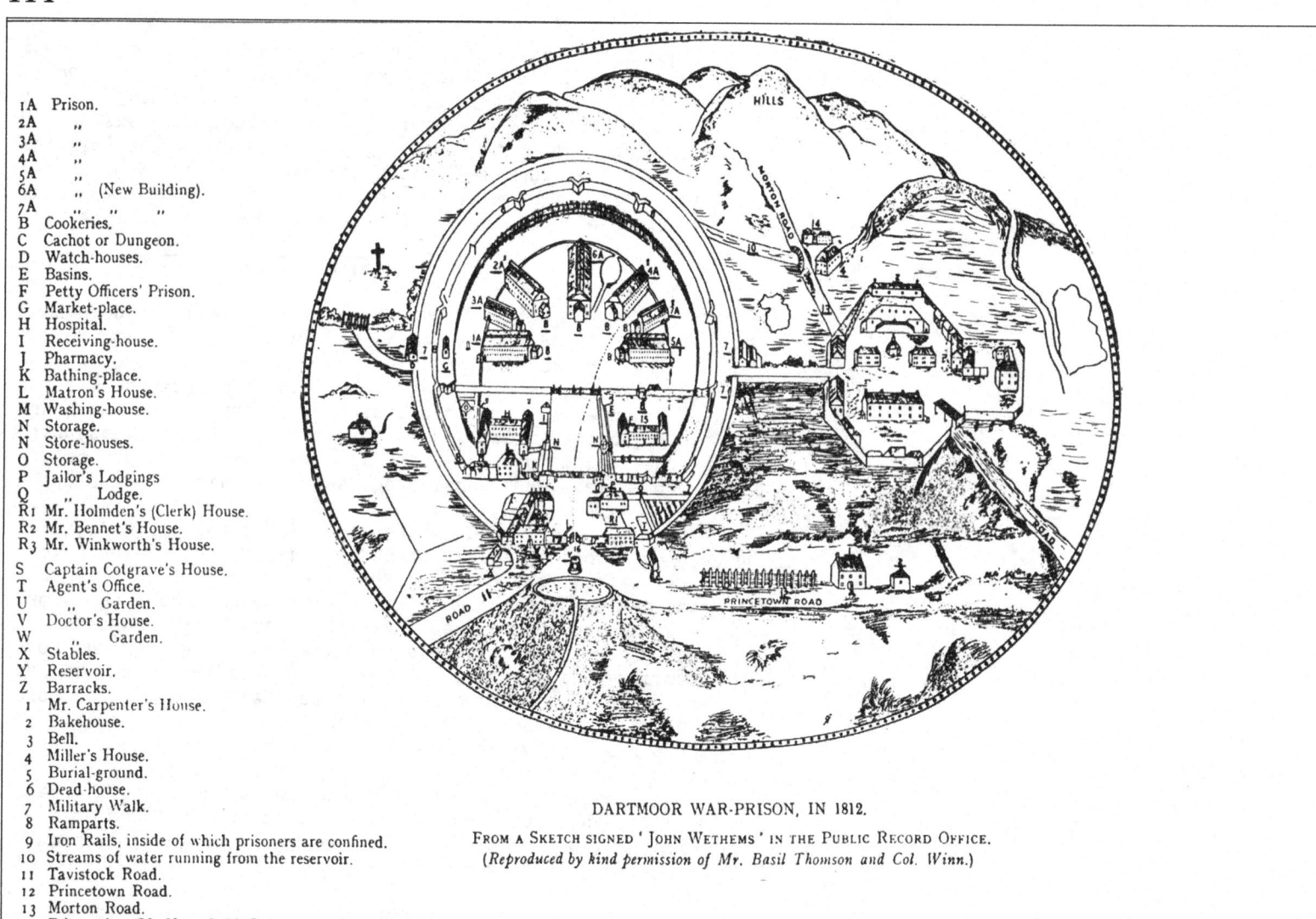

DARTMOOR WAR-PRISON, IN 1812.

FROM A SKETCH SIGNED ' JOHN WETHEMS ' IN THE PUBLIC RECORD OFFICE.
(*Reproduced by kind permission of Mr. Basil Thomson and Col. Winn.*)

they sold outside and thereby got some little income and
others had credits in London by which they obtained all
needful supplies. From these several sources a pretty large
sum was disbursed, both in the market and at the shops kept
in the prison. A large number of the prisoners being thus
furnished with the means lived well enough, but many really
suffered from hunger, for in the elevated position of the
prison the air was exhilerating and the appetite keen. The
regular allowance was 1½ lbs. of bread (soft) and ½ lb. beef
and some vegetables daily except one day when they had dry
or pickled herrings instead of beef. The beef and
vegetables were made into soup, and then served out, but any
prisoner could receive his allowance uncooked, if he chose.
On the whole, neither the provisions nor the treatment of
the prisoners by the officials could be complained of. The
most violent altercation that occurred between them while I
was there arose on account of two Americans who it was said
rather than be made prisoners attempted to blow up their
vessel after she had been captured by the British.

They were brought to Dartmoor and there put in solitary
confinement in a building in one of the yards called the
Cachot surrounded by a high iron fence. By some means they
got out of this, and were concealed. To find them Capt.
Shortland (the commandant of the prison) marched a company
of soldiers into the yard. The prisoners hustled them and
finally drove them out, and threatened to kill any others he
might send among them. He did not attempt to do this, but
in order to coerce them stopped the market. This was a loss
to the country people and they grumbled. The soldiers,
always ready to turn an honest penny, assisted to pass other
things, besides spirits, over the walls. Finding his plan
not effectual, Shortland proposed to negociate and offered,
if the prisoners would allow the soldiers to search...

Mode Of Living Peace of Ghent 1815 Release From Prison

...the prisoners without molestation to open the market,
whether they found the proscribed men or not. This was
agreed to. The soldiers marched in and marched out again

"A Green Hands First Cruise, to-gether with a residence of Five
Months in Dartmoor", Josiah, Baltimore, Dushing and Brother,
London, 1841

Dartmoor, Arrival, 1814
-Clerk office-registered, given number, a hammock, bed and
blanket, followed turnkey (guard) to the "lock-up" (cell)
-stood in upper end of first story of building, in one
compartment: 250' X 60' studded with light and people,
cooking, reading, walking, dancing, singing, fiddling,
fifing, gambling or clustered around tables watching - all
were in good spirits
-one man searching out pedigree lice so as not to have them
cross-bred with others
-parties of 6, large portion of bread
-rigged up hammock highest place for privacy, 14ft. up,
climbed a stanchion and then a beam to reach it
Uniform: blue or yellow stout woollen cloth, no regard for fit so
many swappped later
Industries:
-cobbler made a pair of wooden shoes, inch in thickness
- another covering a worn out hat body with a canvas to be
smeared with wax, blacked and polished, a tarpaulin
(waterproof covering)
-sewing a cast-off stocking into gloves, coarser yarns worked
into caps, suspenders and stockings to be sold
-selling a sailors suit of navy blue broadcloth
-selling a dark beverage, 1 pot tea, twice price of coffee
but tasted the same
-cook for the day washing mess dishes
-merchant laying out a pound of butter, plug of tobacco, half
dozen pipes, skiens of thread, paper needles 8 to 10 rows of
pins
-prison crier also painter
-old clothes pedlar-Jew pedlar with hats on head, loaded down
with commission goods
-Negro with pan of fritters, best in prison
-better living section: suckling pigs, goose market being
the faro table winners, gambling tables

-some over spellers, number, musicians, dancers, actors stock
companies on things like wine caskets
-ornaments made from beef bones
-beef bones reduced to powder to be used as a pastry flour, 1
schilling per lb.
-cooks assistants paid with food
Rough Alley: group known by wickedness; No. 4, blacks and
outcast whites, Big Dick boss,

Final Week: sold birthrights for bedding etc. so after Treaty of
Ghent would be amongst first to be free to go home
-when named called, 3 times, freedom exists but if person not
there by third, often someone sneaks out and real person
denied exit
-some whites and blacks remained, black fearing slavery on
return
-mosquitoes horrendous
-given shoes and a day's ration for march to Plymouth
-sailed to Carolina as freight.

* * *

and the market was restored, but the men were not found.
They were under ground, in a mine which some few of us were
having constructed with a view of escape sometime or other.
Peace however came before it was completed. I am not aware
that it was ever discovered or suspected by the officers.
My being sent here at all was probably owing to the part I
had taken on board the 'Benson'. Mr. Williams had
interceded with the Transport board for my release and it
was promised, but when the case was enquired into my name
was returned with a black mark against it, and the promise
was never performed. I was not however uncomfortable except
from the uncertainty as to the time of my deliverance. I
was perfectly well and had means for procuring all the
material comforts I required. Every morning early I took a
lesson in fencing for the sake of the exercise. I got my
meals at the coffee shops and eating rooms that were plenty
in the prisons. Between them I walked a good deal, wrote
some, and read considerably having a tolerably good
circulating library in our prison No. 7 owned by one of the
prisoners who had been a petty officer on board a British
man of war. During this time I composed a history in blank
verse (I called it an epic poem) of considerable length of
the American Navy. I don't know what became of it nor can I
recollect a single line of it. I don't believe it was worth
remembering.

Early in January 1815 we heard that a treaty of peace had
been signed at Ghent, and had been sent to the United States
for ratification. Late in March it was returned to London
ratified and on the 31st of that month I received advice
from Mr. Williams, London, that my discharge was granted and
from Capt. Shortland that it was received. The next day,
April 1st, I took my departure, being the first American
prisoner released under the Treaty of Ghent. I procured a
conveyance to Ashburton some Dozen miles over the moor, and
here met a number of Americans on parole, this...

Arrival in Liverpool – Dartmoor Ma[ssacre]

The Consignees of the American Ship Eliza Bar[ker]
belonging to Jacob Barker of New York, but now under
Russian colours, generously offered us a free passage
... the Cabin, to New York. We of course furnishing our
own stores. There were I think some 12 of us, mostly ship masters, but I have entirely forgotten the names of every one of
them and have never since to my knowledge fallen in
with a single individual, of the party. We sailed about
the 15 or 20 of April, Nervous to leaving England, we heard
of the affair at Dartmoor prison, commonly called the
Dartmoor massacre, but I doubt the justice of the term.
Some of the prisoners, were playing ball – which bounded
over the wall into the military walk. They called to the soldiers
on duty there to throw it back, which they refused or neglected
to do. On this some boys commenced to pick a hole through the
... The soldiers interfered, and the prisoners attacked them
The soldiers then fired and some 5 or 6 were
... nded. There was no doubt blame
a time. It was compelled
... nowledge of
... ool

Arrival In Liverpool, Dartmoor Massacre, Remarks

...being appointed residence of prisoners of that class. I
immediately took the mail coach for Liverpool, passing
through as well as I recollect the towns of Exeter,
Wellington, Bridgewater, Bristol, Gloucester, Shrewsbury &
Chester. In Liverpool there were several Americans who were
seeking a passage home.

The consignees of the American ship 'Elija', Capt. Porter,
belonging to Jacob Barber of New York, but now under Russian
colours, generously offered us a free passage in the cabin
to New York. We of course furnishing our own stores. There
were I think 10 or 12 of of us, mostly ship masters, but I
have entirely forgotten the names of every one of them and
have never since to my knowledge fallen in with a single
individual of the party. We sailed about the 15th or 20th
of April. Previous to leaving England we heard of the
affair at Dartmoor prison, commonly called the Dartmoor
massacre, but I doubt the justice of the term. Some of the
prisoners were playing ball - which bounded over the wall
into the military walk. They called to the soldiers on duty
there to throw it back, which they refused or neglected to
do. On this some boys commenced to pick a hole through the
wall. The soldiers interfered, and the prisoners attacked
them with stones. The soldiers then fired and some 5 or 6
were killed and several wounded. There was no doubt blame
on both sides.

I have never since regretted the short time I was compelled
to reside in Dartmoor prison. It gave me a knowledge of men
better than I could have acquired in any other school in a
much longer time. As to treatment by the officials there
was nothing to complain of, but the conduct of the
prisoners, although towards me personally unobjectionable
was in many instances outrageous. There was a good deal of
intemperance and gambling prevailed very generally. There
was nevertheless a strong resistance to the introduction of
the latter into some of the prisons and in No. 7 where I was
it was for a time effectually stopped. There was also a

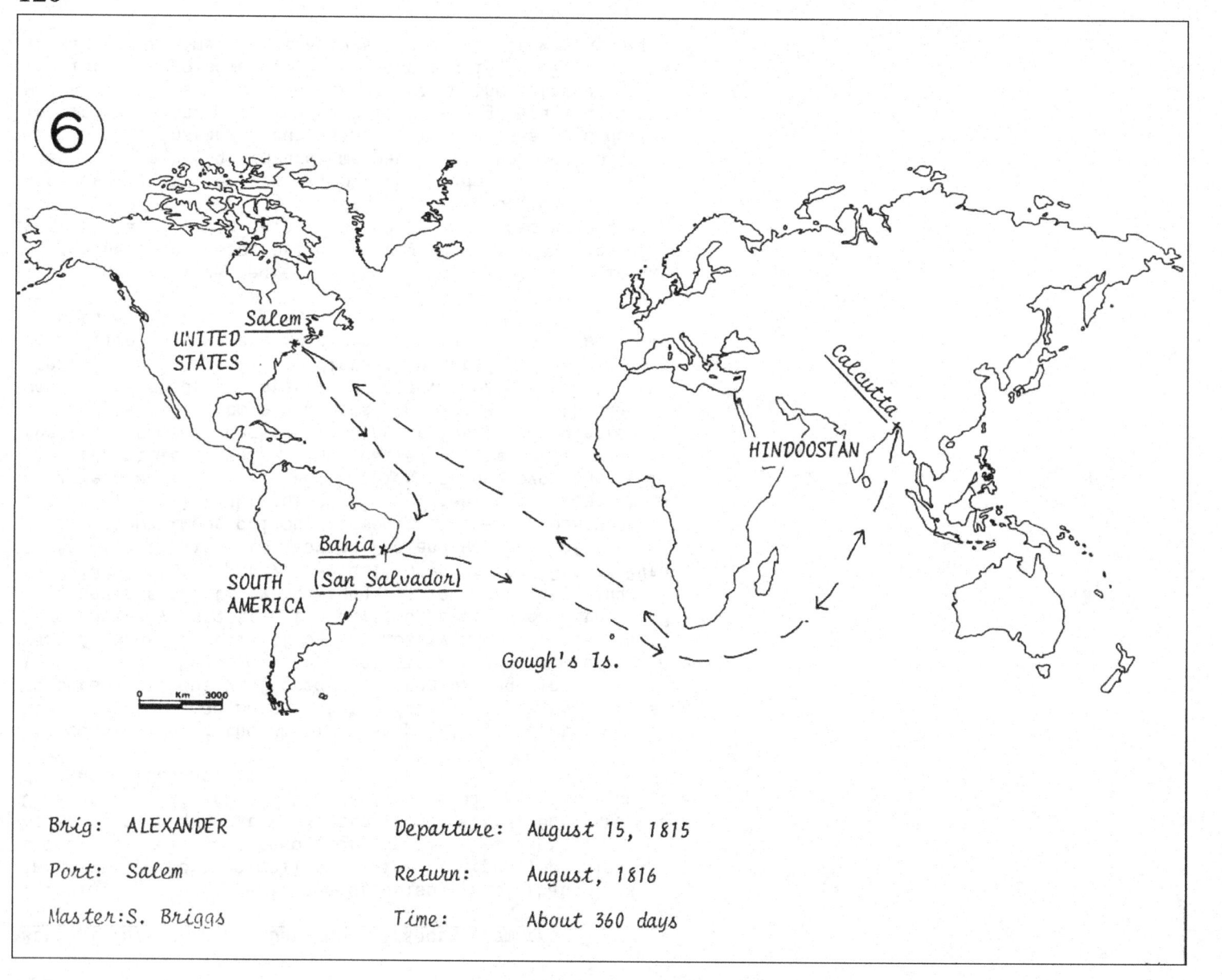

⑥

Salem

UNITED
STATES

Calcutta

HINDOOSTAN

Bahia
(San Salvador)

SOUTH
AMERICA

Gough's Is.

0   Km   3000

Brig: ALEXANDER   Departure: August 15, 1815

Port: Salem   Return: August, 1816

Master: S. Briggs   Time: About 360 days

good many men of high rank, principles and probably more
real patriotism among them than is usually found among the
same number in any class of life.

Arrival United States, Voyage Brig 'Alexander' to Calcutta

We arrived on the American coast late in May and being off
Block Island with a head wind, three or four of us who were
bound north chartered a fishing boat to take us into Newport
where we took stages for our several homes.

I was now just 22 years of age and of course desirous of at
once engaging in some active business. After a good deal of
search my Father and myself bought an Eastern built Brig of
about 240 tons, called the 'Alexander', a poor carrier and
not coppered. It was however the best vessel we could
find. I took 1/4 and my Father 3/4 of her. We loaded her
with spars and some other articles and specie, and I
proceeded in her as supercargo to Calcutta.

spars: a general term for any wooden support used in the rigging of
a ship; it embraces all masts, yards, booms, gaffs, etc.
(OCSS p. 820)

Samuel Briggs was master and his brother Henry 1st mate. We
sailed Aug. 15th, 1815. On the 5 Oct., in lat. 7135 S long.
30.11 west in a heavy squall & head beat sea we sprung the
foremast so badly as to induce us to put into St. Salvador
for repairs. We arrived there on the 10th of the same
month. This place (called also Bahia) is of considerable
commercial importance, exporting large quantities of sugars
in boxes of enormous size. It is in Lat. 13 South Long. 42
West. Having procured a new mast we sailed again on the
17th Nov. 1st made Gough's Island. From this time our
passage was very tedious. We had very light winds most of
the way and the vessel's bottom being very foul, we made
slow progress. At length after a passage of (including the
delay in South America) 191 days, we took a pilot on the
sand heads on the 21st of Feb. 1816. In Calcutta after
various negotiations I employed Ram Chuder Meter as my
Banian. The spars on cargo sold well. They cost about $170
and brought between 8 and 9,000 rupees. We were in port
only 30 days, having taken a full cargo of ginger, tumeric,
goatskins, indigo and piece goods and then sailed for the

bottom being foul: since the ship's bottom was not coppered, it
collected a great many weeds and barnacles that slowed
progress considerably especially in the tropics (OCSS p. 323)

piece goods: bolt goods such as cotton fabric etc. (Ed. note)

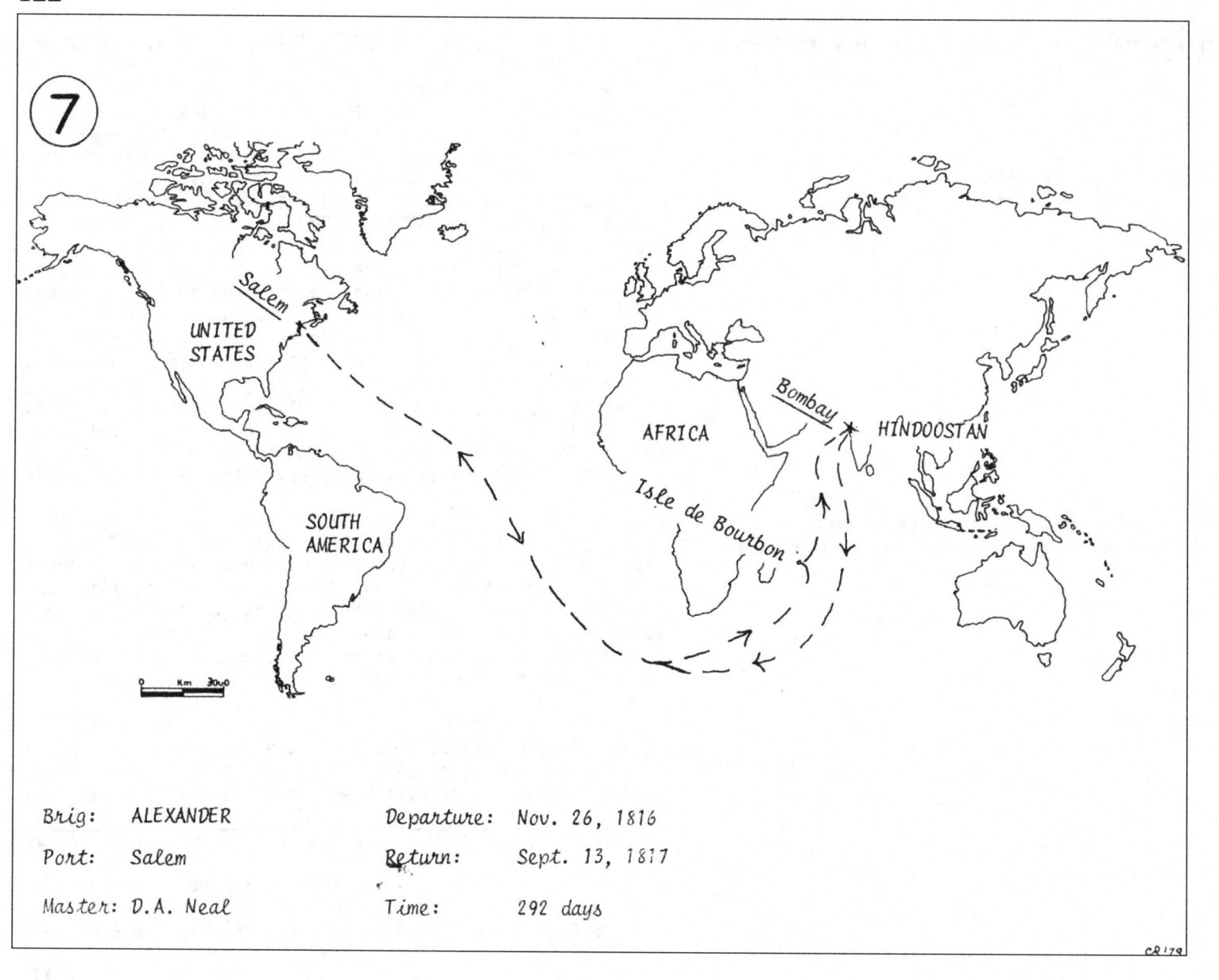

⑦

Salem

UNITED STATES

SOUTH AMERICA

AFRICA

Isle de Bourbon

Bombay

HINDOOSTAN

0   Km   3000

Brig: ALEXANDER

Port: Salem

Master: D.A. Neal

Departure: Nov. 26, 1816

Return: Sept. 13, 1817

Time: 292 days

CR179

United States. We arrived in Salem in August. The voyage proved very profitable for the size of the vessel and the capital employed. The ginger of which we had a large quantity cost about $3.05 per lb. and sold for $15.00 per lb. I now felt myself fully competent to the task of managing and navigating a ship and there were many reasons for taking the whole business into my own hands. I therefore took charge of the 'Alexander' on her second voyage, having John Derby as my first and John Preston as my second officer and with some cargo and specie enough for a ...

Voyage of 'Alexander' to Bombay - First Voyage Master 1816

...cargo of coffee or cotton, sailed on the 26th Nov. 1816 for the East Indies. I first touched at Isle Bourbon March 6, 1817 but finding coffee too high for my purposes, kept on to Bombay, where we arrived on the first of May. My brother William accompanied me on this voyage as clerk, being his first attempt at a sea life. Here I employed Norajee and Masseruanjee Parsee, merchants through whom I purchased a cargo of Sweat cotton with some ginger for loose storage.

While in Bombay I visited the celebrated caves or temples on the Island of Elephanter. They exhibit in their sculpture the evidence of great antiquity and some considerable skill, having been the work and elucidating the mythology of the hindoos. The collossal figure of an elephant carved rudely in stone and at a considerable distance from the caves gives name to the island.

The commerce of Bombay was very considerable. It exported mostly cotton to Europe - cotton and opium to China, and had considerable intercourse with the Red Sea and Persian Gulph from which it imported coffee and dates for which it paid in English manufactures and specie. It also carried on a considerable coasting trade with Surat on the north and smaller ports on the Malabar coast to the south. The house of Forbes & Co. was the most important English firm there but there were several very wealthy persons who carried on a

sweat cotton: since sweat means to remove moisture I can only guess that it is a dried cotton possibly to prevent rot during the voyage. (Ed. note)

The Island of Elephanta was a Hindu temple dedicated to the god Shiva who was the fertility god as well as the one of power not yet proven in the form of lingums or phallic symbols. The elphant he later mentions is not religiously significant. However the elephant was around even in the earliest stages of India's history and was regarded with deep respect and predominantly owned by kings and chief.(Basham, "The Wonder that was India" Grove Press Inc., New York, 1954)

China at this time was in the Manchu Dynasty. Its biggest import until 1840 was opium. At this time the Opium War broke out because the government finally had the power to stop it, to the financial loss of many other countries and to Chinese officials who took in a percentage, since it was illegal. The main reason that the opium trade was finally banned was not for moral reasons so much as it was for financial ones. Contraband paid no taxes and the import of opium was more than the profits made in exports.(C.P. Fitzgerald, "China, a Short Cultural History" Praegar Publishers, New York, 1961, p. 565)

Rogers, Wm. Augustus, "Journal containing Remarks and Observations during a Voyage to India, A.D. 1817, 1818," Salem, Ship Tartar, 401 tons

Sept. 1817:   Salem - passes Thatchers Island lighthouse
Sept. 20:   Hurricane, split our topsail
Sept. 26:   vegetables rotting fast owing to these being taken on board when not ripe
Sept. 29:   calm, water has thick appearance like sand - thought brought by Gulf steam, swallow came on board completely exhausted - caught 3 fish, 8 - 9", lead colour like a perch, sailors call them Old Wives since they are so snappish
Oct. 1:   struck a devil fish, length 6 ft. head in 2 parts like a prong, unable to get aboard (hammerhead shark?)
Oct. 4:   vast numbers of flying fish 8-12" bright mackeral colour with wings (fins) which it extends half his length rapidity amazing especially when pursued by dolphins
Oct. 5:   saw porpoise and blackfish, could not harpoon
Oct. 9:   heavy rain, we caught about 1000 gal. in about 2 hours
Oct. 10:   say many little birds called Mother Carey's chickens, by sailors, small, larger, than a swallow, feathers dark brown and black, white spots on wings, fed on little pieces of fat that fall overboard, of the GENUS PETREL and the smallest aquatic bird I have seen - have been used as candles, wick being passed through their body, it being so full of oil sailors believe they appear before a storm and fly in ships wake for protection but often runs or walks atop the waves when gale at height - caught a hawk in the rigging, had befriended our pigeon (kate) is 18" beak to feet and young
Oct. 13:   caught a French shark with a sucker fish attached to her belly, a species of basking shark, 5 ft. long, 5 apertures of gills on each side of neck
Oct. 14:   Englishmen hang themselves in March and November because of the horrid weather
Oct. 19:   spoke to a brig out of Boston, and beat her by at least 4 days (def: spoke to refers as coming alongside to actually talk)
Oct. 29:   Magellan Islands, Nebula clouds
Nov. 3:   spot Trinidad

Nov. 25:   gale continues, sea is mountains high literally, ship lying badly in the trough, 3 p.m. a heavy sea struck our quarter, dashed our stern boat from our stern with such force, drew the bolts from her keep, stayed in sight for 2 hours when the ship outdrifted her and lost sight much to the regret of all, a fair boat and breasted the siege nobly - cook had deposited whole stock of onions in boat - set a new top mast, staysail reefed, ship lay abroad in a most dangerous position
Nov. 26:   heavy seas, winds calming , worst storm he'd ever experienced
Nov. 28:   caught an albatross with small baited cod hook, took 2 men
Nov. 29:   blue substances like jelly on surface of water
Dec. 5:   caught jelly: called Portugese men of War - create great itch when handled - old sailors tell young they are good to wash with
Dec. 7:   Cape pigeon - have tried to take on but unsuccessful, look a great deal like the domestic pigeons
Dec. 8: housed masts, heavy gale, hove to, shipped some water, set reft foresail and found her lie to better

Bombay:

- harbour easily entered through 2 islands
- walls of fort have 400 cannons, troops: red coats, short drawers, white, reaching half way down
- centre: vendors selling cotton bales, peppers, coffee, should ask 3 times what an article is worth and bargain
Dock: 4 docks, 2 entrances, 2 for frigates, 1 for sloop of war
- most elegant ships built here (teak) juggles, troupadours, men carrying serpents, dancing girls, bears, monkeys and goats, parcees next in line after English in rank

Elephanta: climbed steep hill, gate pass required but liquor would do as a bribe - awed by magnitude of figures and pillars (half of which was destroyed by Portuguese who believed equated with devil) 4 ft. diameter, 7 ft. high, gods and goddesses in relief at end of Hall, fugeres of Supreme diety, several heads of Bramha, face of dignity, Sishnoo, head of blandness and Sura
- lotus in one hand, the other a pomagranate, on the wrist a ring as do the Hindoos
- left for Boston Apr. 25, 1818

large trade and owned many vessels. One of the wealthiest
perhaps the wealthiest among them was Homojee Bonojee, an
uncle of the young man with whom I did business. Jansitjee,
who was a ship builder and constructed some ships of war for
the British East India Co. and also for the government was
also very rich, and was afterwards knighted by the king.
The government docks here were capacious and well
constructed, and the vessels built in them of the teak of
the country were very durable. I saw a vessel there in
active service over 100 years old.

We sailed *from Bombay on the 23rd of May for the United*
States, having discharged and sold one cargo and purchased
and taken in another in three weeks.

Bombay arrival Home, Voyage to Havre, Paris 1817

I took also a passenger Luke Ashburner, Esq. late mayor of
Bombay and a gentleman of high respectability there. His
wife and children were in England but he had conceived a
very favorable opinion of our institutions and wished to
settle in the United States as he subsequently did at
Stockbridge, Mass.

We arrived in Salem Sept. 13, 1817 in 113 days from Bombay.
On this voyage everything went on very smoothly. It was I
think the first one out of the U.S. carried through without
rum. It being my first voyage as master and having come in
(as the sailors say) through the cabin windows, the men had
a notion of trying me, so when a few days out they sent back
their usual allowance of grog saying that if they could not
have more they didn't want any. I directed the steward to
cut off the tap and not open it again till I gave him
orders, which were not given during the voyage. The rum
came home all safe and so did the men.

Our cargo of cotton, not being suitable for our markets, I
proceeded in the 'Alexander', my brother and some officers
with me to Havre de Grace, having sailed on the 6th and
arrived on the 28th of October. Here I did my business with

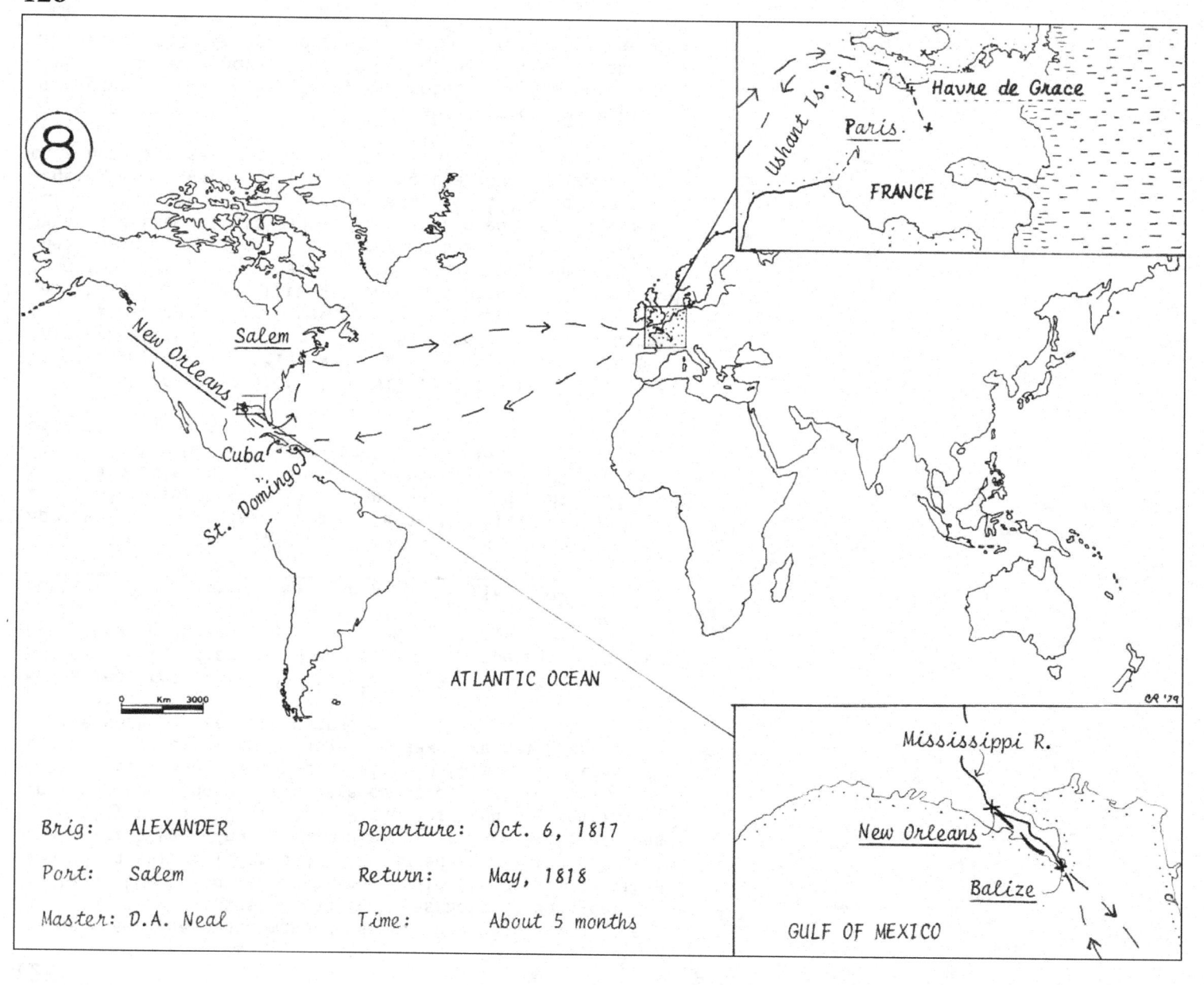

⑧

Havre de Grace

Ushant Is.

Paris.

FRANCE

Salem

New Orleans

Cuba

St. Domingo

ATLANTIC OCEAN

0   Km   3000

CR '79

Mississippi R.

New Orleans

Balize

GULF OF MEXICO

Brig: ALEXANDER   Departure: Oct. 6, 1817

Port: Salem   Return: May, 1818

Master: D.A. Neal   Time: About 5 months

the house of Willis & Greene, a branch of the Paris house of
Willis, Williams & Greene. My cargo sold well, realizing
24¢ per lb. for a cost of 11¢ in Bombay. We were
quarantined ten days. After that I visited Paris and there
found Mr. Willis who had just arrived from the U.S. with his
new wife. I took a room in a house where Mr. Henry
Fettyplace was lodging, met here also Cap. Wm. Story of
Salem and at a dinner party at Mr. Willis, Mr. Theodore
Lyman and John C. Gray of Boston. At this time Louix XVIII
was in the zenith of his power, having in 1815 been replaced
on the throne by the combined armies of England, Russia and
Prussia. Everything now bore the marks of their conquest of
Paris. The Louvre had been rifled of its choicest gems of
art, the statue of Napoleon had been hurled from its proud
eminance on the pillor in the Place Vendome, but the bronze
which encircled it still remained to tell in alto relievo
the story of...

Havre to New Orleans

...his battles and his victories. Paris was draped in
white, the white flag of the Bourbons waving everywhere, but
it was the white dress of the funeral mourner, for Paris had
lost in Napoleon its greatest benefactor. The imperial
eagle was but half effaced on the public offices, and the
tricolour was often shaded but not concealed by the daub of
white that had been passed over it. Who then would have
believed that before one generation had passed away all
would have been restored, the statue to its place, eagles to
their eyrie, and the flag to the front of a new imperial
army led by another Napoleon.

It seems to lengthen out life to contemplate that events
that would seem to be the work of ages were condensed within
the experience of a single individual.

After a visit of about 10 days I returned to Havre and
prepared for a voyage to New Orleans. Before I left however
I returned to Paris to arrange some credits to be used there

clear...

on the 7 of ...

...go, Jamaica, y Cuba. ...

...ed in a violent squall or tornado...

being scarcely felt on deck, and twice ...

first about ... the rigging, taking the foretop m...

This was about a week before we took a pilot. On...

15th I left the Brig in the river just below the English turn.

There were no steam tugs in those days, and it was often

a tedious work to get a vessel from the Belize to the City.

The country was, at this time everywhere overflowed

and except on the levees impossible except in boats.

I found a French planter who let me have a canoe

and a negro to take me round by the bayou and the over-

flowed country to a point opposite New Orleans.

Here I found Cotton, which was the

Return to Salem — Marriage — 1818.

object of my voy-

age, altogether too high. the best red river qualities

... high as 35 cts perlb. I therefore loaded a part

... balance of cargo on freight, of tobacco

... and despatched the Brig in charge

... ...ther William as supercargo.

... passage to Boston...

me

in case of need, but spent only one day in doing it to my
satisfaction. I had already by letter made a similar
arrangement with Saml. Williams of London.

We sailed from Havre on the 10th Dec. for New Orleans,
having heavy gales ahead in the channel did not get clear of
Ushant until the 22nd and arrived at the Bulize on the 7th
of Feb. 1818, having passed in sight of St. Domingo, Jamaica
and Cuba. In the Gulf of Mexico we were dismasted in a
violent squall or tornado, which pased over our heads, being
scarcely felt on deck, and twisted off the mainmast just
above the rigging, taking the foretop mast with it. This
was about a week before we took a pilot. On the 15th I left
the Brig. in the river just below the Englishturn. There
were no steam tugs in those days, and it was often a tedious
work to get a vessel from the Belize to the city. The
country was at this time everywhere overflowed and except on
the levees impossible except in boats. I found a French
planter who let me have a canoe and a negro to take me round
by the bayou and the overflowed country to a point opposite
New Orleans. Here I found cotton which was the ...

Return to Salem - Marriage 1818

...object of my voyage, altogether too high, the best red
river qualities being as high as 35¢ per lb. I therefore
loaded a part and took the balance of cargo on freight of
tobacco for St. Andros in Spain and despatched the Brig in
charge of Mr. Derby, sending my brother William as
supercargo. She sailed in April. I then took passage to
Boston in the Brig --- Captain R. Pedrick, where we arrived
late in May. We had several passengers but the only one I
fell in with or knew afterwards was Cap. Phineas Sprague of
Duxbury.

Marriage

I have already mentioned my engagement to Miss Harriet C.
Price. She had continued to reside with her Aunt Ward to
this time. I was now 25 and she 24 years of age. I had

English turn: I haven't been able to confirm this but I suspect that
since the mouth of the Mississippi River was not deep enough
for these ships to sail up that the Englishturn was an
unloading dock somewhere in the channel. It probably was a
colloquiallism since New Orleans was predominantly French
speaking that it was a pun on their trading partners who were
mostly English speaking. (Ed. note)

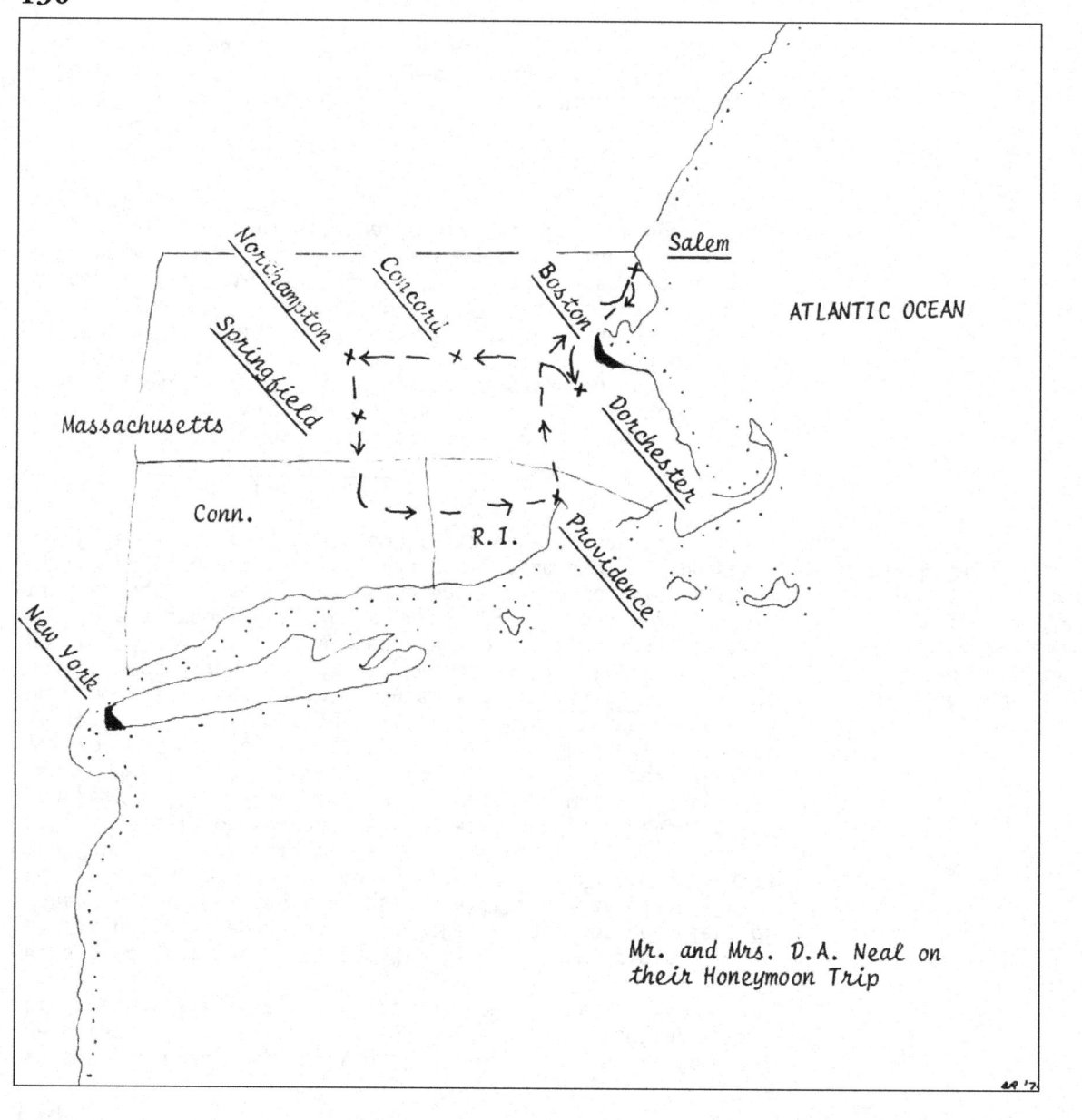

ATLANTIC OCEAN

Salem

Boston

Concord

Northampton

Springfield

Massachusetts

Conn.

R.I.

Dorchester

Providence

New York

Mr. and Mrs. D.A. Neal on
their Honeymoon Trip

accumulated by my own earnings about ten thousand dollars.
We had concluded that our marriage should take place on my
return from New Orleans and having hired a tenement in
County (Now Federal St. No. 23) and furnished it at a cost
of less than $1,000 but with every comfort and convenience.
We started in a buggy on the 25th of July for her
grandfather's place in Dorchester, where we were married the
next day by the Rev. John Codman, about 10 o'clock in the
morning. It is now upwards of 42 years since that event and
I can truly say that during all that time she has been the
kindest companion, the most affectionate and devoted mother,
the most accomplished housewife and the kindest friend to
all with whom she has been connected or who have claimed her
sympathy. More than any one that I ever knew she has always
been ready to sacrifice her own comfort for the happiness of
others. With more power of endurance under the severest
pain than I ever witnessed in any other person, she has
shown a sensitiveness to the slightest ills of those around
her equalled only by the keenness of her attachments and the
strength of her love. She is not one who in affliction
could say "let the cup pass from me" if any portion of its
bitterness would thereby be transferred to another.

Almost without fault herself she never found fault with
others. If she ever speaks of them it is to defend or to
applaud. If she can do neither she is silent.

Voyage of Ship 'Stag' 1818

There were present at our marriage only her immediate
relations. Immediately after the ceremony we started in our
buggy and went to Concord, Mass. This was her residence
from the time she was 18 months until she was 9 years old,
and she had never been there from the time she left it at
that age, until this the day of her marriage. The next day
we drove by her old residence but did not stop and proceeded
towards the Connecticut river, visited North Hampton, then
to Springfield and down the valley of the Connecticut a
short distance and through the northern part of that state
into Rhode Island, stopping at Providence and from there
home.

132

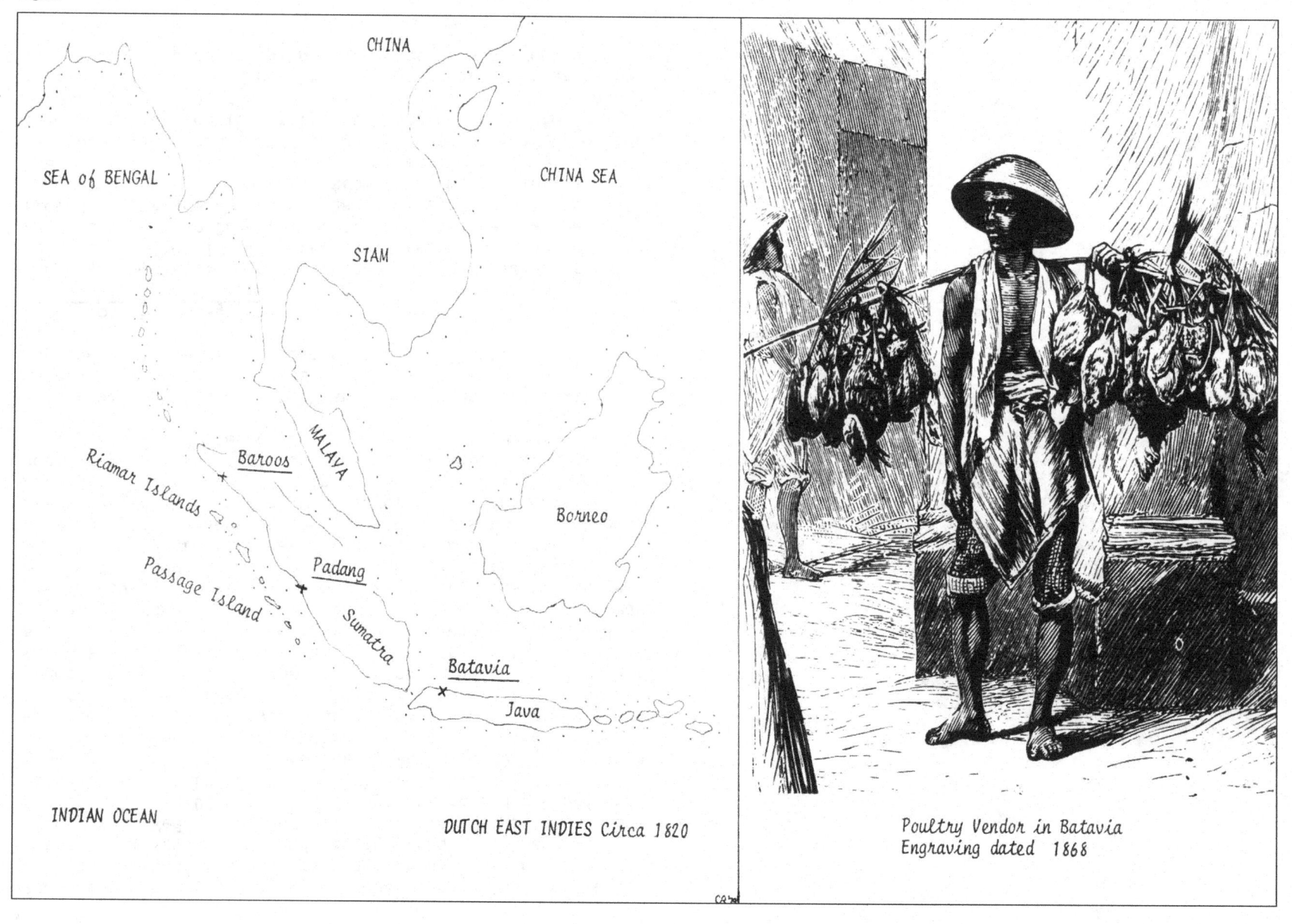

SEA of BENGAL

CHINA

CHINA SEA

SIAM

MALAYA

Baroos

Riamar Islands

Padang

Passage Island

Sumatra

Borneo

Batavia

Java

INDIAN OCEAN

DUTCH EAST INDIES Circa 1820

Poultry Vendor in Batavia
Engraving dated 1868

Shortly after this my friends Henry & Rob. H. Osgood, then
established in a flourishing commission in Baltimore
proposed to me to take charge of the ship 'Stag', belonging
to themselves, Christopher Deshon, Amos A. Williams, James
Beatty, and Doct. Schuarts on a voyage to the coast of
Sumatra. This ship was 435 tons, sharp built and supposed
to be a very fast sailer. Unfortunately I accepted the
offer and proceeded to Baltimore, where I arrived on the
23rd of Sept. 1816 and I proceeded to prepare the ship for
the voyage. Got my officers from Salem, chief mate Jacob
Agge - 2nd do Thos. Sleusman, and as clerks I took my
brother Theodore and Wm. Schwartze the son of one of the
owners. The crew also were from Salem and were named James,
Rowell, Carpenter, Hunt, Smith, Osborn, Price, Land, Tufts,
Poor, Crapen, Johnson, Thayer, Turner and Torrance (late of
Balt.) seamen Chas. Charlester, steward Dan Fuller cook.

sharp built or sharp up: the description of a square-rigged ship
with her sails trimmed up as near as possible to the wind
with her yard braced up as far fore-and-aft as the lee
rigging will allow (OCSS p. 777) or to put it another way, a
design technique to offer the best possible angles for sails
to catch the maximum amount of wind to heighten speed
potential.

On the 10th Oct. took on board 50,000 Sp. dollars, and on
the 11th proceeded down the Chesapeake Bay but did not get
clear of the pilot off the Capes till the 20th. Nothing of
importance occurred on the passage. We arrived on the coast
of Sumatra and anchored near the Riamar Islands on the 30th
Jan. 1819 being 103 days from the capes of Virgina.

Arrival on Coast of Sumatra 1819

I immediately started in my boat for Padang, the principal
Dutch town on the coast, about 10 miles south of our
anchorage which was as near as may be on the equator.
Shortly after leaving the ship fell in with an English
schooner, the 'Courier', Capt. Lautser with a cargo of 1,000
piculs of coffee which I purchased to be delivered at some
native port up the coast. At Padang no trade was allowed
except the Dutch. I procured some supplies, returned to the
ship then proceeded in company with the 'Courier' up the
coast. Touched at Tappanooly and Mensulardsland where we
fell in with the schooner 'Happy Couple', Capt. Savage of
Salem waiting for a vessel from Padang (The brig 'Traverse')
with coffee for her. I left my brother Theodore on board
the 'Happy Couple' with 10,000 Sp. dollars with orders to

piculs: a weight equal to 136.16 pounds (Ox.D.), a weight between
133 to 143 pounds (ACD)

THE 8 MAN BILGE PUMP

JUST ABAFT THE MAINMAST THE BILGE PUMP IS PLACED OVER THE DEEPEST POINT OF THE SHIP. WATER WAS PUMPED OUT OF THE BILGES BY MEN WORKING THE PUMP HANDLES. BILGE WATER WAS THEN ALLOWED TO FLOW ACROSS THE DECK AND OUT THE SCUPPERS. IT HELPED KEEP THE DECK MOIST AND PREVENTED THE DECK FROM SPLITTING. (U.S.S. CONSTITUTION)

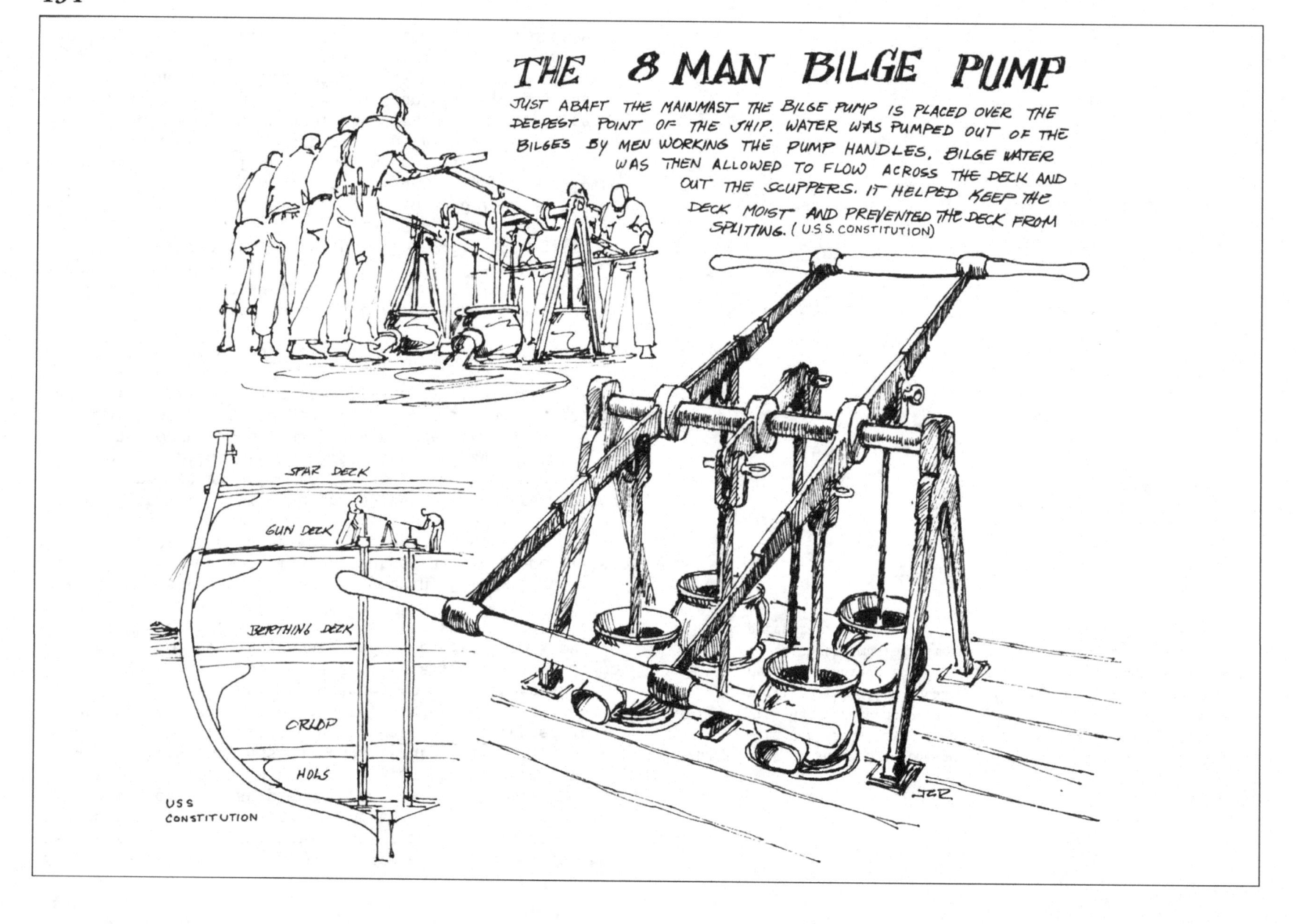

SPAR DECK

GUN DECK

BERTHING DECK

ORLOP

HOLD

USS CONSTITUTION

return in the 'Traverse' to Padang, and there purchase a
cargo of coffee for her to be delivered on board the 'Stag'
on the coast. We went to Barrous and there took in the
cargo of the 'Courier', Barrous being a fine harbour. We
then proceeded with the ship for Tremain bay, a large pepper
port, and arrived there on the 27th of February.

Here we found the ships 'Oscar', Capt. Briggs, 'Malay
Endicott', Falcon Fairfield, and at a short distance of at
Salecut the 'Restitution', Capt. Maservy, James Briggs
supercargo, all of Salem.

So many vessels made it difficult to obtain as much pepper
as was required to load them. We agreed to divide and all
kept good faith but Capt. Briggs. He tried to get more than
his share but being found out he went off with part of a
cargo. Having got all I could at the price I was willing to
pay. On the 25th April I left and returned to Baroos where
we arrived on the 17th of May, having touched on a coral
reef on the way down, but sustained no injury. At Baroos
took in the cargo of the ship 'Argo' which had been bought
by my brother at Padang. Thence to Tapuse where we took in
another small cargo of coffee which I bought from a Chinese
junk. Thence we proceeded to Poo Carong where we got
another cargo of coffee from the Argo that had been brought
to Padang for it. This was obtained under a contract with a
Mr. Smiles, an English Merchant...

Disasters - On the Coast 1819 - Ashore - Sailed

...at Padang. Being now loaded we proceeded towards Padang
for supplies and to settle accounts. On the night of the
21st of June while lying by were set by the current upon a
coral reef inside of Passage Island. Made sail and forced
the ship over, but in getting into deep water found the ship
leaked badly and our rudder broken. Rigged a jury rudder.
On the 23rd fell in with the British ship 'John Bull', Capt.
Bean. Having the chief mate and several men sick. Our
temporary rudder worked badly and the ship leaking some 200
strokes per hour, contracted with Capt. Bean to assist us

rigged a jury rudder: a makeshift arrangement to give a ship the
    ability to steer when she has lost her rudder, (OCSS p. 438)
    In the Peabody Museum there are examples of jury rudders on
    models, the simplest form seems to be a cannon or cannonade
    attached to a rope. The principle on which it worked was
    that if the boat aimed in one direction the weight which
    originally would go opposite would eventually cause the stern
    to reverse. There would not be the control of a fixed rudder
    but definitely better than none at all. The same principle
    works in a small boat using a bucket on a rope behind (Ed.
    note)

leaking some 200 strokes per hour This is the amount of strokes
    on the bilge pump it took to keep the ship afloat. (Ed. note)

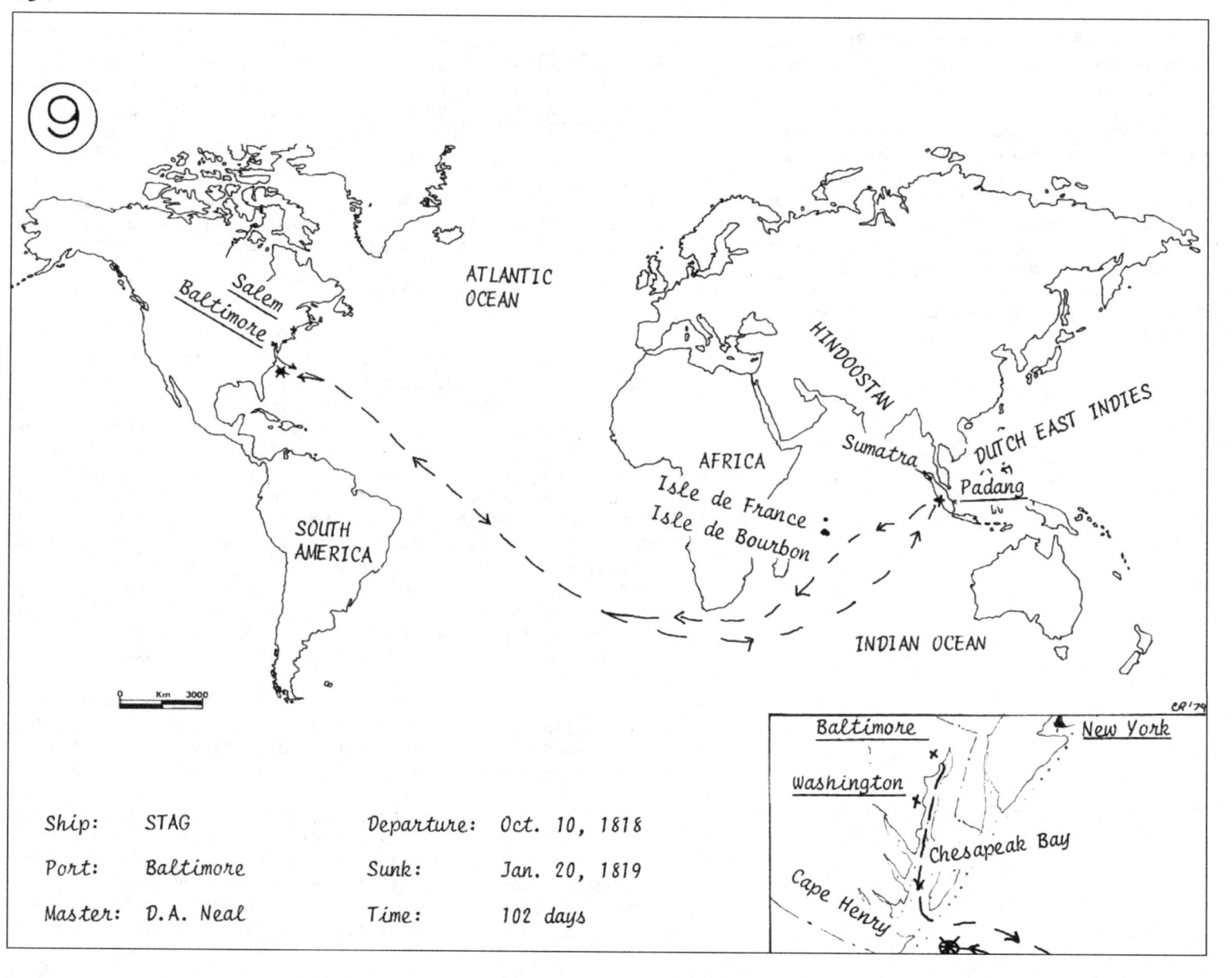

Ship: STAG	Departure: Oct. 10, 1818
Port: Baltimore	Sunk: Jan. 20, 1819
Master: D.A. Neal	Time: 102 days

137

with men and proceed in company to Padang. The next day we anchored under Pooloo Pisang off Padang. After the requisite surveys proceeded to Pooloo Quay an island about seven miles from Padang where could lie in smooth water near the shore.

Here we discharged the cargo, putting the pepper on the island, and the coffee into vessels chartered for the purpose, hove her out and repaired the damage as well as we could, got a new rudder made, reloaded except so much of the cargo as we were obliged to sell to pay expenses, and on the sixth of Sept. finding we should all die if we remained on the coast, having already buried the carpenter and two seamen, and all the rest being sick and off duty except the second mate, one old man named John Price and myself. I shipt two Chinamen and having got a parcel of coolies to reef the sails and heave up the anchors sent them off and proceeded to sea under double reefed topsails. On the 13th seven days out Wm. Schwastre the clerk, a young man of most amiable disposition died and was buried in the ocean. On the 6th of Oct. being still under short sail and most of the crew continuing sick, passed in sight of the Isle of France, where I ought to have stopped, but thinking the crew were mending I was unwilling to lose the time and incur the expense. On the 21st however one of them, James Land and on the 4th Nov. another Elijah Thayed died, and the rest continued very feeble. The carpenter and one man died on the coast. Nov. 8th we doubled the Cape of Good Hope and on the 23rd hove too off the island of St. Helena, but Napoleon ...

Death on Board - Storms Shipwreck, on Cape Henry 1820

...being then a prisoner on the island no foreign vessel were allowed to anchor in the roads. We were boarded by H.M. Sloop of War 'Redwing' from which vessel we obtained some medicines, but could get no other assistance. We could see the residence of the Emperor but not near enough to distinguish persons on shore. Failing to get supplies at St. Helena we got quite short of provisions and water before

The sickness is not given in any detail but it is believed to be malaria which infected by germs carried in the air and could infect even men who did not touch land. (Editor's Note)

shipt: believed to be the taking aboard of people or things (Ed. note)

parcel of coolies: labourers hired for cheap service. (ACD) The fact that he refers to the labourers as a parcel and the Chinamen as people offers proof of the attitude of the skilled to the unskilled is akin to slavery. (Ed note)

reef the sails The amount of sail taken in by securing one set of reef-points. It is the means of shortening sail to the amount appropriate to an increase in the strength of wind. In square-rigged, sails up to the topsails normally carried two rows of reef-points, enabling two reefs to be taken in, sails set above them usually had no reef-points as they would normally be furled or sent down in a wind strong enough to require the sails to be reefed. (OCSS p. 695) reef-points: short lengths of small rope set in the reef-bands of square-rigged sails used to tie down a reef. (OCSS p. 696) Summary: Reefing the sail was a protection against the sails ripping in a strong wind by reducing the areas exposed to the wind. If the sail was fully let out the it might pull the ship over in a violent wind or tear it as previously mentioned. The reefed sail maintains stability and speed. (Ed. note)

double reefed sails: see above. It would only be done with very large sails (Ed. note)

138

Deaths on board - Storms - Shipwreck on Cape...

two of which were alongside ~ Loaded them both ~ ... giving orders to keep the pumps going & proceeded in one of the... to Norfolk for assistance to save the cargo. After I left the... men continued to pump until 10 a.m. of the 20 ~ when the... water being over the Cabin floors, they gave up. At 4 a.m. the...

Loss of Ship Stag - Arrival at & departure from Baltimore.

careened on her beam ends and filled. The officers and crew then left her in the long boat, and landed on the beach close to the light house on Cape Henry. From the fact of the ground being covered with snow I was deceived in my estimate of its distance, and when we shoaled so suddenly supposed we were on the middle ground and intended to anchor and wait for ... that we had unsuccessfully sought the day before. ... at 5 a.m. of the 20 ~ where I obtained ... by R. Harwood a merchant there & ... man of high standing ... the associated

I engaged

139

we arrived on the coast of the United States. It was mid-winter. Another man Daniel Osborn died on the 15th January 1820. The rest of the crew were either worn out by continual pumping or incapacitated from work by continued illness. We were on short allowance. The gales as we approached the coast were tremendous and directly ahead. Most of our sails were in a bad state, some of them blown from the yards. On the 17th in a severe squall split all three topsails. On the 18th we had moderate weather and struck soundings working to the westward in 14 or 15 fathoms. At 4 p.m. of the same day saw the light house on Cape Henry, Va. from aloft. At 8 it bore W by N having 11 fathoms, wind light and baffling. Fired repeatedly for a pilot and stood to the north & west going about two knots till 1 a.m. of the 19th (civil time) hauled up foresail and trisail (main sail being furled) having 10 or 11 fathoms - lead wind going all the time Light W 1/2 North. At 1:30 suddenly shoaled to 5 fathoms and while letting go the anchors, the ship struck the ground. Tried all means in our power to get her off, but were unsuccessful. At 11 a.m. a pilot came on board. Again tried to force her off without success. In the afternoon the ship sprung a leak and the bilge pumps could not keep her free. At 8 p.m. the men left the pumps and got their chests out on board the pilot boats, who of which were alongside. Loaded them both with coffee, giving order to keep the pumps going I proceeded in one of them to Norfolk for assistance to save the cargo. After I left the men continued to pump until 1 a.m. of the 20th when the water being over the cabin floor they gave up. At 4 a.m. she careened on her beam ends and filled. The officers ...

Loss of Ship 'Stag' - Arrival & Departure from Baltimore

...and crew then left her in the long boat and landed on the beach close to the lighthouse on Cape Henry. From the fact of the ground being covered with snow I was deceived in my estimate of its distance, and when we shoaled so suddenly supposed we were on the middle ground and intended to anchor and wait for a pilot that we had unsuccessfully sought the

short allowance or **petty warrant:** a naval expression to indicate that, because of the victuals (food rations) on board running short, six men were to exist on the scale of victuals for four. (OCSS p. 798)

yards a large wood or metal spar crossing the masts of a ship horizontally or digonally from which a sail is set (OCSS p. 959)

struck soundings a name give to a depth of water obtained by a lead and line. (OCSS p. 817)
lead line: a means of finding the depth of water near coasts and probably the earliest of the devices used by coastal navigators to facilitate safe navigation, especially in thick or hazy weather. It consists of a hemp line to which is attached a loop holding a lead weight of plummet of about seven pounds. The lower end of the plummet is cup-shaped to accommodate the arming of the lead, this being a lump of tallow pressed into the hollow at the base to indicate the nature of the bottom deposits. Sand, mud, shingle, etc. would adhere to the tallow and tells the leadsman the type of bottom he is finding; when the tallow comes up clean, he is finding rock (OCSS p. 471)

shoaled: indicating a patch of water in the sea with a depth less than that of the surrounding water. (OCSS p. 471)

struck the ground: or ran aground: when the ship is resting on the ground (OCSS p. 12)

careened on her beam ends and filled: the operation in older days of heaving a ship down on one side in order to expose the other. Beam ends: the tranverse measurement of a ship in her wides part. Summary: she fell over to one side and sunk. (OCSS p. 139, 169)

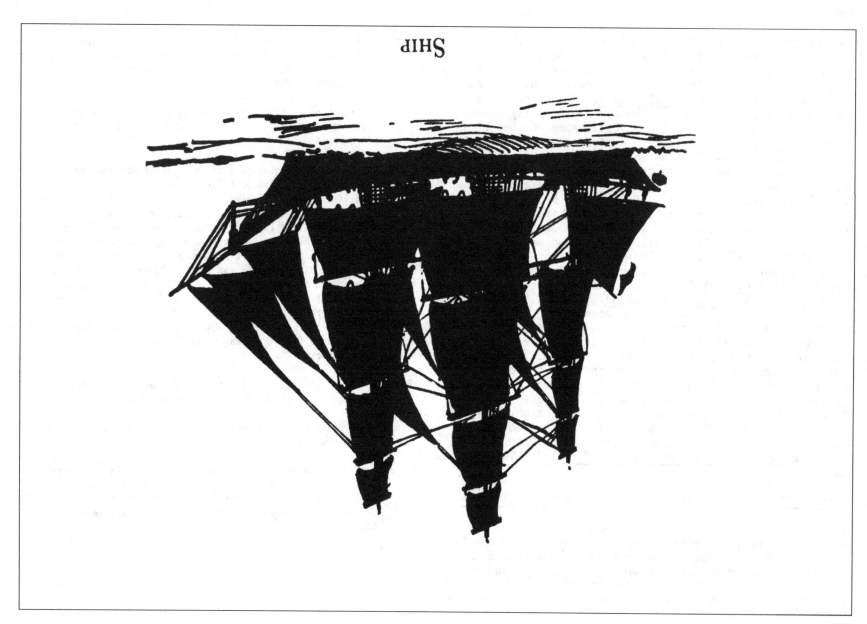

141

day before. I arrived at Norfolk at 5 a.m. of the 20th
where I obtained the assistance of Mr. John R. Harwood a
merchant there and also of Mr. Christopher Frye, a gentleman
of high standing there whom Mr. Harwood wished should be
associated with him in the business. Having noted protest,
I engaged a sloop and schooner and proceeded with them to
the wreck, leaving my brother who came up in one of the
pilot boats to look out for the property. Arrived at the
ship at two a.m. of the 21st and went immediately on board.
The hatches were off and the sea making a breach over her.
During the day cut away the masts when she righted and we
were enabled to get out about 1,200 bushels of wet pepper.
The next day Sunday 22nd had a N.E. snow storm and we could
do nothing.

The result of this illfated voyage was about a total loss of
the ship and cargo and rather more than that to the
underwriters. After doing and saving all that I could at
the cape I proceeded through the country of Norfolk and
thence by steamer up the bay to Baltimore where I remained
until the whole matter was settled with the offices and then
proceeded on my way home. It was now the beginning of
March. The boats had not commenced running to Havre de
Grace and Philadelphia but the stages had been taken off.
There was no communication but by mail wagon, an uncovered
vehicle and could take but one passenger. After waiting
some days for a chance I finally left Baltimore by this
conveyance in the evening. The driver was my only
companion. About midnight we passed through a pile of brush
stuff...

Incident on Way Home - Arrival Home 1820- Voyage of 'Nereus'

...and lumber of trees thrown directly across the road. We
passed through it without difficulty, but it seemed so
evidently placed there for some purpose that I enquired of
the driver if he had any arms to defend himself if
attacked. He said no that the government did not furnish
any, and he did not want them for if attacked and he
resisted, he should undoubtedly be killed, whereas if he

noted protest: a formal document drawn up by the master and a
proportion of the crew of a merchant ship at the time of her
arrival at a port, and sworn before a notary public, or a
consul in a foreign port, that the weather conditions during
a voyage were such that if the ship or cargo sustained damage
it did not happen through neglect or misconduct on their
part. It is a safeguard against the owners of the ship being
held accountable for the damage, if any, if the cause of it
was stress of wind and weather. One of the conditions of
such a protests is that the cargo hatches must not be removed
until a survey has been carried not. (OCSS p. 672)
Note: Since the hatches were removed on D.A. Neal's ship,
the protest must have been finished or 'noted' as he states.
(Ed. note)

breach: the breaking in of the sea, either in a ship or a coastal
defence such as a sea wall. A sea which breaks completely
across a ship is called a clean breach. (OCSS p. 105)

Harris, Walter B., "A Journey through the Yemen and Some General
Remarks upon the Country," Wm. Blackwood and Sons, Edinburgh
and London MDCCCXC111, 1893

Terrain: West: Red Sea, South: Gulf of Aden, interior, mountain
          ranges and elevated plateaus some over 8000' above sea level,
          seaboard on west and south consists of sandy deserts and
          plains, ranging from 30 to 100 mi. wide, head land of Sisi
          Sheikh, southwest corner of Red Sea, mountains reach the sea,
          plains called Tehama, drought, little rain, water from oasis
          and mountain torrents which are usually exhausted by the time
          they reach the sea - believed riverbeds will always have some
          water, plains breed camels, some cereals
          Jibal or highlands: mountains rise abruptly from the Tehama -
          split by wide fertile valleys - coffee grown here, indigo and
          related dye making species, all types of European vegetable
          and fruit trees

          - vast temperature differences - Aden average 85 degrees F.,
          Sanaa in the mountains averages 61 degrees F. (S. capital of
          Yemen) plains dry, mountains produce two wet seasons per
          year, mountains produce also gums

Mokha: peak export city of the coffee - berry but is shipped from
        the mountains by caravans, originally English and Dutch
        created trading factories - a flourishing town containing
        numerous nationalities - French followed Eng. and Dtuch in
        1803, Americans commenced to trade directly
        - British occupation of Aden in 1839 and because of the
        immense superiority of Aden as a port, Mokha fell into decay
        - during first 20 years, constant trouble with the fanatical
        natives (Wahatables according to D.A.N.) and Christians
        augmented by jealousy of European trading habits with which
        they co-operated-was tolerated by the British government
        until 1820, a force under Capt. Bruce was sent to propose a
        treaty with the Iman's Amir along with Capt. Lumley of H.M.S.
        'Topaz' and bombarded Mokha and forced entry into the town -
        resulted in a British factory, agreeing with the treaty of
        commerce with the Yemen government.

Man and Woman of Yemen

made no resistance robbers would probably take the mails and let him go. But he reckoned without his hard. This was Monday. On the next Thursday night he had no passenger, was attacked, the mail robbed, and he tied to a tree and shot dead. Two men named Hutter and Hull were afterwards arrested, convicted and hung for this crime, and one of them, in a confession, made just before his death stated that they had intended and were prepared to commit the robbery on the Monday previous, but finding there was a passenger with the driver and fearing resistance, defered it till the Thursday following which determination probably prolonged the driver's life three days and mine some 40 or 50 years.

I arrived home about the middle of March. Business was now very dull the prospects of foreign trade so poor that many vessels were laid up. Thinking that the darkest time is often just before dawn, I at any rate determined, in spite of my past bad luck, to persevere in the life I had commenced. I took up the Brig 'Nereus' belonging to Mess. N. L. Rogers & Brothers and with my Father and some others undertook a voyage to the Red Sea and Europe with a stock of 50,000 Spanish dollars. Andrew Ward was my first and Joseph Webb my second mate. We sailed on the 2nd of October 1820 and arrived in Mocha Noads Feb. 10, 1821. The place had shortly before been bombarded by a British (E.I. Co.) squadron and the Forts demolished. A treaty was then made with the Imaum of Java who has jurisdiction over this part of Arabia in which it was provided that the Company should have a Resident here and among other privileges, one never before conceded, the ...

Mocha 1821

...very important one of the Resident being allowed to ride through the Mecca gate (the Eastern) if he chose. This office was now held by Capt. Robson of the E.I. Co. marine service who had with him a surgeon Doct. Fay. On my first arrival I hired a house on shore, but shortly after, finding it would be some time before I should get a cargo, I

reckoned without his hard: may be a reference to "hard up in a clinch and no knife to cut the seizing": a sailor's saying indicating that he is overtaken by misfortune and can see no way of winning clear of it. (OCSS p. 374)

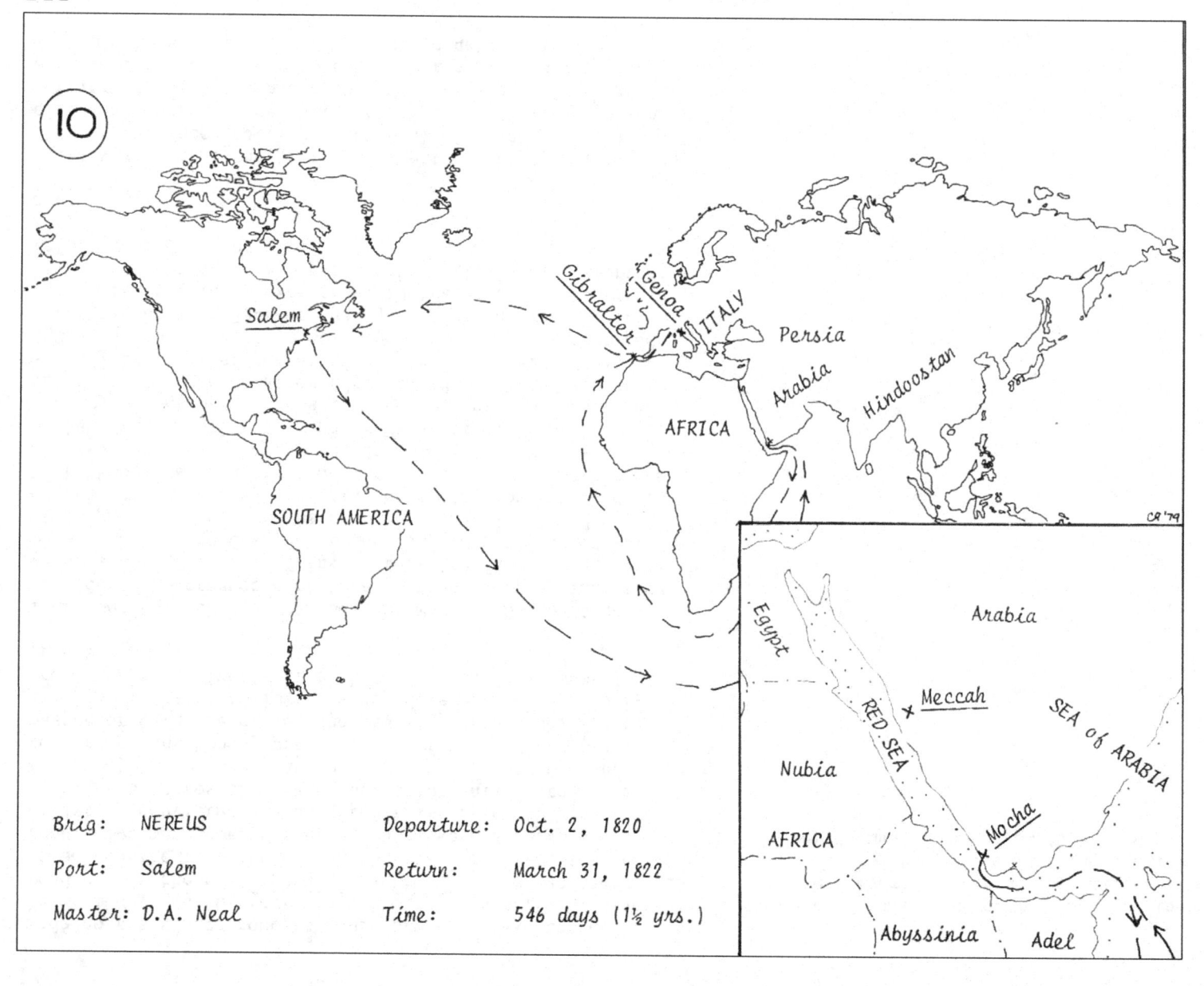

10

Salem

Gibralter · Genoa · ITALY

Persia

Arabia

Hindoostan

AFRICA

SOUTH AMERICA

Egypt

Arabia

RED SEA

× Meccah

SEA of ARABIA

Nubia

Mocha

AFRICA

Abyssinia

Adel

CR '79

Brig: NEREUS

Port: Salem

Master: D.A. Neal

Departure: Oct. 2, 1820

Return: March 31, 1822

Time: 546 days (1½ yrs.)

accepted Capt. Robson's invitiation to live with him. Capt.
Robson also gave me the use of the old English Factory or
Residency, an old delapidated building, but exceedingly well
adapted to the purpose of cleaning and repacking coffee. I
used one room as a sleeping apartment. I then contracted
with Beniger, a resident Parsee merchant, for a cargo of
coffee at $60 per bale of 305 lbs. net, but just at this
time a war broke out in the interior with the wahables, a
tribe who inhabited or rather infested the country between
Mocha and Hodeida, so that for a considerable time all
intercourse was stopped. Beelhopacker is the town in the
coffee country where it is first collected. Sana is the
capital of Arabic felix and the residence of the Imaum who I
believe admits some allegiance to the Pacha of Egypt and
through him to the Grand Sultan of Turkey. The coffee is
ripe in December and begins to come in in January. The
principal export of it is to Judda up the Red Sea and to the
Persian gulf to which places it is taken in the Doans or
native craft. It is brought to Mocha in an unclean state in
bales of 500 lbs. each on the backs of camels, two on each
camel. Those animals are really the ships of the desert.
Mocha is a walled town with some tolerably decent houses,
built of brick and plastered with flat roofs and court yards
in the Spanish style, but they are mostly in a state of
delapidation. There are several small Mosques in which the
Mohamedans are continually worshipping. The country about
Mocha is a desert, the soil of baked clay, with some short
stubble on it, with the exception of a date grove on the
south side about two miles in length and here is the only
drive for a wheeled vehicle. About ...

Pilgrims to Mecca - Parsees

...6 or 8 miles off the hilly country commences, and there
is found a good soil, producing fruits and vegetables in
abundance, but I never had any means of getting to it. I
usually drove out in a horse drawn carriage in the evening
with Capt. Robson through the date grove, but that was the
extent. One evening he thought he would for the first time
exercise his right under the treaty and pass out by the

Water – Heat. continued.

All that can be procured from wells within the walls is blackish. At Baleila some 2 or 3 miles out, there is a spring of very good water & this is brought in in skins & sold for a small sum to those who could afford to pay for it. It cost about one dollar per 100 gallons.

The heat at Mocha is proverbial, but it is only in the month of June, that it is so excessive, & then it is because of the dead calm that prevails & its continuity day & night, than of its very high temperature months from 1st Sept to the last of May, there is generally a good breeze from the water & the air is not disagreeably hot. From Feb to May I did not find a cloth coat uncomfortable. In June in a well shaded room at the English Residency occupied by Lieut Fog, who kept the stone floor wet all the time, the thermometer never indicated, night or day less & it never rose above 98°. Outside however it was much the heat was unbearable, & in the night the desert were like those from the mouth exposed to the sun would For drinking by simply

147

Mecca gate. We did so, but were saluted with stones by the
boys who saw probably for the first time white men driving
towards the Holy City.

Mocha is the rendezvous or rather stopping place of the
numerous pilgrims that every year come to Arabia from all
parts of India to pay their devotions at the alter of
Mahamet (Mohammed) in Mecca. There is a large caravansery
here which is free for their use, but they must bring and
cook their provisions in it themselves. There is not in
Mocha and probably not in Arabia anything like our hotels,
where travellers can find sustenance. None but Mahamotans
are tolerated as permanent residents of Mocha, except under
the treaty with Great Britain and some few parsee merchants
from India. There is a colony of Jews who live about a mile
outside the city. They never mix with the Arabs. Indeed I
believe any intermarriage would be punished with death.
They are blacker than the Arabs, but not so black as the
African, but they retain all the distinguishing features of
the Jewish race. They are a miserable set of outcasts,
living in wretched huts, and subsisting on the little trade
they can carry on and by the distillation of a spiritous
liquor from dates, which though prohibited by the Koran is
used by the more unscrupulous of the Moslems. The parsees
are not allowed to have the female part of their families
with them, and consequently few consider it as their
permanent residence. They retain the Persian worship of
fire and the Bramincal horror of shedding blood. They
cherish everything that has life and the wealthy among them
take turns in distributing bread twice a week equally among
the beggars and the dogs and it would be difficult to say
which were the most numerous, or the most ravenous on these
occasions. On the day that Benjee entertained them I often
stopped at his house to observe them.

Water - Heat

The beggars would arrange themselves around in a semicircle,
and the dogs would occupy the area. The beggars were first
served by handing a loaf for each person and then the dogs

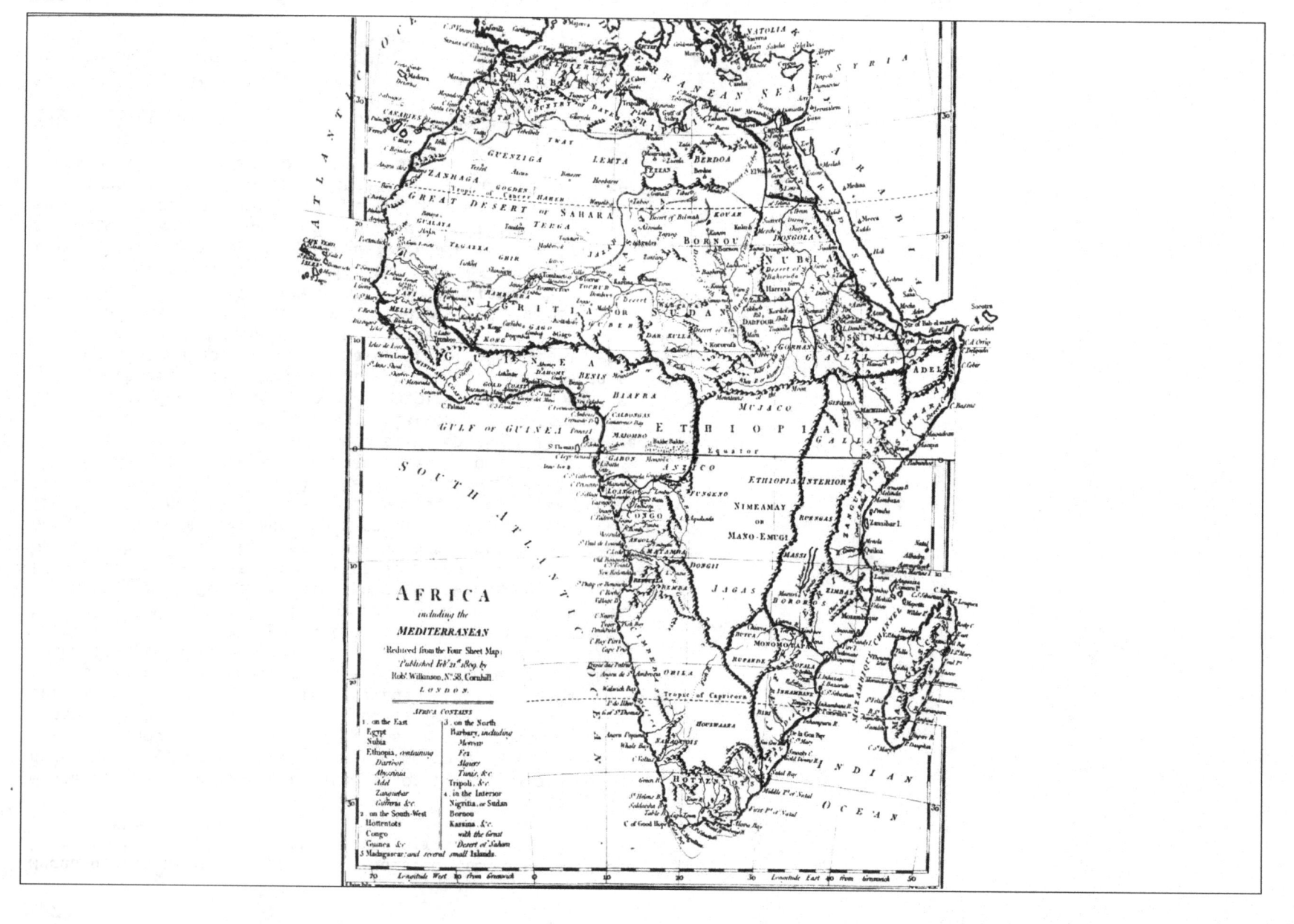

by emptying baskets of bread among them, but for these there was always a general scramble both by the beggars and dogs and each carried off all he culd get.

The want of good water is very much felt at Mocha. All that can be procured from wells within the walls is blackish. At Baleila, some 2 or 3 miles out, there is a spring of very good water and this is brought in in skins and sold for a small sum to those who could afford to pay for it. It cost about one dollar per 100 gallons.

The heat at Mocha is proverbial, but it is only in the month of June that it is so excessive, and then it is because of the dead calm that prevails and its continuity day and night, than of its very high temperature that it is so oppressive. In the Southerly Monsoon, which lasts 9 months from 1st Sept. to the last of May, there is generally a good breeze from the water and the air is not disagreeably hot. From Feb. to May, I did not find a cloth coat uncomfortable. In June in a well shaded room at the English residency occupied by Doct. Fay, who kept the stone floor well wet all the time, the thermometer never indicated night or day less than 92° but it never rose above 98°. Outside however it was much, hotter, and in the sun the heat was unbearable and in the night the night airs that came from the desert were like those from the mouth of a furnace. Water for bathing exposed to the sun would become uncomfortably hot in an hour or two. For drinking however we were able to get deliciously cold water by simply hanging the porous clay goblets that contained it in a draft of air. The rapid evaporation did for it what Wenham Lake ice does for it at home. In May, coffee began to come in plentifully in fulfillment of the contract, and I cleaned and packed it under my own inspection, but when I began to ship it, I was met by a demand for a new export duty of two dollars per bale.

This I resisted and as Benjee the contractor was the Banian of the E.I. Co. and of course under the protection of the English Resident, I had all that influence in my favor. I

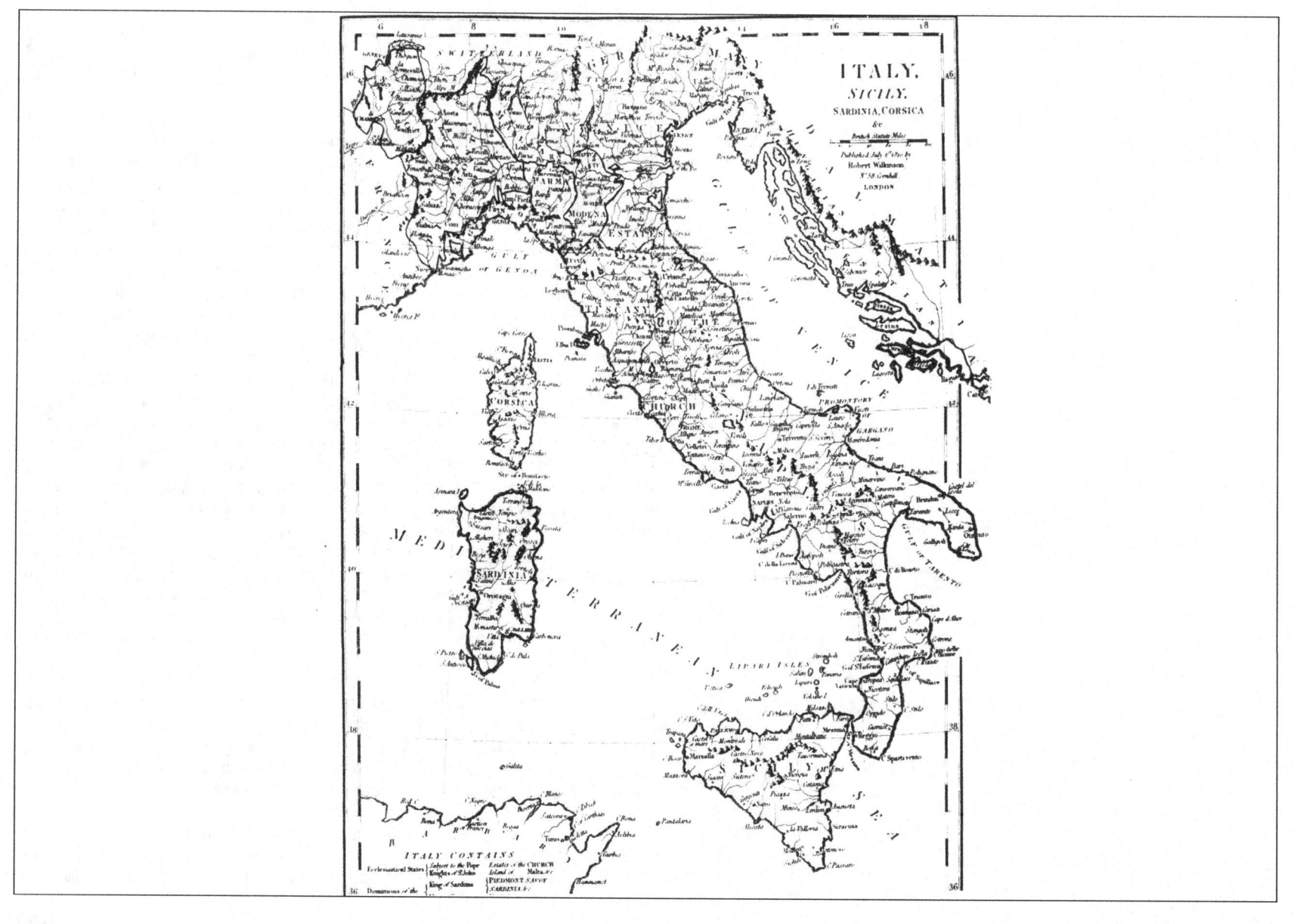

sent a messenger on foot to the Imaun Sana 100 miles
distance. He returned in about a fortnight with orders to
the Dola to permit my cargo to go off on the old terms, but
to enforce the new duty in all future cases.

We sailed with my cargo of 1,000 bales on the 3rd July 1821
for Gibraltar, and arrived after a passage of 135 days on
the 19th of November, got pratique the same day and called
on Horatio Sprague (my old friend of 1811-12) where I found
letters from home communicating the sad news of the death of
my youngest brother Theodore Frederick at Havana, where he
went as supercargo of the Sch. 'Geo. Brooks'. He died on
the 14th of June 1820 of the yellow fever, taken in
consequence of his exertions in the business in which he was
engaged in that pestiferous climate. He was scarcely 19
years of age, having been born Nov. 3rd 1802. He was a
young man of the most kindly disposition, of the purest
conduct, of great industry and uncommon intelligence.
Troops of friends mourned his death and to his immediate
family his loss was irreparable. His Father wore a lock of
his favourite son's hair next to his heart for sixteen
years, and with his last breath directed it to be buried
with him.

Mr. Sprague when I left him in 1812 was first establishing
the first American house in Gibraltar. I now found it as
flourishing and as highly respected as any house in Europe.
He was married to a French lady from Marseilles and had a
young family growing up around him.

Finding no market here for my cargo, I sailed from Gibraltar
on the 22nd of of November, and arrived at Genoa on the 6th
Dec. 1821. Hauled into the quarantine side of the harbour
and were condemned to lay there 35 days but finally got off
in 27. Mr. Lawes of the house of Campbell Lawes & Co. to
whom I consigned and Capt. Curtis of ship 'Cyrus' of Boston
(now the agent of Brown Brothers in Boston) met me at the
Lazrarette on the day of our arrival. After ascertaining
the state of the markets elsewhere I sold the whole cargo at
a price that netted 33¢ per lb. Being allowed to discharge

Attached to the leaves of the family "Neal Record". An obituary for
Theo. F. Neal possibly from a Salem paper

"Died in Havana, June 14, Mr. Theodore Frederick Neal, aged 19,
youngest son of Jonathan Neal, Esq. of this town. Possessed of good
natural talents, which had been cultivated and developed by a proper
education with the stability of character, and discretion wonderful
for his year, he was just coming into life under the most favourable
auspices-the pride and delight of his friends-esteemed wherever he
was known-a favourite with the aged-and a fair example to the
young. He was a son, of whom a father might be proud-and brothers
and sisters were attached to him, not merely from the common
anstinet of natural relationship, but because through many years of
the most intimate intercourse, in sickness and in heatlh, at home
and abroad, he had exhibitied such a conciliating disposition, so
much attractive generosity, and such an unwearied attention to the
most trivial claims of friendship, that not to love him, were to
resist the strongest impulse, of which the worse nature is
susceptible. His friends esteemed him, because he was so true a
friend. He never violated the sanctity of mutual confidence - he
never wantonly injured the feelings or invaded the rights of
another. He was respected, because his industry, which never
allowed him for a moment to be idle - his probity, which was founded
upon principle, and not upon convenience - his careful discreet
management of whatever he undertook, are the very qualities which
fit a young man for the duties of life, and insure to him reputation
and success."

in quarantine, I did so, but was obliged to land the cargo
in the quarantine depot on the coast outside the harbour.
Fearing that the dampness of the lower ...

Gale at Genoa - Description of the City

...floor might injure the flavor of the coffee I had it all
taken up into the second story and luckily enough for on the
24th of Dec. one or two days after it was all landed, we had
the most tremendous storm ever experienced in Genoa. The
<u>stone mole</u> which served as a breakwater on the western side
of the harbour, was much injured, and several hundred feet
of it washed entirely away. The vessels at quarantine being
under a point of land and moored stem and stern, were with
two or three exceptions uninjured, but every vessel of every
description in the harbour and on the city side were driven
on shore, or dashed to pieces.

The next morning the whole bay was covered with the
fragments of vessels, and the merchandise they contained.
The depot where my cargo was stored stood about 100 feet
from the seashore. The waves rolled in with tremendous
force, and reaching the building stove in its heavy doors
and completely flooded the whole lower floor. Had I not, to
avoid an entirely different danger, put my cargo aloft every
pound of it would have been wet and about a total loss have
accrued to the owners, for being on shore it was no longer
covered by the insurance. As it was, not a bag was
injured. We were admitted to <u>pratique</u> Jan. 2nd 1822.

Genoa is too well known to need any description here. It
has not probably altered for the last 100 years, except to
deteriorate.

It has only two streets where carriages can pass, and these
are streets of palaces, but palaces that indicate poverty
rather than wealth. Most of them have been abandoned by the
renowned families to whom they belonged, from inability to
meet the expense of living in them, and they have been
rented to merchants for their residences or compting rooms

mole: a long pier or breakwater forming part of the sea defences
of a port. It can be built either in the form of a detached
or constructed entirely in the sea or with one end of it
connected to the shore. (OCSS p. 553)

pratique: a certificate given to a ship when she arrives from a
foreign port, the port health officer of the point of arrival
is satisfied that the health of all on board is good and that
there are no cases of notifiable disease in the ship. A ship
remains in quarantine on arrival in port until she has been
granted her certificate of pratique (OCSS p. 668)

Its Commerce — Return to U.S. 1822.

a small, but well constructed entrepot, where all dut...
goods are landed and stored, until the duties are paid. This entrepot has a good quay for landing merchandize, a number
of fire proof stores and a wall around it, from which there is
expressly only one gate on the side of the city.

I took in a cargo of Smyrna fruit, Rays &c on freight &
sailed on the seventh of February for Boston, where we arrived
on the 31st of March 1822 —

While at Genoa I corresponded with my brother William, who
was in Antwerp with a cargo of coffee from Batavia —
also with John Well & Co, Leghorn, who were sorely disappointed
that I had not chosen that place instead of Genoa for the sale of my
cargo, and with Sam. Williams, London, to whom I remitted part
of the proceeds of my cargo — and part I took home in Specie.
J. Campbell Lawes & Co. did my business very much
but they were afterwards unfortunate &
to the house of Grant Bros & Co. Trieste.
I remained at home till the
chased one quarter of
retained the

155

and in many cases for much meaner purposes. All the other
streets are so narrow as to render a passage through them
impossible, except on foot or in sedan chairs carried on
men's shoulders, and those are the only modes of passing
from one place to another in the city. The most beautiful
part of this city is located on the side of the mountain
which overlooks the ...

Its Commerce - Return to U.S. 1822

...city and is included within its walls. It is studded
with beautiful villas and gardens laid out in terraces
rising one above the other, and affording a picturesque view
both of and from the sea.

Genoa has always been a commercial city, as the birthplace
of Columbus should be, but it has lost much of its ancient
importance in this respect, though still it has a
considerable trade in the foreign supplies required in Savoy
Piedmont & Lombardy, and exports hemp, silk and silk goods,
velvets, rugs, etc. Its conveniences for business are
exceedingly good. It has a splendid harbour, a small but
well constructed entré port, where all dutiable goods are
landed and stored until the duties are paid. This entre
port has a good quay for landing merchandize, a number of
fire proof stores and a wall around it, from which there is
egress by only one gate on the side of the city.

I took in a cargo of Smyna fruit, rugs, etc. on freight and
sailed on the seventh of February for Boston, where we
arrived on the 31st March, 1822.

While at Genoa I corresponded with my brother William who
was in Antwerp with a cargo of coffee from Batavia - also
with John Webb & Co. Leghorn, who were sorely disappointed
that I had not chosen that place instead of Genoa for the
sale of my cargo, and with Saml. Williams, London, to whom I
remitted part of the proceeds of my cargo   and part I took
home in specie.

entré port: or entrépôt: a description often used for the
particular type of trade of a port. The strict meaning of
the word is a place to which goods are brought for
distribution top other parts of the world, and when used in
connection with a port is generally taken to mean the centre
to which local manufacturers or produce is brought for
export. It is frequently used, however, to indicate trade in
the opposite direction; a port is said to be an entrpot for
the goods imported from overseas for distribution in its
immediate neighbourhood. (OCSS p. 288)

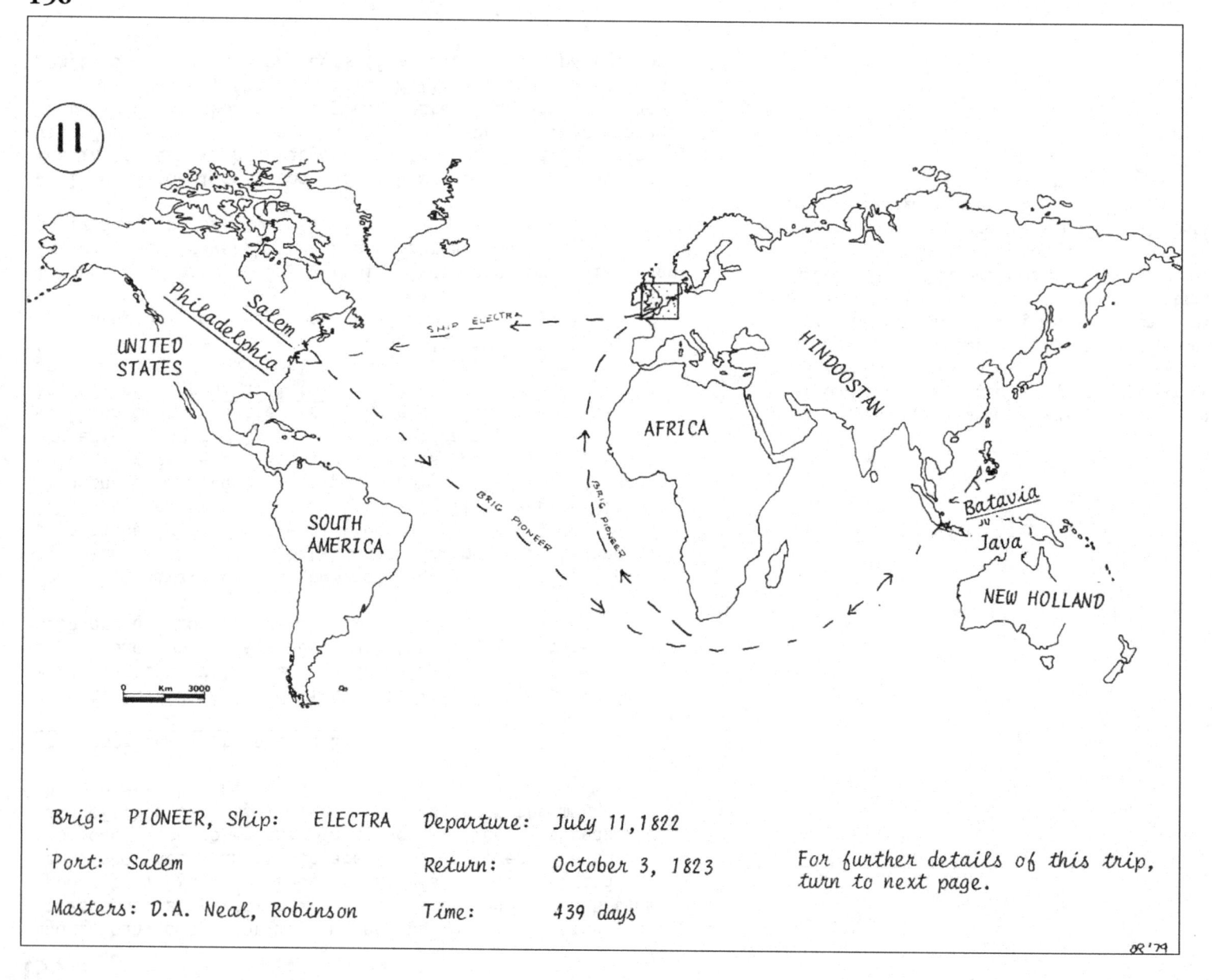

Brig: PIONEER, Ship: ELECTRA   Departure: July 11, 1822

Port: Salem   Return: October 3, 1823   For further details of this trip, turn to next page.

Masters: D.A. Neal, Robinson   Time: 439 days

157

The house of Campbell Lawes & Co. did my business very much
to my satisfaction, but they were afterwards unfortunate &
failed. Campbell went into the house of Grant Bros. & Co.
Triests, and Lawes, I believe, died poor. I remained at
home till the 11th of July following when having purchased
one quarter of the new Brig. 'Pioneer' of the N. L. Rogers &
Bros. who retained the balance, I sailed for Batavia in
ballast with specie for a cargo of coffee. Mr. Andrew Ward
was my chief officer. We arrived in Batavia roads Oct.
23rd. Not being able to procure a cargo at once I took a
government freight to Rembung and back to Batavia and sent
the vessel in charge of Mr. Ward. She sailed the 3rd
November. On the 9th arrived at Rembung loaded salt for
Packalongon, sailed on the 16th and on the 24th sailed from
Packalongon for Tagal where she loaded rice and arrived back
to Batavia the 7th of December.

roads: a protected place near shore where ships may ride at
anchor (ACD)

While the Brig was away, I, in company with Mr. John
Shillaber (who did my business) and two other gentlemen made
a trip to Beutenzing (the seat of the Governor General of
Dutch India) and thence into the hills 20 miles beyond the
plantation of an Englishman, an acquaintance of Mr.
Shillaber's. We had a carriage we hired in Batavia and took
gov. horses, which are stationed every five pauls (4 1/2
miles) along the great road which extends the whole length
of the Island of Java. The climate in the interior is very
salurious and not too warm. At Beulenzing, ever, we found a
blanket at night not uncomfortable. We met with great
hospitality everywhere, and were much delighted with our
trip. The horses were the small breed of the island, and a
driver belonged to each stud of 4, which number we took at
each station. They would go the distance in from 15 to 22
minutes and were then walked back without being put up to
the place they came from.

I loaded the Brig with coffee bought at the Gov. public sale
and left for Europe on the 2nd April 1823 and arrived at
Cowes (Isle Wight) on the 17th of April 1823. From Cowes I
went over to Portsmouth and there took a coach for London to
consult with Mr. Williams - remained only one day, though it

Crawford, John "History of the Indian Archipelago", 3 Vol.
      Archibald Constable and Co., Edinburgh 1820
Vol. 1
P.7:   brown and negro peoples, brown being superior
       - brown: short, squat, robust men, 5'2" women 4'11", lower
       limbs heavy

P.35: Manners: vegetarian, slow, not active, unclean, but bathe
      frequently due to climate in foulest or purest water: often
      washwater dumped under bamboo flouring boards and give rise
      to maggots and noxious smells - don't change often so wear
      dark garments - relieve themselves in holes in their floors
      if sick or rivers if well, washing in the same water
      - eat fish, rice, spices
      - habitual drinking
      p. 53 hospitality practised widely
      - roads created not to cross water with no regard for
      peoples property, windy and often upsetting houses and trees
      along the way - revenge: never forget - a "muck" is an act of
      desparate excess i.e.: a series of impetuous murders for
      which he seeks homage since he was not responsible for his
      actions, etc.

Marriage:
      - women eat with men, come at a price into marriage, not
      secluded, good deal of equality, active in business life, can
      be raised to the throne, eats from the right side of her
      husbands bowl, better classes have more seclusion but not
      rigidly enforced, simply as a point of manners
      - first wife is mistress of the house, second and third
      wives, etc. little better than handmaidens
      - divorce available - women as wanton as husbands
      - good parent-child relationships

      - marriage at age of puberty but arrangements can be made
      much earlier for woman, men, two to three years older, -
      women old maids at 18 yrs., but age does not stop possibility
      of marriage.

Courtship: arranged by parents and youthful interference would be
      scandalous, fathers get to-gether, then mothers, then if
      succesful, youths betrothed - gift presented by future groom

to future bride, a ring, cloth, etc.
- family and friends of future groom visiting brides father
and bringing fruits, viands to give publicity to event
- price paid night before nuptials, gifts of money, jewels,
cloths, kine, buffaloes, rice etc.
- money or goods going to parents of bride usually
- ceremonies solemnized at the house of brides father
- public processions, horses included, groom astride, bride
in a litter, music, gay attire
- many ceremonies connected with births, but little
importance give to names - circumcision on men, 8 - 12 yrs.,
women, about same age

Funerals buried same day or next, wrapped in white cloth, no coffin,
      simple mound of earth and an unmarked stone
      - respect for ancestors and property of forefathers, annual
      visit to the grave with flowers

Mannerisms: respectful to cover the head, turn's one back on a
      superior, to sit cross - legged on the ground, an inferior
      addresses a superior, palms joined, thumbs touching nose, end
      of each phrase, bows, little class distinction
      - embracing
      - use intoxicating narcotics, prepared areca and betel nuts

Areca: a species of pepper vine plus terra japonica, a bitter
      astringent plus quicklime plus fruit of areca palm

Betel Nuts: highly narcotic and leaves a red colour covering teeth,
      gums, lips, a brownish red, believed a sign of beauty
      - smoking tobacco adopted 1601
      - opium, liquor

Commerce:
      Indigo: exported in liquid in large jars, Dutch monopoly,
      manufactured at 2 sch. 3 d. and exported at about same price.
      -Pepper: Penang and west of Sumatra best, 4 Spanish
      dollars/picul 1 (Indonesian) picul: 136.16 lbs., 61.76 kg.)
      -Coffee: Java, 4 Spanish dolls/picul

                            . . . . . .

Earl, G. Windsor "The Eastern Seas in the Indian Archipelago in 1832, 33, 34" Wm. J. Allen and Co. London, 1832

Aug. 1832 p. 3
- trade winds in higher latitudes very changeable - water colour change and disappearance of the flying fish indicated land (near Java) - prevailing easterly - sailed along shore to the westward and when mist cleared - lined by a range of hills sloping to the beach - slides covered with trees
- high peaked mountains 50 miles inland - Dutch forbidden merchants to land on south end of island (Java)
- however needed water provisions so entered
- entered small creek on which bamboo huts were erected for natives to collect water - houses low, 2 rooms fishing PRAHU
- local craft - houses shaded by large trees mostly palms - native SARONGS draped clothing - often morning free of Europeans in Java

Ayer: fishermen or occupations connected with the fort - inland villages grow sweet potatoes, yams etc. and sell very cheaply
- schooner soon surrounded by small canoes having turtles, ducks, foul, cockatoos, monkies and numbers of animals and birds for selling to passing ships
- monkeys believed to prevent sickness in houses if kept near the stables
- wind high as they proceeded to Batavia - winds off land brought aromatic smell of decaying vegetation, created a chilly damp sensation and probably contained malaria germs
- monsoons upon us - difficult navigation among low islands and coral reefs

Batavia: approach covered with ennumerable islets clothed in uxuriant vegetation - native boats - Prahus with yellow mat sails shoot out from behind them - tops of trees can be seen sails of stately sails of merchant ships in harbour rounded Ontang, Java's point Sept. 2 and bore up for Batavia road, occasionally viewing island shipping between them number of fishing boats, large, were standing with us into the roads, 14 or 15 tons each, graceful with 1 immense square sail - since breeze strong, thick plank thrust wind ward for an outrigger on which several of the crew sat to prevent capsizing

anchored - visited by guard ship - observed neighbouring ships, mostly Dutch, American, English
went into harbour next day, in a boat covered with a canvas awning - river is carried out about a mile into the sea between 2 piers to keep the channel from silting in
when near one pier, boat's crew jumped on one with a rope to pull boat up since current too strong to row

- fever has carried off many Europeans since vapours cover the ships at night, spreading the germ - remedies proving as harmful as the cause-just returning to ships in the damp night air has proven harmful
- coffee and pepper heavily taxed and and monopolised by Dutch sugar close behind - natives being paid pathetic amounts and often burned crops in desparation

Spices by Regions: Moluccas: coffee, pepper, Celebes and Sumatra: gold dust and diamonds, Borneo: tin, Banka: tortoise-shell, bees wax, dye wood, Timor: and Subawa, and other east ward islands, rice the mainstay of their diet Chinese, Japanese etc. amount to at least 100 thousand, most of Mallay extraction

- natives are slaves boatmen, servants, labourers, no wealthy ones due to the Dutch and heavy taxes

. . . . .

Water Carrier in Batavia

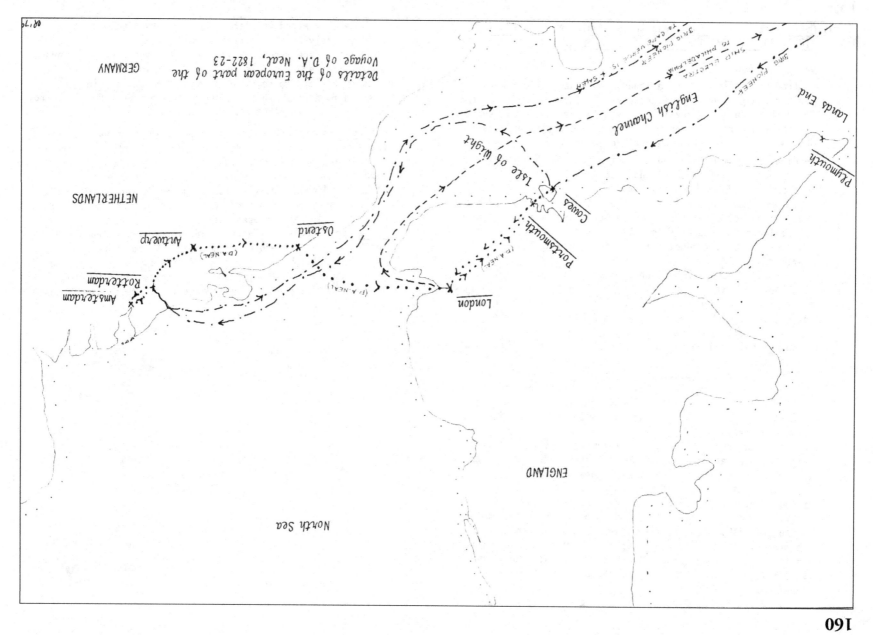

Details of the European part of the
Voyage of D.A. Neal, 1822-23

GERMANY

NETHERLANDS

Antwerp   Ostend   (D.A NEAL)

Amsterdam
Rotterdam   (D.A NEAL)   London   Portsmouth

Isle of Wight

Cowes

English Channel

To CAPE VERDE IS → SALEM

3rd PIONEER

SHIP ELECTRA
to PHILADELPHIA

BRIG PIONEER

3rd PIONEER

Lands End

Plymouth

North Sea

ENGLAND

161

was my first visit to London. Stopped at the New England coffee house near the Exchange. Having got the requisite information returned to Cowes and proceeded to Rotterdam, where we arrived in 3 or 4 days and hauled alongside the Bumpties opposite the residence of Mr. Cellings of the house of Cellings and Maingy to whom I consigned the cargo and by whom after holding it some time it was finally sold.

Not however being willing to detain the vessel until this could be done, I dispatched her in charge of Mr. Ward to the Cape de Verds for a cargo of salt, remaining behind to look after the cargo. During this time I visited Amsterdam to see Messrs. Hope & Co. (Vanderhup, Selin & Labouchere the partners) and corresponded with Messrs. Muteus Russelman & Co. Antwerp, before I ...

Antwerp - London - Passage to Philadelphia 1823

...decided to sell in Rotterdam. I then took Bills of Exchange for the net funds of my cargo and proceeded to London via Antwerp & Ostend in July. In Antwerp I became personally acquainted with Mr. Mosselman, Mr. Solens and at Brussels with Mr. Mertus and his family. In London I had lodgings at the London Coffee house, Ludgate hill. Found Mr. Josh Bates residing here as the agent of Mr. William Gray in Broad St. Buildings. Saw a good deal of Mr. S. Williams at his house 14 Finsbury Square. After stopping at the London Coffee house, I went to a boarding house where there were several Americans living in Tinsbury Street. I took part of my funds in specie, and the part belonging to my Father and myself in U.S. Bank Stock, and with these took passage for Philadelpia in the ship 'Electra', Capt. Robinson. I went down to Cowes to join her, and there having a day to spare drove across the Isle of Wight to the south side, in company with some other of her passengers. We arrived at Philadelphia on the 28th of Sept. thence home, stopping one day in New York where I sold my U.S. Bank Stock to Prome Ward & King at a handsome advance. I arrived in Salem on the 3rd of October.

New England Coffee House: a business exchange for trading Bills of Exchange and other merchantile pursuits. There was a coffee house per colony in England. (Ed. note)

Bumpties: believed similar to the modern bumpers to prevent hulls of ships from rubbing against the dock plus some place to attach a mooring line, thus bumpties. (Ed. note)

United States Bank Stock: stocks issued by the National Bank of the United States, partially backed by specie and the majority backed by federal bonds at an attempt to stabilize the American dollar. At this time Pres. Hamilton's ideas were very new and somewhat speculative. Thus the bonds could be recalled for specie at any time, in theory. As it happened, in the 1837 depression the bonds were recalled and thousands of independent banks went under. (H. May, "A synopsis of American History", C. Sellers, N. McMillen, Rand McNally, U.S.A. 1976, Page 108)

162

Brig: ACTIVE	Departure: March, 1824
Port: Salem	Return: April 29, 1826
Master: T. Tunison	Time: 633 days (1 2/3 yrs.)

SOUTH AMERICA Boundaries Circa 1813

During my absence on the above voyage my first child, Theodore Frederick was born - to wit on the 18th of December 1822, but lived but a few hours, his mother having at the time a severe fit of sickness from which at one time it seemed doubtful if she would recover. She was however quite well when I got home. We were now living in a house belonging to Mr. John Dodge on Essex Street, standing where the new building of Capt. Bertram's 110310 has since been erected.

I remained at home during the winter of 1823-4 during which time I agreed to take an interest in a new Brig called the 'Active' with Mr. Charles Saunders, Mr. Wm. P. Richardson & Messrs. Pearce & Nichols with the view to a voyage to Europe and thence to the west coast of South America. We dispatched her early in March in charge of Mr. Junis Tunisin who was to act ...

Brig 'Active' - Passage to Liverpool in 'Emerald' - 1824

...as chief officer, after I should join her in Europe. With that view I took passage for Liverpool in the ship 'Emerald', Capt. Fox, and sailed from Boston on the 21st of March 1824. The 'Emerald' was a fine ship, one of the regular line of packets across the Atlantic and Capt. Fox had a great reputation for making some of the shortest passages ever known. His last had been less than 15 days from Liverpool to Boston. We had several passengers, some of them ladies. I recollect among them the late Doct. Robbins, his wife and a Miss --- afterwards the wife of the Rev. Mr. Ward. I soon found that Capt. Fox was excessively intemperate and the greater the difficulty he was in, the worse he was. His wife and child were on board. Her brother was his chief officer and perfectly dreaded him, being afraid to move except in accordance with his orders. Capt. Fox carried sail very hard and frequently alarmed the passengers, but I saw no particular danger, except when we crossed the Banks of Newfoundland where we fell in with ice islands. We had a good breeze, not very foggy, and in the day time there was no danger. That night however it blew

Published in June, 1824, this etching illustrates the arrangements
in the best passenger accommodation in the contemporary short
voyage packet ship. The sexes aren't segregated and those
who can handle food have to fight against the motion on the
central table.

strong from the west, and we run at the rate of ten miles an
hour. But for the vigilence of the crew, not one of whom I
believe closed his eyes, the risk would have been imminent
of being dashed to pieces against the icebergs. It was <u>hard
up and hard down</u> all night to avoid them. The Capt. was <u>of
course drunk</u>.

The passengers did not know of the danger and were not
alarmed, till the next day when we passed a number of them
close to. But then we could see and the danger was over.
We had a good run to Cape Clear. Going up Irish Channel we
had a fresh gale from the northwest, reducing us to double
reefed topsails. A little after dark we pased the small
lights on our starboard hand, <u>close hauled</u>. The Capt. by
this time had got pretty mellow. He gave orders to keep on
the course we were steering (about NNE) and went below. I
was on deck with the 1st officer who had the first watch.
From 8 to near 9 I watched the bearings of the light and
found the ship was drifting or carried by the current almost
bodily to leeward. Being so near the wind under short sail
she of course made some leeway, which with the tide would
eventually carry us upon the rocks off the coast.

Incident on Board 'Emerald'

I pointed this out to the mate. He tried repeatedly to
rouse the Captain and finally rolled him off the sofa onto
the floor, but it did not wake him. He was dead drunk. I
then told the mate he must put the ship on the other tack
and stand out. He said he did not dare to do it. I at once
sung out all hands about ship - the men jumped on the word.
I took the helm, put her round and then was obliged to haul
close on a wind to weather the rocks on which the small
lights were placed and we hardly did so. The second mate
who was of course on the forecastle told me that when the
word 'hard alee' was given by me, he thought he could have
tossed a biscuit ashore, so near were we to the iron bound
coast of Wales, and where had we struck, not a soul could
have been saved. Once more clear I gave up the ship to the
mate who let her jog on till the Capt., having slept off his

hard up and hard down: believed to mean tacking or similar
sailing technique to create veering motions, a combination of
steering and sail handling techniques, up meaning into the
wind and down, down from the wind. Hard means it was done
fast as is most sailing in winds of any caliber. (Ed. note)

very hard and close hauled: a condition of sailing when a vessel
trims her sails so that she proceeds as close to the wind as
possible with all her sails full and not shivering. (OCSS p.
173)

The par... ... had occured, ...

afterwards (and he lived ...

did not remind me how his life ...

were saved on this occasion. I went ...

London, and called on Mr. H. Williams, and ...

his house some of our own passengers, and also seve...

Boston gentlemen, who had been waiting to take pas-

sage in the Emerald, home, so great was the reputation

of this ship and her commander, for short passages.

But they got some hints and took some other convey-

ance. Fox was discharged as soon as he returned to Boston, & finally died

Arrival in London — Hamburg — Bremen

I believe, a common hand, in some fishing craft out of Hingham.

After spending a few days in London, part of the time at

Highgate in the family of Mr. Josh. Bates, he continuing the

special agent of Mr. Gray in Europe. I took passage on the

24th April in the P. O. packet for Hamburg. Here I engaged

Messrs. Strain Brodie & Co to assist me in my proposed in-

... I proceeded to make my purchases of Silesia &

... here & in Bremen for the Octive which

... from Charlestown S.C. on the 2d

consigned by agreement

... Taking in

grog, came on deck, probably about 12 o'clock and enquired
how she headed, and finding she had her starboard instead of
her larboard tacks on board, angrily enquired why she had
been put about without his orders, but on being told who had
done it, slunk back and let her jog till morning. As soon
as I saw him after breakfast I took him aside and told him
the danger we had been in and what I had done, and assured
him that if he took another drop of spirits till we got a
pilot I would take charge of the vessel and confine him a
prisoner in his state room and so take him into port. He
was exceedingly humble and begged hard that he should not be
exposed, and promised all that I required. The next day,
April 13.th, we arrived at Liverpool. The passengers found
out from the second mate all that had occurred, and I
believe Doct. Robbins never met afterwards (and he lived
several years in Boston) that he did not remind me how his
life and that of his family were saved on this occasion. I
went immediately to London and called on Mr. S. Williams and
found at his house some of our own passengers, and also
several Boston gentlemen who had been waiting to take
passage in the 'Emerald' home. So great was the reputation
of this ship and her commander for short passages. But they
got some hints and took some other conveyance. Fox was
discharged as soon as he returned to Boston, and finally
died,...

Arrival in London - Hamburg - Bremen

...I believe, a common hand, in some fishing craft out of
Hingham.

After spending a few days in London, part of the time at
Highgate in the family of Mr. Josh. Bates, he continuing the
special agent of Mr. Gray in Europe, I took passage on the
24th April in the P.O. packet for Hamburg. Here I engaged
Messrs. Pitcain Brodie & Co. to assist me in my proposed
investments. I proceeded to make my purchases of Silesia
and Westphalian goods here and in Bremen for the Active
which vessel arrived at Hamburg from Charlestown S.C. on the
2nd of June, with a cargo of rice, consigned by agreement
(being partly on owners a/c) to Mess Merck & Co.

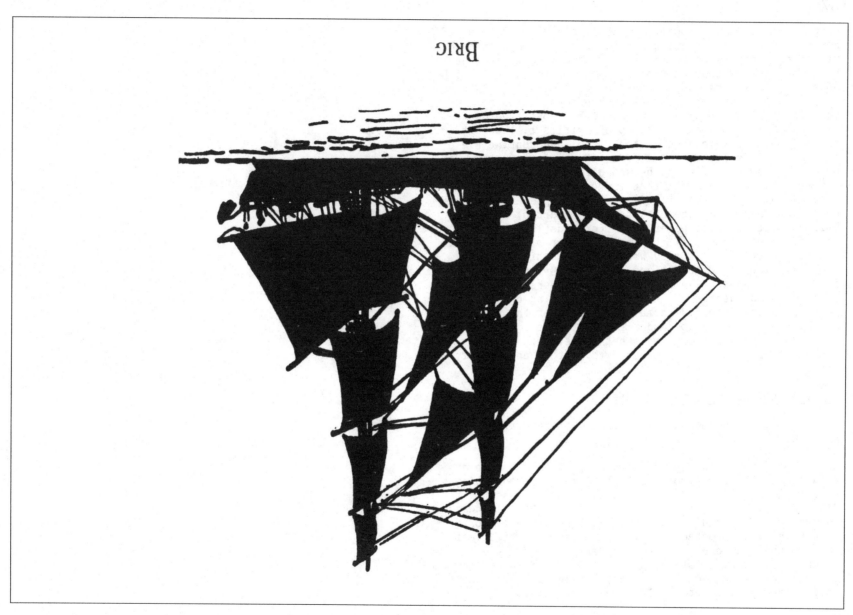

On the 5th she was discharged and commenced taking in her
outward cargo. Having done so, on the 20th she proceeded
round to the Weser, and anchored at Bremerhaven where she
took in the goods purchased at Bremen and on the 4th of
August I took charge of the Brig and proceeded to sea.

The three months thus spent in the two cities of Hamburg and
Bremen gave me an excellent opportunity of acquainting
myself with the commerce, the manufactures and the customs
of these free cities of the Hanseatic league. Though under
the influence of the German diet they are practically
independent. Each has its own exclusive territorial
jurisdiction and government. The Senate of Hamburg was one
of the most respectable political bodies in Europe, being
composed of citizens of great wealth and character. Though
despoiled of its commercial importance and prosperity by the
French invasion, it was at this time recovering rapidly and
becoming again the centre of the trade of some of the most
populous districts of Germany while Bremen absorbed
spacially that of Westphalia. Mr. Pitcain, the head of the
house of Pitcain, Brodie & Co. with whom I conducted my
business in Hamburg, and Mr. Fred Deleus of the house of
Fred and Edward Deleus, who purchased for me in Bremen, both
exertd themselves in an extraordinary manner to enable me to
effect in the best possible manner the objects I had in
view, besides lavishing on me the most gratifying personal
attentions.

The old town of Hamburg, like nearly all European cities
consists of narrow, crooked and ill paved streets, but the
newer parts are laid out with liberality and convenience.
What was once the site of immense fortifications is now in
both Hamburg and Bremen laid out into the most beautiful
walks & gardens in the English style, every vestige of the
ramparts, except their height above the surrounding country,
having been obliterated. The environs of both towns, but
especially of Hamburg are delightful, being the residence of
most of the merchants, or the site of splendid public or
private gardens,...

Fracker, Geo. "Voyage to South America with an Account of a
Shipwreck in the River La Plate in 1817", Ingraham and Hewes,
Boston, 1826
Buenos Ayres: P. 98
- tides in river - bed of river hard sand, low tide, no
boats get near shore and many gain a living conveying goods
between ships and shore

Montevideo: eastern side of river, houses low, 2 stories in front,
1 story in rear forming a square and a court in centre,
strongly fortified - Portugese, taken in 1813

Buenos Ayres: capital of the provinces of the Rio de las Plata -
ancient and gloomy appearance - streets at right angles,
paved, good sidewalks, street runs along the beach parallel
with the river, extent of city and many pedestrians enjoy in
the early morning - blacks washer women along shore brought
down on trays on their heads and select a natural hole in the
tuskers of sand, pipes or cigars in mouth and beat the clothes
- bathing: mixed sexes wantingly and promiscuously both in
evening as is custom, women who are accompanied by a female
slave
- women while enveloped in a sheet, disrobe beneath and slip
into the bathing costume - no impropriety
- Bull baiting in Plaza de low Toras
- Carnival, women pour water on strangers below, boys sell
egg shells filled with scented water, closed with wax and
thrown at females
- horses, bullocks, dogs and sheep in vast regions run wild,
swine small and black, dogs in great numbers and often
dangerous to the traveller
- milk in earthen jars carried by boys 7 to 14 yrs. old
- horses NOT ridden through town as would be bad manners
- leopards, lions, wildcats, ostrich,
- melons, grapes, peaches
- mild and peaceful people, smokers fond of "Yerba"
- women, black eyes, hair, flute-like voices, flirt with
fan, fair complex - country girls smoke cigars, flowers
presented as hospitable

- country carts: awkward, singular, as tall as a 2 storey
house, sides and roof of cane, bottom of solid wood, front
part under an arched roof sits the driver, stout pole
suspended over his head extending to the foremast of the 6
oxen, in hand a shorter pole used to spur nearer cattle on
(longer pole spear pointed and by touching it at the cart
end, can direct oxen) lashed at back is a large earthen jar
of 20 gal. of water - no grease in axle so squeaks incessantly
- when caravan halts, cook meat overfire, resting on stakes,
squatte in a circle with a matte to drink
- custom to kneel at a venerable carriage going to
administer last rites, old fashioned carriage pulled by half
starved mules - even strangers enforced to do this
- priests have extreme powers over the simple people,
numerous religious figures and generally well off
- beef sold at 75¢ a quarter, a sheep dressed, 25¢
- slaves well fed and leisurely, fleas abundant
- Paysanos - cattlemen - saddle a few pieces of square cloth
and leather, triangular wooden stirrups, green hide straps
for big toe
- lassos - iron ring instead of slip knot, estancias: large
farms

Peru

Funerals: after twilight-each person carries a lighted candle,
hearse folowed by priests chanting-corpse left in church all
night and interred next day-mass for the soul celebrated
months later-
- Negroes sing-expensive ceremony

Marriage: 2 parts: first a simple benediction on joining hands,
second parties go to Church and the veiling, bride covered in
a veil, and kneels with the groom before the alter, after
mass places the ring on brides finger and presents her with
13 pieces of money then given to the curate

continued....

Environs - Left for S. America - Arrival at Montevideo

...in the latter of which, especially on Sundays, it seemed
as if all the population was gathered together in social
groups enjoying themselves in a most rational manner. The
house of Pitcain, Brodie & Co. was dissolved some few years
after I left Hamburg by the death of Mr. Brodie and the
removal of Mr. Pitcain to New York with his only daughter
who married a German and lived there several years. He must
have been dead a long time, but I never heard of it. The
house of Deleus at Bremen, I believe still exists, conducted
probably by some of the younger members, though I have never
been advised of the death of those partners that I knew then.

On our way to Chile we stopped about the 24th of October at
Montevideo and stopped a day or two, but found the country
in a state of civil commotion and nothing to be done there,
or at Buenos Ayres, and therefore proceeded on, passing
through the straights of Le Mane, round Cape Horn and
arrived at Valparaiso on the 29th Nov. 1824.

I found there four American vessels. Markets were
depressed. The metallic currency had been much diminished.
The Government under Freyre was undisturbed by intestine
conflicts, but was without energy, without money, and
without any efficient army or navy. Commerce was of course
languishing and rendered more so by the Estance System by
which a monopoly of all liquors and tobacco was given into
private hands. I employed here Mr. Schultze, a German
acting for the house of Huth, Gunning & Co., London and Huth
Coit & Co. Lima. During the first three weeks in December
made some considerable sales. On the 23rd or 4th, being in
treaty with Don Ramon Dios, a Spanish merchant of Valparaiso
for a large portion of the cargo, the result of which would
depend on some parties at St. Jago de Chile. I went up to
that city in company with Don Ramon, Mr. Schultze and
several Spaniards. We left Valparaiso on horseback on April
the 23rd.

FRACKER, 'VOYAGE TO SOUTH AMERICA...' PART 2

Huanchaco or Guanchaco
- ships cannot land so met by Balsas, consists of 2 large
bundles or straw or rushes of a conical shape, bound close
to-gether leaving a hole towards the large end in which
parcels are sometimes carried-apex of the cane turned up like
shoes of antiquity-wore a straw hat, coarse shirt and
trousers, a double paddle

Indians: short, stout of a sleek copper colour, small black eyes,
coarse black hair, small topknot in the middle of the
forehead and temple locks hanging down in line with the lower
part of an ear. - wore coarse white shirts and
trousers-employed carrying bales of goods from the launches
or loading others with sugar and bales of tobacco
- G. consists of a storehouse, church, 2 dozen huts

Truxillo
- 7 miles off-road good, passes through ruins of Chimu, a war
prince at
the time of the Incas, called Libertad now
- stands in a sandy plain 6 mi. north of G. and 3 miles (1
league) from the sea-founded by Pizarro in 1535
- streets intersect at right angles, dusty dirty roads
- houses adobes 2 stories high with balconies looking into
streets and inner courts-6000 people
- city surrounded by an adobe wall originally for protection
against indians-a cathedral 2 convents, hospital
- immediate countryside barren but a valley is rich with
sugar cane, corn and wheat
- silver is smuggled out regularly.

···END···

Women of Lima, Peru

Valparaiso - St. Jago - Journey

At 8 p.m. arrived at Casa Blanca where we spent the night at
an inn kept by an Englishman. Started at 4 a.m. on the 24th
and after going over a level country 5 or 6 miles we began
the ascent by a good zig zag road the Querto Zapatas, a high
rugged mountain range from which we descended into a valley
called the "Caxon" from its narrowness - then passing over
some hills and fording a rapid river, we stopped at
Bertamento for dinner and a siesta. At 2:30 pursued our
journey over another mountain range called the Questo del
Prado. We took the steep mule path being the shortest, in
preference to the main road which was very good but very
winding. From the top of this we got our first view of the
Cordilleras, the chain of mountains that separates the
valley of the St. Jago from the pampas of Buenos Ayres.
Descending we pursued our journey and arrived at St. Jago at
8 p.m.

In St. Jago I made several pleasant acquaintances Messrs.
Post Ingram (of the house of Winter, Britain & Waddington of
Valparaiso) Reynold, Ross, Patrickson, Sewell, Sewall
Buxton, Clarke Mr. & Mrs. Dupateau, etc. It being here mid
summer, the weather was very hot, although the snows of the
Cordilleras seemed almost over our heads, St. Jago being
located at their foot. During the middle of the day, say
from 12 to 3 or 4, the stores are all closed, and the
inhabitants take their siesta - from 8 to 12 p.m. are their
visiting hours and the morning only is devoted to business.
My negotiation with Ramon Dias having failed, I left St.
Jago very early on the morning of the 3rd of January 1825 in
company with Mr. Schultze, rode on horse all day and arrived
at Valparaiso at 11 p.m., a distance of 96 miles, a feat
that I had afterwards reason to regret, as it produced an
inflammation of the bowels, and a stoppage that was overcome
only by alternate doses of 5 grains of calomel and a cup of
senna every half hour for 24 hours, and these then assisted
or rather started a large blister on the abdomen.

....,"Three Years in the Pacific Containing Notices of Brazil, Chile, Bolivia Perua in 1831,2,3,4, by an officer in the U.S. Navy", Richard Bentley, pub. (London,) 1835

Chile

- Valparaiso: 49 days from Rio, mountains capped with snow, Cordilleras - midwinter - rainy, season, mid-summer dry

Monte Alegre: high bluff, also called Jew's hill, English and American dwellings like a separate colony
Quebrade de San Francisco are ruins of a former castle after earthquake of 1822
- plantations of olive trees
- small fort under the guns which, 1814 USS 'Essex' captured by the British
- beef butchered by dissecting large muscles out instead of cutting at joints, carried around on asses followed by the butcher with knife shouting out his product

- principal fruits: grapes, oranges, apples, pears, peaches, plums, apricots, nectarines, lemons (sweet and sour), limes, figs, strawberries (5 or 6" in circumference but inferior) and the best musk melons
- madeira nut, chestnut
- potatoes, yucas, cabbages, cauliflowers, cucumbers, radishes, pumpkins tomatoes, lettuce, celery, peas, beans as fine a quality as European
- variety of shell fish

Water carriers: Aguadores: donkey carried 2 kegs suspended, 1 per side in a wooden frame, carriers sits bareback in front-coarse cone-shaped hat drawn over his face shirt with rolled sleeves, learther apron and loose trousers reaching below the knee-carried a pole 6ft. long armed with an iron curve lying cross-wise,-small bell on his saddle

Muleteers: wear ponchos-spurs usually iron but silver is preferred, mules covered in sheepskins upon which the lad is dashed by thongs-mule blindfolded so will stand still-strung to-gether by a halter, 10 ft apart.

- muleteers wear short jacket of white or blue cloth, seasonal choice, felt or straw hat, Maila or Guayaquil manufacture

Ladies walking dress: arrange hair with several natural flowers, parasol, church dress is black with a veil or mantilla
evenings: chandler makes his appearance - load or dirty tallow candles, tinker with tin objects, Saturday night plaza filled with flat baskets of shoes lighted by a tallow candle-an old custom by which ladies buy shoes as judged by the spreading of fingers

Furniture: tables, mirrors, sofa, piano, chairs in 2 rows facing a thick straw mat or Petate on the floor, carpet under chairs on one side of the room

Ladies covered in large shawls-warmth in winter by placing a copper pan of well-burned charcoal near the sofa with a basket upon to rest their feet or sit upon
- tallow candles lit in evening
- tortoise shell combs 18"-24" around shawls of Canton crepe, hand embroidered with silk, dresses of French muslin, rose in their hair

yerba mate: tea substitute, greenish yellow dust, mixed with lemon and cinamon-drunk from a mate, silver or a small gourd supported by a stem or plate of the same metal-cover included a 12" tube with a bulb at the end and pierced with holes-liquid sucked up in, older ladies especially passed from mouth to mouth and spicey
- on emptying, replenished with sugar and hot water from a silver kettle placed upon coals-guests given live flowers as a token of welcome on departure for first 3 or 4 visits
- ladies wash hair in a suds solution of quillai, a tree bark that mixed with water makes a soap, also useful for cleansing cloth, silks, crepes without harm.

* * *

As my business was closed before I was attacked, I was detained only a day or two, having the day after my medicines operated, the 30th inst, been able to go on deck and get the vessel under way for Chorillos, Callas (port of Lima) being held by the Spanish under Rodell, who had possession of the Castles.

Lima - Heranchacel, Truxillo - Guayaquil - Lambayeque

We arrived on the 29th at Lima. I employed Mess. Huth Coit & Co. Bolivia was now in the supreme command of Peru, having driven out the Spanish forces from every part of it except the Forts at Calleo.

I remained in Lima until the 6th of March, when having made all the sales I could I sailed for Hunanchao, the seaport of Truxillo, distant in land 6 miles, and containing about 6,000 inhabitants. At Truxillo (then called Boleia in honor of the president) I employed Mr. Cramond an English merchant resident there with his family and connected with Mr. Barnard, also an Englishman, but not in partnership. Here I sold some goods and took in a cargo of sugar, chukaka and rice and sailed on 12th April for Chorillas and arrived 30th. Remained in Lima till the 15th of June, when sailed again for Heranchao, arrived on the 19th. Sailed on the 26th for Payta, arrived there on the 29th, made some considerable sales of outward cargo, sailed on 2nd July and arrived at Guayaguil on the 5th. At Guayaquil I employed Messrs. Bartlett & Swett, the former son of sherif Bartlett of Haverhill, Mass. and now a wealthy merchant in New York. The latter was a nephew of Horatio Sprague of Gibraltar and afterwards died in South America. At Guayaquil discharged all the cargo remaining and hove the Brig out and recoppered her - reloaded all I could not sell and the specie and sailed on the 20th of August.

Guayaquil is in the republic of Ecuador, situated on the right bank of the Guayaquil River, 40 miles from its mouth in Lat. 2.20 S. Lon 79.43 W. It had then a population of 18,000. It is on low level ground and considered

Mathison, G.P. "Narrative of a Visit to Brazil, Chile, Peru and the
Sandwich Islands during the years 1821-2", Charles Knight,
Publishers, London, 1825

Chile

Rio de Janeiro, 12 days later, Faulkland Island through
straits of Le Maire, but current too strong against so went
around Staten Is.
- neighbouring shore - mountainous, rugged, sloping towards
the sea or rising in peaks and precipices - a scene of "awful
desolation"

Jan. 27: passed southward of Cape Horn and weather changed
drasticly westerly gale - averaged 40 degrees F. in cabin,
freezing on deck and saw floating islands of ice covered with
snow, a brilliant appearance in the sun.

(Valparayso point) Feb. 22: anchored, 45 days out or Rio -
inspected by Custom House officers and captains of the Port
who were dressed in a smart blue uniform and favourable
manners - suggest we present ourselves to the governor

Landing Place: space between the beach and the custom house
filled with goods and merchandise i.e. timber, boxes, iron
bars, barrels bales etc. - all exposed without any method or
arrangement in the open street - interspersed with mules
standing, some loaded some with unloaded paniers, drivers
called PEONS dresses characteristicly - noisy shouts -
porters carrying packages
- boatmen stood ready to importune you with incessant demands
- large group of soldiers added greatly to the general effect
- English and American constituted bulk of the population of
the town - naval officers, mates of merchantmen, sailors, men
of business, except for the mean and dirty appearance of the
place, might have been a British settlement

Government House: proceeded towards, mean looking edifice of
small dimensions, Excellency taking a SIESTA and could not be
disturbed - 2 hours laters, his aide - de - camp dresses in a
loose linen jacket and cigar gave us permission to proceed to
St. Jago

Valparayso: dirty sea port, small mud houses, 1 storey, situated on
the declivity of a hill - slopes gradually to the sea -
- surrounding country barren and unattrative - name
translates into the interior and perspective of the ocean was
considered beautiful
- 5,000 people most being of the second rate and lower class
inhabitants - some English and American merchants have houses
of business but more at St. Jago, the capital

St. Jago: (Santiago) went by horse back, horses kept by peons who
serve as guide, guard, and servant - horses changed every 10
to 15 mi. and could gallop the whole distance if required -
could average 12 mi. per hour but very fatiguing - danger of
robbery great
- wise to be armed - a peon has fidelity towards his
employer and acts as the best protection despite the
lawlessness they generally practise.
- ferocious and unsettled habits been increased by the
disturbed state of the country and war of revolution - public
justice encourages rather than checks the growth and
continuance of evil

Peons: said to live on horse back, costume the same over all
parts of Spanish South America: over a common jacket and
pair of trousers - wear a PONCHO manufactured locally - made
of strongly woven cloth, striped and variated with different
colours - 6 ft. to 8 ft. square, a small aperture being made
in the middle sufficiently large enough for the head - hangs
loose from the shoulders - like a blanket and protests from
wind and rain and cold - black cloth gaiters are buttoned
over the trousers as high as the knee and a clumsy pair of
spurs with rowels that bruise not prick at the horse,
attached to the heel - large high peaked Spanish saddle
covers whole back of horse which being wrapped round with a
number of cloths conveys a convenient travelling bed when the
rider chooses to sleep
- attached is the LAZO, a leathern thong, 30 to 50 ft. in
length strong enough to endure the most violent jerk without
breaking

CONTINUED...

unhealthy. The principal export is cocoa. The island of
Puno lies off the mouth of the river and has some population.

On the 4th Sept. anchored at Lambayeque. This town is some
4 or 5 miles from the landing which is an open road stead
where the serf is always so heavy as to prevent landing in
ordinary boats, and the only mode of communication between
the ships and the shore is by balsas which are made of logs
of a very light wood, and cobbed up together, being
lengthwise about 60 feet, and atwartships 20. These are
lashed together with ropes forming a sort of cobwharf. A
mast is put in the centre and a large lug sail is used, and
these square rafts are sailed either before or by the wind
and pass through the heavy serf in perfect...

Return to Chorillos & Lima

...safety. On them are taken off and on all persons and
goods. The country about Lambayeque is fertile, being
watered by several mountain rills and produces sugar, rice
and cotton. Soap is manufactured and exported from here.
There is seldom any rain in this region, and all cultivation
is the result of irrigation as in other parts of Peru. The
cotton plant is perrenial and gives two crops every year,
but its cultivation is limited and it is seldom exported.
Sugar of a coarse quality is exported to Lima and other
southern ports. From the landing to the river, nothing is
to be seen but loose sand, sometimes level, and at others
blown by the wind into banks like snow. The horses feet
leave no mark behind them, and yet I was told that after a
single shower of rain (which happens once in two or three
years) these sand banks become covered with plants and
flowers that spring from the seeds that are preserved by the
dry soil, blossom and then die away and are entirely lost or
covered up in the drought that follows. The town is a
miserable village of some 2,000 inhabitants. I made some
sales here through Mr. Tanning, an American located here and
took away some Pina and some soap.

178

- one end fastened to the saddle, the other a slip knot and
the lazo is conveniently folded up in the hand of the peon
for use
- thrown with such dexterity and precision as to entangle
the animal with a slip knot and render escape impossible
- herdsmen use it for cattle and the strongest bull is laid
prostrate by the jerk - robbers often catch victims from
horse back this way then knife them

Landscape: no trees, no cultivation, downs covered in FURZE
and bushes, 1 solitary post house

Casa Blanca: small village, decent inn, 10 leagues from port
(1 league: circa 3 miles)

March 25: arrived St. Jagos travelled 20 leagues, 60 miles, port to
city is 90 miles - good road made carefully over steep hills
called Cuesta de Prado - magnificent view - extensive valley
embosomed amid precipitous rocks and hills while the
Cordillera de los Andes with snowy summits

St. Jagos: extensive and fertile plain elevated high above sea level
and at the base of the Cordillera de los Andes so view on
principal streets terminate by snow clad mountains - streets
at right angles (as in other Spanish American towns) good
pavement, streams flowing in the middle - 1 storey mud houses
being less endangered by the frequent earthquakes - built of
unbaked clay, white washed and painted in Spanish style of
different colours - better quality homes have a spacious
courtyard enclosed within a large portal and a few steps
which lead up to the entrance door
- principal square: there are several squares, stand the
Government House and Cathedral

Government House: spacious and handsome edifice and covers 1
entire side of the square, His excellency the Director of the
Republic Don Bernando O'Higgins resides and other government
officials - on walls in front "Libertad" emblazoned in large
letters inscription purporting the building finished 1818
after Chilean independence - another part is a prison

entrance door engraving reads "Hate the offence, pity the
offender" in Spanish

Cathedral: another side of square, unfinished and without
steeple,

Mint: handsome stone edifice - most complete coining
apparatus in South America - average amount of bullion coined
$600,000 to $800,000.

Peru

March 17: set out for Lima - anchored at Callao, Peruvian coast
rugged and mountainous - island of St. Lorenzo separated by
an earthquake in 1746, forms southern boundary of the bay, 2
to 3 mi. around, sand and black rock - snowy summits of
Cordillera mountains
- country in the immediate neighbourhood low - patches of
verdure (Oxford Def.: greeness and freshness of vegetation)
-towers of Lima, on entering harbour suggests a large city

Port of Callao: disgrace to Peru's capital - after anchoring Capt.
of the port came aboard

Fri. Mar. 29: landing place well guarded by sentinels - proved a
garrison town, few hundred houses, small wretched dirty, an
inn kept by an American of the worst description - castle -
actually a fort covering an extent of ground, surrounded by
thick walls, a moat, drawbridge, barracks, chapel, governor's
house, smaller buildings, large square in the centre
- remains of hundreds of uninterred soldiers shot during the
revolution creating a fowl air, bones, bits of clothes,
shoes, caps, etc. lay scattered - very painful to see

Mar. 30: rode to Lima, 8 miles from Callao, each side of road were
filled of mandioc (poisonous reed, meal made from leaves) and
maize, pastureland, enclosed by mud walls and cottages on a
small scale - met many loaded mules and asses

CONTINUED...

On the 15th Sept. proceeded to Haunochoa and went up to
Truxillo, thence to Chorillos where arrived Oct. 5 - and
went to Lima. Here I closed the sales of all the goods I
left on shore and most of those that remained on board, took
up the proceeds in Chappa ... (adulterated) old silver ware
and utensils in Pince and some gold. Part of the time the
Brig lay at a point north of Callao ostensibly for the
purpose of ballasting, but really to be able to take on
board the bullion which the shifting and shiftless policy of
the government obliged us to smuggle. In going to this
anchorage from Lima the only road was the one that went in a
straight line to the castles, not turning off till we got
within 1/4 or 1/3 of a mile of them. Once on returning from
the vessel with 2 or 3 others by this road Rodill opened his
guns on us, but as we then were a mile or more distant we
could see the flash, and observe where the ball would come,
and so easily avoided it. We sailed from Chorillos on the
---- Nov. and on the 3rd Dec...

Coquimbo - Mines of Aoqueros - Huasco - & Sailed for U.S.

...arrived at Coquimbo, where found Mr. Delano, chief clerk
for Mr. Edwards the Am. Consul., contracted with him for a
cargo of coffee to be taken in at Huasco at $16 per quintel
on board some three months before this time rich silver
mines said to be richer than those of Potosi - were
discovered in the Sierra back of Coquimbo. Capt. Palmer of
ship 'Galess' of Baltimore. Mr. Gerald, a resident of
Coquimbo (an Englishman) and myself determined to visit them
on horseback.

We took our beds and provisions with us and with two
servants forded the river and proceeded up the quibrada
arrived in the evening of the same day at the mines which
were distant about 40 miles. Slept in a ranch at the mine
owned by Mr. Edwards and Mr. Frost. We found the scenery
most magnificent - the top of the mountains, where the mines
were being worked were said to be 11,000 feet above the sea
which was in full view from them, and with a spy glass the
vessels in Coquimbo roads were plainly visible.

180

- peons dresses similar to Chile but the straw hats with broader brims and higher crowns, rode armed with cutlass, blunderbuss, horse pistols and CUCHILLO or knife - avenue of trees - entrance is ña archway, now dilapitated

Lima: streets full of bustle - large proportions of negroes,
- most striking difference between Lima and St. Jago - Lima on a commercial footing - smart shops abounding in French silks, jewellery and British goods - houses larger that St. J. but similar including water flowing down streets
- public square of large dimensions - 2 sides covered with shops and piazza in front, Gov't house former Viceroy's palace on third side and cathedral on south side, the finest church in S. America but none of the buildings have remarkable architectural design
Dress: Sayo and manto principal peculariarities of female dress
Manto: black silk attached to the waist, brought over the head and held by a hand in front to allow one eye only to show except on formal occasions
Saya: outer garment of a thick elastic stuff fitted so closely as to be considered indelicate elsewhere - certain degree of padding to heighten the effect and show off a slender waist
- Banda Patriotica - worn by some females in order of the newly established Patriot government, colour usually brown, also blue, pink, green
- females who wear a Manto over their faces called TAPADAS live in a perpetual masquerade - to remove mask, an unpardonable sin despite constant flirtation with gentlemen

April 2, rode to public baths - 1½ miles from city - rude construction, extensive scale, commodious - long row of buildings, mud walls, flat reeded roof - 30 baths partitioned through which passes a stream of water from a spring from the hill beside, each bath 5' deep by 6' square, also a plunging bath for swimmers - ladies often frequent these in the summer
- roads around evidence of ancient ruins of Indian tumuli.

Chorillas: 100 mud cottages, 2 churches and deserted villas originally country residences of Limanians, sea bathing in the summer, houses mostly by Indian fishermen, comfort or convenience left wanting - live on fish, maize, sugar-cane, men dress like Spanish creoles in ponchos, women in a loose petticoat, a thick woolen shawl from llamas - jet black hair plaited down back, no attention to their persons loathsome and dirty, small eyes, broad flat nose high cheekbones, black shaggy hair, coppered complexion
- above the village, a lofty promontory juts out into the sea affording a magnificent view - remains of a fort and telegraph to be seen - good smuggling place

Revolution erupting between Lord Cochrane of England and San Martin of Peru over certain Prize ships

- bull fight (baits) exhibited every Sunday though not as frequently as during the revolution (in Chile: 1810)

Population: Truxilla: 230,967
          Lima: 149,112 (1790)

Lima's population consist of:

Spaniards and Creoles	17,215
Mestizoes (½ Eur. ½ Ind.)	4,631
Quarterans (¼ Ind., 3/4 ?)	2,383
Quinterans (1/5 Ind. 4/5 ?)	219
Indians	3,912
Negroes	8,960
Mulattoes	5,972
Zambos (Indian, ½ Negro)	3,384
Chinos (½ Indian, 3/4 Negro)	1,120
	47,796

··· END ···

Whatever may have been the height, it was clear we were
above the line of vegetation, nothing growing but furze but
not into the region of frost at this season, which was the
middle of summer, the sun being about vertical at noon.

On the 21st proceeded with the 'Active', Mr. Edwards with
us, to Huasco, a small port about 100 miles north of
Coquimbo, at the mouth of the river of the same name. Next
day we visited the towns of Freynina and Ballemore, the
former a village of about 1,000 Spanish inhabitants some 10
or 12 miles, and the latter a town of 3,000 people and about
30 miles from the coast, both on the Huasco River. At
Fayrina we found a son of Mr. Edwards and a Mr. Havilland,
nephew and clerk of Mr. Frost of Coquimbo. Spent the night
there, visited some copper furnaces and next day returned to
the vessel. We disposed of all the balance of our cargo
except a little iron, took a cargo of copper and sailed for
the United States on the 29th of December 1825, having been
13 months on this coast. I have not since known much of the
parties with whom I was connected in business or social
relations during this time, except Mr. Bartlett, already
mentioned and Mr. Coit, who some five years after returned
to the United States with a good property, but lost it -
then went out to San Francisco - made some money and
returned and is now living at Norwich, Conn. quite wealthy.
Mr. Schultze has since been in the United States, but I did
not see him. I believe the ...

Arrival at Philadelphia & Salem Ships 'London' & 'Paris'

...house of Huth, Gunning & Co. still exists in Valparaiso
but am not sure. In 1832-33 I became acquainted with Mr.
Huth in London, and again called on him in '51. He was a
merchant of high standing there. Mr. Delano married a
daughter of Mr. Edwards but I don't know what became of
him. I think he went to Valparaiso and established a flour
steam mill there. Mr. Wheelwright (whom I then knew as
supercargo of a small trading vessel on the coast) has since
been the originator of steam navigation on the coast, built
water works for the supply of Valparaiso, and built a

182

Harriot C. (Price) Neal Account Book, 1824 (wife of David A. Neal)
Presented by her brother Fitz J. Price

Memorandums: "Mrs. Wallace's daughter sick - sent her grapes, Orange
custard twice, 30 Feb.: custard, roast beef Old Mrs. Holmes
sick sent her custards, 30 Feb. pie and custard, roast beef
Aunt Robinson sick, sent her baked apples, ginger custard
twice, sponge cake, ---veal Feb. 9
Drew the pattern of a collar from Miss Shillab
Feb. 30 sent Mrs. Gravitt custards

January, 1824
1: at Mrs. Cunninghams, spent the afternoon and evening at
Mrs. Powers, Boston
2: went shopping, bought a rug for Mrs. Checker and 1 for
myself at 3 dollars each
3: returned to Salem, dined at Mrs. Dodges, p.m. Sarah Ropes
called
4: Went to ride with Brother William, Mehetable and Mrs.
Cheever spent the evening
5: Invited to Astronomical lecture, went walking could not go
6: D.A.N. at home writing
7: Took tea at Mehetables with the Miss' Shillabet and Sarah
Ropes called at Aunt Wards
8: Sister returned from Boston, Mrs. Grafton Mrs. F. Foster
Sarah and Maria and went to Mr. Stephens lecture
9: Mrs. Blagge, Mrs. Jarvis, Mrs. Ward afternoon and Mrs.
Storey called, took tea at Hetty's supped at Aunt Ward's
10: 3 lb. figs at Mrs. Dodge at 9 cents, Brother William
dined
11: Mrs. Dodge came spent the evening
12: Mrs. Cheever paid for the rug and paid for quinces a
schilling a buschel
13: Miss Shillaber sent me two bottles of Soya, in the
evening Henry O. came, D. is at home.
14: (Wed.) Mr. Kinsman called, Brother William dined,
Margaret went to Aunt Ward's
15: Brother William invited H. Gibbs to the assembly,
Husband and wife went to Miss Shillaber for tea

16: Sick head ache, Sarah Ropes called, Aunt Robinson called
17: Mrs. N. Rogers called and Margaret came home from Mrs.
Ward, we spent evening at Dodges
18: Henry Cheever came to tea
19: Played chess with D.A.N.
20: Mehetable and Father Neal took tea with me, played chess
with Hetty (Menetalbe)
21: Sarah and Maria to tea, Hannah Gibs came to stay a few
days
22: Mehetable S.E. Doliver call and W.N. they W.G. and S.D.
went to the assembly
23: S.E. Doliver and Wm. H. Neal dined and took tea, company
in the evening, B. William
24: We all call on Aunt Ward and Aunt Robinson, took tea
with Mrs. Ropes, made the flower patch
25: Wm. Shearns - - - after he left we all went in the
evening to Mehetables
26: Capt. Cheever called in evening
27: Margaret and Hannah were at Aunt Ward's and Miss
Fairfield called
28: Mrs. Ropes and Maria Ropes called, Ann Gray called - - -
Hannah, D.A.N. and myself had a fine sleigh ride
29: Finished my crape turban Capt. Cheevers and his wife
spent the evening
30: We all went to the astrology lecture with Capt. Cheever
and wife
31: Dr. Treadwell, Holyoke, called, had just come from Mrs.
Peabody

February, 1824
1: Sun. Read the "Pilot" all day except when the people were
going to meeting, then we looked at them (*Pilot some sort of
Religious pamphlet, not a regular newspaper)
2: Had mutton chops for dinner, Ropes concerned called - - -
3: Boil'd mutton not half done - Wm. dined here went to
astronomical lecture, began Work collar
4: Beef stakes - called on Mrs. Cheevers - - - - a lie
5: Margaret and myself spent the evening into Mrs. Dodges,
Wm. H. Neal dined, H. Gibbs ...
6: M. Fairfield, Sally Deveriau, Ann Williams called, we all
passed the evening at Miss Shillaber

183

Feb. 7: Capt. Cheever called, <u>Backgommon with husband,</u> Wm. Neal supped

8: Heard that the "Pioneer" arrived at Rio (D.A.N.'s ship on last voyage) stormy

9: S. Ropes and Mrs. Cheevers called, Mrs. Hawthorne died, we all took tea with Mrs. Dodge, Capt. Cheever called

10: <u>Made a black gown for Mrs. Hawthorne,</u> W.H. Neal dined and drank tea with us

11: H.A. Gibbs went to the assembly <u>I mended D.A.N's coats</u>

12: Sent Susan, Phebe, Mary C. <u>9 yds. of thread edging - - yard 1/2 of nice muslin</u>

13: Friday *the Husband went to New York*, Mrs. Rope, Mrs. Cheevers took tea, Mrs. Cheevers called

14: We took tea with Mrs. Cheever - - Prince and W.H. Neal came in and supped

15: Father Neal called, W.H. Neal dined with us. Mrs. Dodge came in the evening

16: W.H. Neal dined with us and took H.H.R. Gibbs home, wrote to Fitz

17: <u>Sick Headache</u> Hannah Osborn dined, Miss Shillabar and Sarah Ropes called, letter D.A.N.

18: Mehetable, W.H. Neal and S.E. Doliver dined, Miss Ropes to tea in the evening, Miss Shillaber

19: Maria Ropes called, <u>finished my work collar'd billet</u> from Mrs. Rogers

20: wrote to Husband, Mrs. Taylor and Miss Chadwick called, walk down to town, W.H. Neal took tea, Mrs. Dodge came in a moment

Monies:
paid Mrs. Wallace	90¢	
Henry Osborn	12¢	
<u>Yerusha</u>	6¢	(* possibly a young servant)
<u>Sausages</u>	90¢	
<u>eggs</u>	36¢	
Henry	12¢	
H. Gibbs	12¢	
<u>Yerusha</u>	12¢	
<u>Letter Paper</u>	25¢	
<u>volatile</u>	30¢	(* evaporates, possibly smelling salt of a type)

eggs	38¢
Sausages	90¢
tea S. tea	1.95
cord	12¢

21: a letter from D.A.N. Hetty S. Ropes, Capt. Cheevers all called took Mrs. Ropes and Hardy prince and W.H. Neal <u>supped with me 12 o'clock</u>

22: W.H. Neal dined and took tea, Stephen called

23: <u>cut out shirts</u> Dodge came, <u>in turkey, counterpanes washed</u>

24: Called Mrs. Ropes, Mrs. Lees, Mrs. Cheevers, Harriot and Mary Osborn, Capt. Cheevers call'd

25: dined at Father Neal, went to ride with W.H. Neal and called at his relations and called to Mrs. Rope

26: Aunt Ward called, W.H.N.

27: W.H. Neal called and Capt. Cheevers Miss Shillaber sent for us to tea

28: W.H.N. took leave of us and handed me a letter from D.A.N. <u>meat pies and cake,</u> Aunt Ward passed the afternoon, Mrs. Kennedy called

29: Nathan called went with sister to Mr. Bracer, evening went into Mrs. Dodge

Accounts: $100 to Manuel
Henry	12¢
<u>Yerusha</u>	6¢
<u>B.A. Book</u>	6¢
<u>WH Sugar</u>	6/gr.
<u>Yerusha</u>	6¢
<u>Tea pot</u>	7/6 (*Prices are both English and U.S. Currency)
<u>1 pr. gloves</u>	50¢

March, 1824

1: a letter from D.A.N. -- work'd for sister, S. Ropes called E. Williams in the evening, Miss Shillaber called

2: <u>mending,</u> very cold, <u>washed my tent</u> (*possibly a bed canopy)

CONTINUED . . . .

184

Mar. 3: called to Mrs. Cheever, A. Robinsons Aunt Wards, Hetty's, Mrs. Ropes, Mrs. H. Hawthorne, Sarah, Maria called here in evening

4: Shopping, call'd to Mrs. Chadwick, Mrs. Hawthorne, Hetty, Mrs. Stearnes, Sarah and Maria call'd

5: D.A.N. got home from New York, Hetty E. West for tea, Mrs ---- Mary Ismer and Sarah Ropes called, Aunt Ward in the morning

6: collar Mrs. Kennedy, Aunt Ward and Mrs. Ropes, Hetty West Cheever and Mrs. Ropes called

7: D.A.N. at home most of day

8: _mending pantaloons_ Nathan dined with Mrs. Dodge invited me to Mrs. Cummings

9: called to Mrs. Shillabar and to Mrs. Preston, we all took tea at Mrs. Kennedy's

10: the Wards took tea Sarah and Maria in the evening D.A.N. went to Boston and returned same day

(** This Account Book mentions many visitations for tea, supper or the evening. To facilitate the reading of it, for the rest of this book. I will include interesting items, ignoring visitors other than family. Ed. Note)

11: called with D.A.N., Marie to the Devereaux

16: closets cleaned

17: tins cleaned

18: D.A.N., Boston, returned same day

20: Nathan sailed 20 min. past 10. D.A.N. start from here 20 min. past 7 and 1 got a letter from him 5 o'clock in the evenings

23: Pilot letter from D.A.N. (*possibly a letter conveyed by shore pilot when taking brig "Active" out of harbour)

24: letter from D.A.N.

Accounts: $245 from D.A.N.

23: wrote to D.A.N. by the Active, made 2 cakes for Mrs. Ward

April 1824

1: Nathan came home

3: Father Neal sent a leg of veal

7: Father Neal call'd, I had a bad headache

10: J.R. Neal, leg of veal, Mrs. Cheever a basket of apples

22: F. Mansfield work here

25: Pioneer arrived

29: Mill Shillabar sent flowers

May, 1824

2: _bird_ making nest

4: I had bad cold

7: wrote D.A.N.

18: Fitz and Theodore dines, bird hatches

24: N.W.N. gave me $100 from F. Henry Price

27: D.A.N. arrived in 23 days passage from Boston to England

28: I had a sick headache, Mrs. Schillaber gave me an orange and barley candy

29: rec'd letter from D.A.N. from Liverpool

30: letter from D.A.N.

31: letter from D.A.N., Apr. 20, London

June, 1824

5: M.P. went with me to Boston and took the birds to stay a week

7: we went to Aunt Blagge to see the Governor - - - take the chair

8: we went over the Mitt dam and saw the grist mill and iron factory

11: I had a sick headache

14: Mary Miller came to live with us

22: Nathan call'd and changed a bill gave me small bills for a hundred dollar bill

29: went to have my bonnet fixed

Monies:

22: paid Mrs. Dodge rent for 6 months

Mrs. Choate delivered the address to the Misor (Mission)

July, 1824

2: We went to see the "Wade" a new brig of Capt. Doah's

3: engaged in sewing all day, Canary hatched

5: We went to see the tables set an Fenuil Hall concert and the State House

6: It rained, sewed all day

10: It rained, we were all day sewing, I received letter from Husband

Monies:
    8: received $12 of Fritz
    11: Mother brought me some gingerbread
    16: Capt. Cheevers and wife call'd and took strawberries and cream

Monies:
    15: C.CH. brought letter from D.A.N.
    21: Brother Fritz and father came out to see me
    22: - - - brought some apples
    24: - - it rain'd, no collair
    26: 6 years ago since I was married
    28: Mrs. Cora came to our chambers and the children spoke pieces
    29: I had sick headache

August, 1824
    2: Fitz and Susan came out at night, Susan came to stay a week
    4: received $15 - - - Dan sailed from Breman (*Germany)
    8: Susan went home, a painting from Julian Hickson
    9: reading Red Gautlet

Monies:
    received from Fritz $25
    8: 1 canary
    9: 2nd canary
    10: third canary
    11: Brother Fritz and Susan sent nice cake, mother sent loaf sugar, I had the sick headache
    12: Work'd on my gown pattern
    16: I was sick, cholera morbus (she probably had a stomach ache as cholera morbus is fatal and she recovered quite quickly)
    17: Brother Fritz with a present from Mrs. Kennedy, a pair of corneal (cornelia is an orange semi-precious stone, probably presented here in earrings)
    18: Working on handkerchief
    20: dating a cape

Monies:
    Sunday 15, LaFayette arrived at Staten Island
    21: went into Boston...on this stage

24: we saw General LaFayette enter Boston, I waved my handkerchief (LaFayette made a diplomatic tour of the United States. In the State House in Richmond, Va. there is a bust commemorating his visit)
25: we went down to Long Island in a sail boat...went to the New England Museum
26: rec'd 3 letters from Husband dated June 1 & 8th
28: gave Aunt my canary bird called La Fayette
29: walked in the (Boston) common to see the tents
30: received two letters from DA Neal dated 8 July
31: It rained, Mrs. Emmerson had false teeth put in

Monies:
paid 4/9 stage fare into Boston

Sept, 1824
    3: gave Mrs. Murdock a canary bird, my bird began to lay again
    4: Marg. sick with a sore throat
    6: letter from Husband
    7: dined at tavern, rain'd all day, toothache
    8: rain'd all day, toothache
    9: came out to Mrs. Aldens, made some little presents to the children

Monies:
    rec'd $40 of Fritz
    11: finished my dotted spenser (cape)
    12: read all day
    13: began to work on insertion for my Indian muslin gowns
    18: finished the insertion in my gown
    19: letter from DAN
    23: finish my spenser
    26: Charlotte Murdock gave me 2 goldfish
    30: washed gown bottom

Monies:
    14 d wide, 46 cents

October, 1824
    6: paid Mrs. Alden for (board) $53.43
    8: my bird laid 3 eggs
    11: received $10 from Fritz

CONTINUED....

186

Oct. 12: made dresses

13: went to Hannah Gibbs, wedding visit (during first weeks of being married it was polite to pay a visit to the bride)

14: Sick headache, received a candy and a slice of cake from Mrs. Murdock who married very well

16: went to see the Ladies ride, received $10 from Fritz

17: went to Saint Pauls church

18: went to the glass house in Essex St.

19: got ready'd..got to Salem, went to the glass House in Essex St. Boston

20: received of Fitz $50, thread lace veil from DAN

21: returned to Salem

29: Mrs. Ropes called, box of flowers and had a present of a box of shells from Miss Shill

Monies:

stage fare $12

Mehetable sent bread, cheese, Mrs. Rope sent cakes

sent custard to Mrs. Holmes

Washing 4/

2 dolls (Spanish dollars or specie) for groceries

50 cents for butter

stage boy 25 cents

received 7 cents

fried grease 3 cents

for sirup

$1.58 for the whole

November, 1824

1: sent goldfish to Hetty (Mehetable)

2: p.m. sister went to Boston and I came to Father Neals for the winter

6: at home, fixed the plants and wrote to husband

8: transplanted all my flowers

Monies:

stage $1 dollar

Yerusha 4/

My birds came, Jack or Augusta

11: I washed and iron'd and went to Treelove to try on my Caroline plaid

12: sick headache, my oleander (bloomed,)

13: my inside blinds

16: Hetty gave me a blue ribbon for the neck

17: Hetty went to the working party (similar to a sewing club)

Monies:

little mug for Horace 8 cents

25 cents for winter green and charcoal

Mrs. Harris 3/

25: sent Mrs. Osborn some pickle

26: sick headache

27: it rain'd, we made pies (Note: when it rains, the streets became nearly impassable for the mud which is why she usually stayed home)

29: we made cake and squash puddings

30: Stoned (pitted) raisins for pudding, 18 spoonsful of sugars will fill 16 second sized soup plates

December, 1824

4: washed the plants, it rained

5: I had the toothache and ague (feverish)

7: sick toothache, Mr. Coleman's new meeting house was dedicated (Note: the only cure for toothaches at this time was to pull it out. That is probably why she had not done anything but try and soothe the pain, the cure often being worse)

Monies:

Worsted, 12 cents

ribbon and rust 2/

11: I did up my muslins

14: sent my flowers

16: William arrived at Batavia (Java) I was sickly

18: I received my new white bonnet

Monies:

$5.25 cents forlining my coat

pins 25 cents

Hananaack 12

Mrs. Patman 10/6

gimp

22: I had a sick headache

23: headache, did up muslins
24: received my coat and went to Boston to spend a week at Mrs. Cunninghams
25: Christmas and I went to St. Paul's
26: a.m. went to St. Paul, p.m. went to North Church wrote to DAN and received a letter
31: had a sick headache

Monies:

stage $1 fare

January 1, 1825
    3 collars 5 schillings
    thimble   40 cents
    sealing   12 cents

Memorandums:
June 15: Miss Cabot was so kind as to take care of my flowers while I was away I sent her 1 orange tree, 1 lemon tree, 1 rose bush, 1 geranium, 1 oleander
Two bird for Fritz, one for Mrs. Cory, one for Miss Cabot one for Mrs. Hickson, one for M. Drone

Cure for Chillblains: take double distilled water, put salt in it then put the foot on the iron hot into it and rub in on chill

Bed Bugs: Cayenne pepper rubbed on will kill them

rub pumice stone on corn will cure them

Cure for Toothache: To a tablespoon of any kind of spirits add the quantity of sharp vinegar and a teaspoonful of common salt, mix them well to-gether, let it enter the cavity, it will give almost instanteous relief. (would have numbed the area)

Cure for Dysentry: take the top of a blackberry bush and made a tea of the same, taking 1 to gills of the tea, for 6 times in the course of 12 hours had cured those who have been confined to their beds with some fever, some sugar may be used and the high top blackberry is to be preferred

Prevent Baldness: rubbing the head once or twice a day with the cut surface of a raw onion until the roots of the hair become moistened with it will effectively keep the hair on.

to DAN when he sail'd in the Emerald, 1824
To DAN Second March 21

Fare thee well the ship is ready
And the Breeze is fresh and steady
Fill'd the Sail, the waves are swelling
Proudly round the buoyant dwelling
Hands are fast te anchor weighing
High in air the streamers playing
Fare the well and when at sea
Think of her who sighs for thee
When from home and land receding
And from the Heart that aches to Bleeding
Think how long the night will be
To the eyes that weep for thee
When the land of strangers leaving
Homeward bound the ship is cleaving
Many a billow breaking round her
While the heaven and ocean bound her
May the blast be tempered to thee
Storms and dread no more pursue thee
May the friends who wait to see
Peace and joy return with thee
DAN This fear I have held on with thee untired
                              H.C. Neal

··· END ···

Theodore Augustus Neal
Author of the "Neal Record"

railroad into the interior. He is still living and active. Have met him once or twice since in the United States and I believe he is now wealthy.

April 29th, 1826 we arrived in the Delaware and the next day at Philadelphia where I deposited my silver and gold in the mint for coinage and then dispatched the Brig in charge of Mr. Tunison for Salem, taking the land route myself.

I now concluded to give up the sea as a profession and devote myself in connection with my Father and my brother to mercantile pursuits. We owned the Brigs 'Java' and 'Banien' and took up vessels on half profits to India.

On the 23rd of March 1827 in the house then occupied by us, which stood on the site where now the mansion of Capt. John Bertam No. 370 Essex St. was born my second son, but the only living child, afterwards named Theodore Augustus.

In August of the same year we contracted with Messrs. Sprague and James of Medford, for two ships of about 360 tons each for $24 per ton for wood and work - with Jas. Carter of Boston for the iron and with the Boston Copper Co. for the composition and copper, with Elisha Stateson for the joinering, with Benj. Felt of Salem for the block, with Jones & Sons for the sailmaking, with ... for the spars, and with McCleaver & Sons, Boston, for riggers work. Engaged during the summer in superintending these ships. They were launched in the autumn, and winter, and were called the 'London' and 'Paris'.

In March 1828 the 'London' started on her first voyage to Cuba and St. Petersburg, and in May of same year the 'Paris' sailed in charge of my brother William for Batavia. At this time we had some interest in ship 'Franklin' and Brig 'Plant' on their voyage to California fitted out by Henry Price & Co. of Boston.

Early in January 1829 I took passage in the ship 'London', Capt. John Duyer, who with the assistance of S. Chadwich,

Margaret Maria Neal
(two poses)

Esq. and of Herckenrath & Co. I loaded her partly on owners
account and partly on freight with a cargo of rice and
cotton for Hamburg. I returned home by land route through
Georgetown, Raleigh, Norfolk, Petersburg and Washington, and
arrived in Salem early in March and remained at home during
the remainder of this year. During the year 1830 continued
to manage our foreign business in conjunction with my
brother Nathan. From January to March in Baltimore and
Washington fitting out Ship 'London'.

January 1st 1831. My Father, my Brothers, Nathan, W. & Wm.
H. and myself entered into regular articles of Co.
partnership under the firm of Jonathan Neal & Sons. My
property was now valued at $31,459.33 all of which was put
into the common stock. I now adapted a regular system of
books in which interest was charged on each item, and we
adopted the plan of giving no note except for premiums of
insurance and of never putting our name on any paper, or
becoming responsible for any one.

February 11th of this year my first daughter was born in the
house No. 103 Federal Street where we were then living. She
was named for her mother Harriet Charlotte. She was born
with a hair lip which after two unsuccesful operations by
Doct. Warren, was finally cured by Doct. Walker of
Charlestown. Nothing worthy of notice occurred after this,
during the year nor in 1832, except that our business was
fair and considerably enlarged. My sister Mehitable was
married to Mr. Amos Choate.

Visit to Charlestown, S.C. - Firm of Jon'a Neal & Sons

On the 15th of June of this year 1832 our second daughter
was born in house in Washington Street. We named her after
her aunt Margaret Maria.

On the marriage of my sister Mehitable, who had hitherto
kept my Father's house, he concluded to give up housekeeping
and he and my brother Nathan removed to Mrs. Page's boarding
house in Central Street, where they had separate rooms and
lived by themselves.

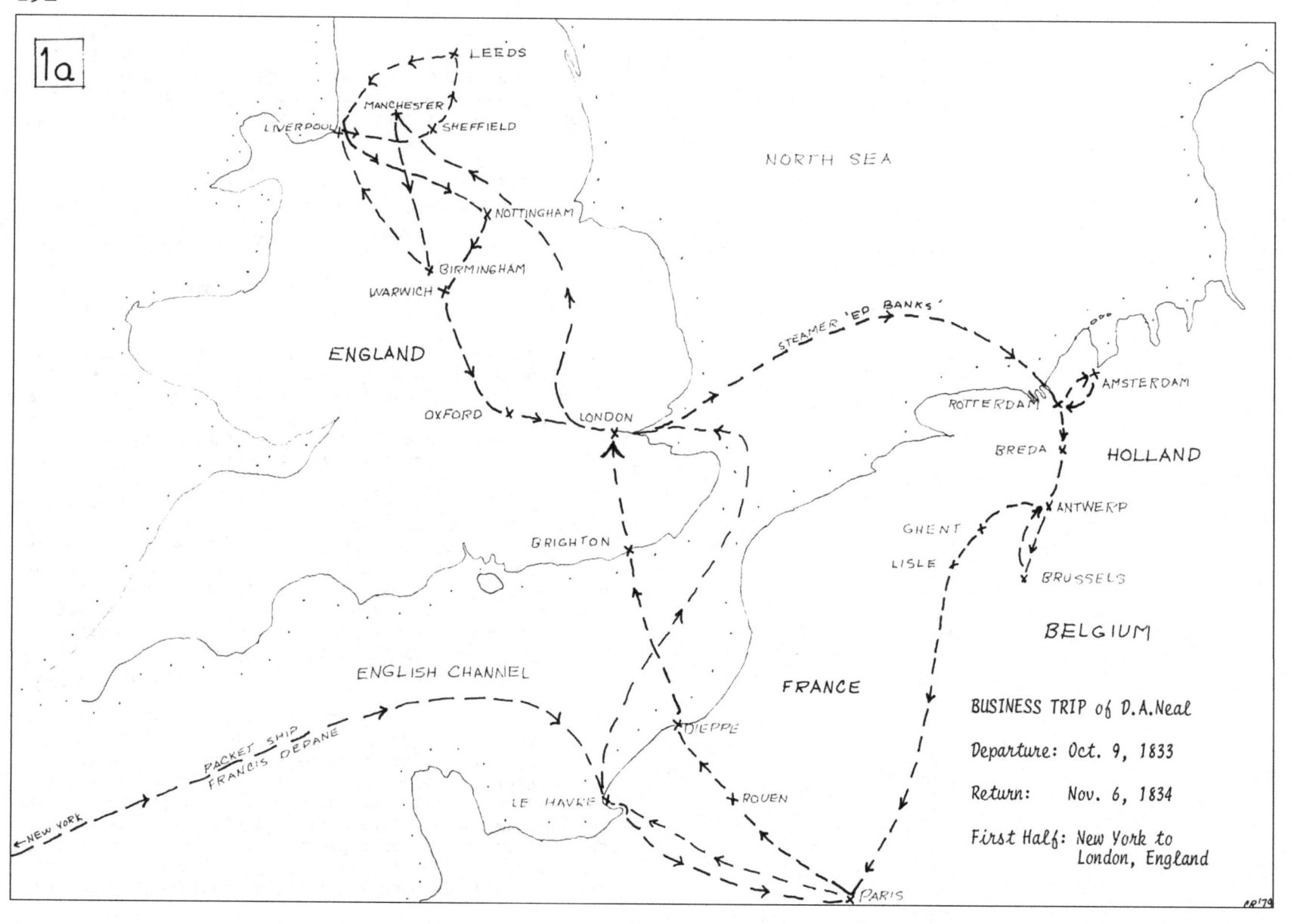

1a

LEEDS
MANCHESTER
LIVERPOOL
SHEFFIELD
NORTH SEA
NOTTINGHAM
BIRMINGHAM
WARWICH
ENGLAND
STEAMER 'ED BANKS'
AMSTERDAM
ROTTERDAM
OXFORD
LONDON
BREDA
HOLLAND
ANTWERP
BRIGHTON
GHENT
LISLE
BRUSSELS
BELGIUM
ENGLISH CHANNEL
FRANCE

BUSINESS TRIP of D.A.Neal

Departure: Oct. 9, 1833

Return: Nov. 6, 1834

First Half: New York to
            London, England

PACKET SHIP
FRANCIS DEPANE
DIEPPE
NEW YORK
LE HAVRE
ROUEN
PARIS

Miss Elizabeth West who lived with Mrs. Page having charge
of their rooms and seeing that they have every
accommodation. On this I took my Father's house in
Washington St. - made some considerable improvements and
moved in, I think, in the spring of 1832.

In 1833 my son had now arrived at an age when I thought it
would best for him to learn the French language, in a manner
that would be sure to give him a correct idiom. He was
between 6 and 7 years old and for this purpose I proposed to
take him for a time to a school in France. I had other ...

Visit to Europe - Paris - Brig 'Hypsea' & 'Jane'

...reasons for visiting Europe at this time. My Father had
a considerable claim under the treaty that had just been
concluded with France, arising out of the seizure and
condemnation of the Brig 'Hypsea' & 'Jane' that belonged to
him, taken under the Berlin & Milan decrees and a document
relating to the cargo was of much importance, and could only
be obtained by some one on the spot. Then we were having
several cargoes from India bound to Holland and Belgium, and
it was well to look after them. Under these circumstances I
concluded to proceed to Europe with my Son and we embarked
on the 9th October at New York on board the packet ship
'Francis Depane', Capt. Robinson, bound to Havre, where we
arrived in about four weeks. There I visited Mr. Greene (my
old friend) of the house of Welles & Greene and then
proceeded to Paris. Here I placed Theodore in an
institution on Rue blanc Montmatre - in which about 150 boys
were boarded and educated - none of the masters or nurses
and but one of the scholars (an English boy) could speak a
word of English, so he was compelled to learn the French.

In Paris I found Mr. Lorenze Draper and family, his wife
having been Miss Sarah E. Dolliver, an old acquaintance in
Dorchester. Mr. Wells afforded me all requisite information
and assistance. I boarded with Madam --- Rue Richelieu.
Mrs. Harrison Gray Otis was a boarder there. After some
difficulty on my part I found Mr. John Lewis Brown at 1106

ENGLAND AND WALES.

E NGLAND and the principality of Wales, which we shall treat as one incorporated country under the former of these names, occupy the most southerly, and at the same time the largest and most fertile, portion of Great Britain—an island, the position of which is at once favourable to commerce, to security, and to national independence. Placed in a medium latitude, it is further preserved by the surrounding ocean from those extremes of heat, and cold, and aridity, to which continental countries, both in higher and lower parallels, are frequently subjected. England, then, is bounded on the north by Scotland, from which it is separated chiefly by the Solway Firth and the Cheviot Hills; on the east, by the German Ocean; on the south, by the English Channel; and on the west, by St George's Channel and the Irish Sea. The space thus included is rather irregular in form, and lies between lat. 50' and 55' 45' north, and between long. 5° 41' west, and 1° 46' east. Measuring along the second meridian, from St

No. 67.

225

Rue Bruyere. He was formerly a merchant in Bordeaux and consignee of th 'Hypesia' & 'Jane', and when her cargo was seized he gave bonds which were finally condemned and paid. It was the receipt for this payment that I wanted to obtain, in order to substantiate a claim for the amount, for the cargo itself sold for so much above the bonds that it shew no loss on the original invoice. At first this document could not be found, but after I had been in Europe some months it was discovered among some old papers in Mr. Brown's bed chamber in Bordeaux. The amount of this bond was I think between $30 and $40,000 all which was subsequently recovered as so much cash paid to the French Government and this recovery was entirely owing to my recovery of this document. The cargo belonged to Geo. Crowninshield & Co. and to my Father for a/c others.

London & Journeys in England - Amsterdam

Early in January 1834, I went over to London where I had various business arrangements to make with Messrs. Baring Bros. & Co. - particularly in relation to shipments of British goods to China. Armed with letters from them I made a journey to Manchester, Birmingham, Liverpool, Sheffield, Leeds, Liverpool and on my return Oxford, Nottingham (the seat of the Duke of Marlborough, Blenheim House) Warwich, and other places which I do not now recollect. At Manchester I dined with Mr. Henry, a gentleman largely in the American trade, who shew me through his warerooms and various places. In the city at Birmingham I visited Rogers showrooms, several of the cutlery and one papier mache establishment, etc. At Leeds I delivered my letters to Mr. Gott, a very extensive cloth merchant from whom I received particular attentions, showing me through his own factories and all the public buildings, cloth halls, etc. At Liverpool I made the acquaintance of Mr. William Browne, and dined with him at his residence at Richmond. Went with him on the railroad to Manchester - met also Mr. Lathan of the house of Maury Latham & Co. and several other merchants. At Oxford went through all the colleges, chapels, libraries, and at Nottingham visited Blenheim House and Park, saw the

celebrated mausoleums of the first Duke of Marlborough, the
cartoons of Titian and the beautiful grounds about the
house, while at the same moment the Duke, who was
overwhelmed with debt, was living in a single room in the
palace and hardly able to command the common necessities of
life. I returned to London on the 10th of Feb. and on the
15th took passage on the mail steamer 'Sir Ed. Banks', from
then to Rotterdam, and arrived on the 17th. I put up at the
Hotel Pays-bas in the Bromties and called on Mr. Collins of
the house of Collins and Maingy. Next day went to Amsterdam
- called on Messrs. Hope & Co. Saw Mr. Stoop, Mr.
Vanderhoof being at the Hague. Made the acquaintance of Mr.
Van Bagger of the house of Van Bagger, Packer & Dixon. Mr.
Crossneedlier of the house of De Cumonelier & Sons and of
Mr. Parker of above house and Am. Consul. Visited Mr.
Siller, the senior partner of Hope & Co. at Harlaem. He
resided in the palace formerly occupied by King Louis
Bonaparte.

Rotterdam - Antwerp - Brussels - Ghent - Lisle - Rheims - Paris

While in Amsterdam our ship 'Paris', Capt. Symonds, arrived
from Batavia with sugar, etc. About this time I gave the
Barings instructions to purchase a ship for a/c J. Neal &
Sons to --------- about £20,000 invoice of British woolen
goods. Dispatched the 'Paris' having employed Hope & Co.
who had always been our correspondents here. At Amsterdam I
stopped at a small hotel called (in Rotterdam) the Hotel du
Paysbas. Remained here until the first of April - had a
most extraordinary winter - no ice - no snow - and not even
a frost till March, but generally very wet and uncomfortable.
At this time war existed between Holland and Belgium and as
I wanted to go to Paris was obliged to get a pass for
Belgium from the commander in chief. Passing a day or two
in Rotterdam where I found Mr. Horace Jenks of Salem. I
proceeded through Breda and West Wessel to Antwerp and here
saw Mr. Maingy, Mr. Mosselman, Mr. Solreur, Mr. Barrow, Mr.
Nottibrahm, Mr. Farue (his son in law) Mr. Patterson, the
American Consul, Mr. Agir, etc. etc.

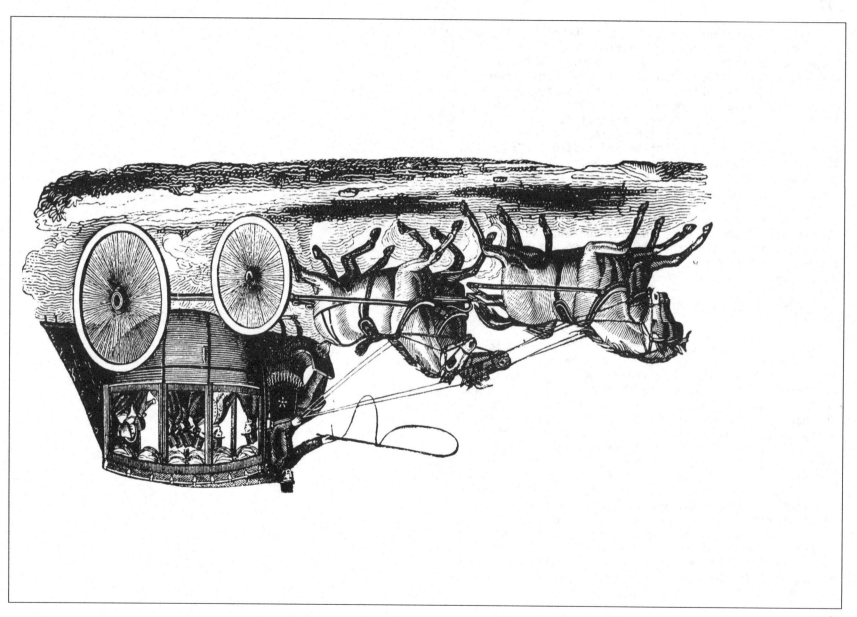

On the 8th April went to Brussels with Capt. Geo. Jenks and
one or two others. Put up at Hotel Flanders. Next day a
grand review of troops, visited the pretty palace of the
Prince of Orange, left in the state in which it was when he
was obliged to fly the Kingdom - the public buildings or the
States General - the museum - theatre - church Geneveive,
etc. On the 12th returned to Antwerps. On the 15th left
Antwerp and proceeded to Ghent, next day passed through
Central to Lisle where lodged - then through Deria, Cambray
and Rheims and on the 18th arrived at Paris. Found Theodore
quite well. Remained here some time - often visited Mr. Sam
Williams, whom I had known so well in London in his
prosperity. He now occupied a small room on the 5th story
of a building in the Boulevard Italion. On the 4th (1st
Sunday) May took Theodore to Versailles to see the water
works which played for the first time that season. An
immense crowd there. On the 11th went to Rouen, thence to
Dieppe, and on the 14th crossed the channel to Brighton.
Here I stopped one day and then proceeded by stage to
London. Found Mr. Bates had contracted for goods under my
order for China to the amount of $13,000.

London, Rotterdam, Utrecht, Hague, Leyden

Called on Mr. Wiggin - went to the East India Co. Docks with
Mr. Bates and Mr. Francis Baring to see their new ship, the
'Alexander Baring'. Dined with Mr. Cryder of the house of
Morrison Cryder. May 29 went to the Epsom races - June 6
went to Richmond and Hampton court. 14 At request of Mr.
Gordon, Sec'y of the Board of control, called on him at his
office. He wanted to enquire into the working of the
specific duties on Teas in the United States. While in
London this time I boarded with Mrs. Fowler, 63 Russell
Square.

Among the boarders I remember Doct. and Mrs. Simpson of New
York, Mr. & Mrs. Chase of Boston, Mr. & Mrs. Mills of New
York, Mr. Moxen Boston, Mr. Craw, and Englishman with whom I
became quite intimate. Misses Mary and Caroline Ayres,
nieces of Mrs. Fowler, assisted in keeping house.

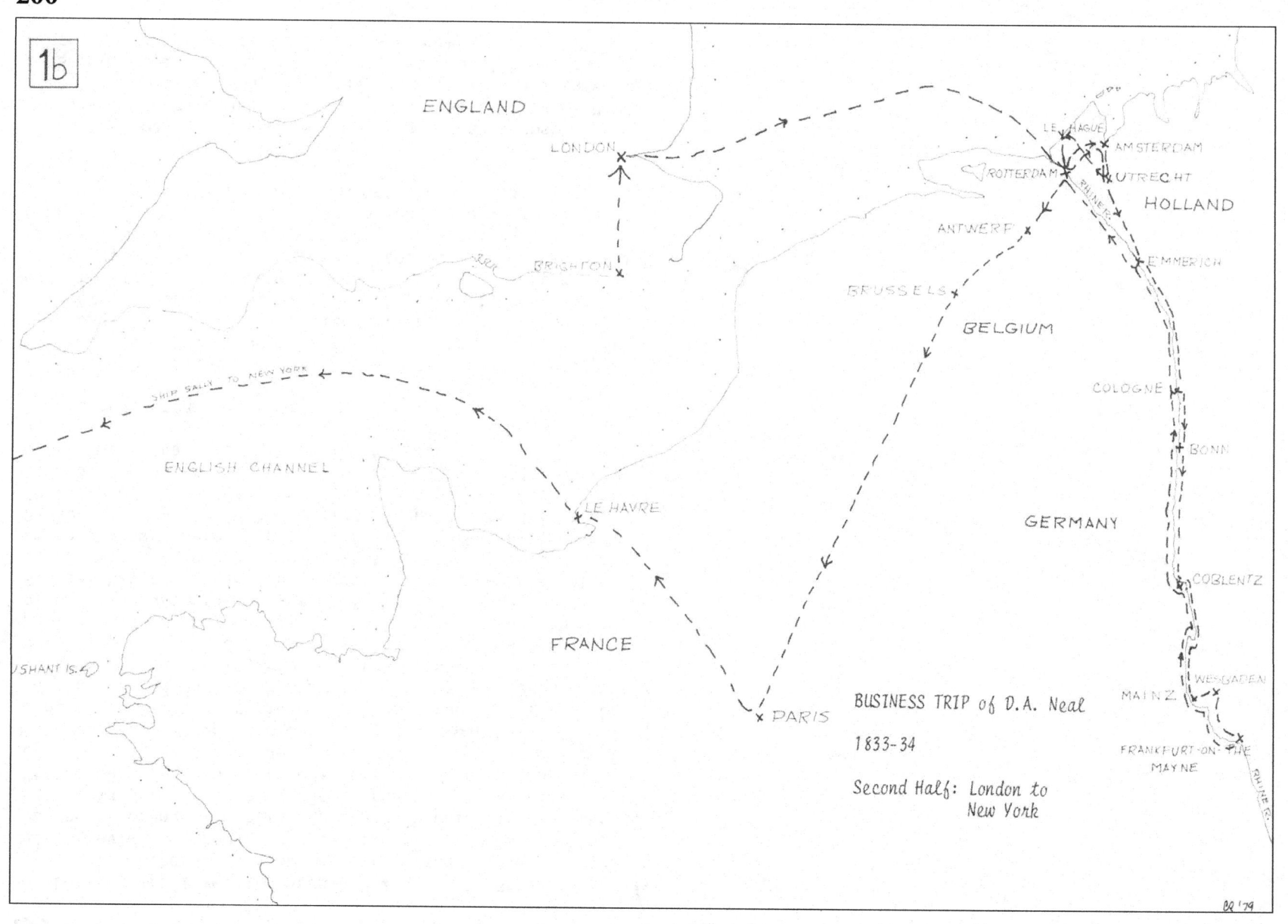

1b

ENGLAND

LONDON

BRIGHTON

ENGLISH CHANNEL

SHIP SALLY TO NEW YORK

USHANT IS.

LE HAVRE

FRANCE

PARIS

ROTTERDAM
LE HAGUE
AMSTERDAM
UTRECHT
HOLLAND
RHINE R.

ANTWERP
BRUSSELS
BELGIUM

EMMERICH

COLOGNE

BONN

GERMANY

COBLENTZ

WIESBADEN
MAINZ

FRANKFURT-ON-THE-MAYNE

RHINE R.

BUSINESS TRIP of D.A. Neal

1833-34

Second Half: London to
New York

BR '79

June 23rd went over to Rotterdam by steamer to arrange
various business matters of the house, and on 24th proceeded
to Amsterdam. Met here Capt. Kurtz of the ship 'Isabella'
of Philadelphia. I had known his sister at Mon Blaw's who
kept an American boarding house in Antwerp. Visited Mr.
Laboucher of the house of Hope & Co.

July 5th went out to the country house of Mr. Van Bagger
near Utrecht and spent one or two days with him and his
family. Went with him and his wife to Utrecht, and visited
a colony of Shakers or some thing of the same sort there.
Mr. Furstenrath of the Rotterdam house of Laboucher called
to see me.

July 16th went to the Hague, made the acquaintance of Mr.
Durisae the American minister at this court and spent some
time there. The Palace in the wood and the bathing houses
at Shavender a mile or two from the Hague are its principal
attractions. Became acquainted here with Mr. Suly and his
wife. Mr. S. was a New York lawyer who detected the robber
who stole the Queen's jewels at the Palace of the Prince of
Orange in Brussels, and he was here claiming compensation,
but I believe he never got any. I saw the thief set in the
pillory and branded at the Hague. One the 23rd went to
Leyden with Mr. Suly and the next day to Rotterdam.

From this a party of four of us, to wit, Mr. T. B. Wales of
Boston, Mr. Smith of Batavia, Mr. Reeves of London and
myself made a journey up the Rhine. I have no memo of the
dates and write from memory. We took a carriage from
Amsterdam, passed through Utrecht, Emmerit and the low
country of Cologne. Here we stopped over one day and then
took river steamer for Bonn, lodged there and in running
across the square in front of our hotel broke a tendon in my
leg which made me very lame, but I kept on. From Bonn we
went by land to Coblentz and had a fine view of the famouse
castle of Ehrenbreitsen but I was too lame to go into it.
From this we took river steamer and having fine weather was
enabled to enjoy in perfection the well known views of the
Rhine. From Coblentz we went to Mayance where we stopped

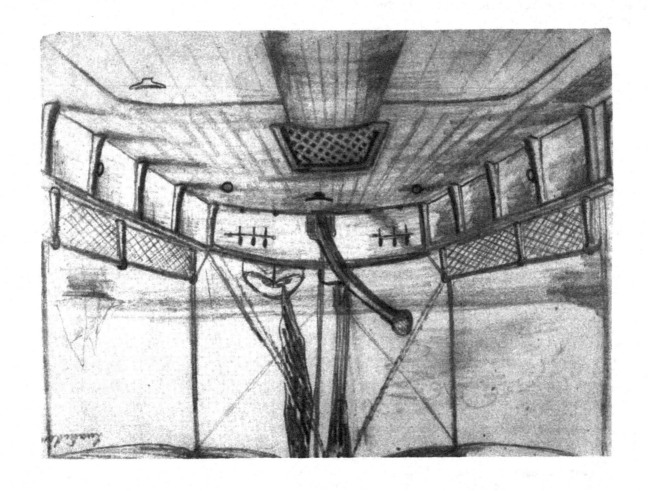

203

one day and night, thence by land to Wesbaden, the famous
watering place, and celebrated for its hot medicinal
springs, used both for drinking and bathing. Remained here
two or three days, then went to Frankfort on the Mayne and
there also spent two or three days visiting every place of
interest and every part of the city and its environs which
are laid out in gardens all round the city. We returned by
the way of the Rhine and the Meuse by steam boat to
Rotterdam. Thence I went to Antwerp and spent some time,
thence to Brussels, and in company with Capt. Geo. Jenks of
Salem, T. B. Wales and Mr. Messenger of Boston, and one or
two others from there by 'Dilijence' to Paris, where we all
took rooms at the Hotel des Princes, Rue Richelieu - and
visited all places of consequence worth seeing in that city
and its neighbourhood. In October I embarked with my son in
the Ship 'Sally', Capt. Forbes, at Havre for New York and
arrived Nov. 6th 1834. My expenses during this trip of 13
months including board and schooling for Theodore amounted
to about $2,900 of which charged to claimants of 'Hypser' &
'Jane' $380. to the House $1,700 and to my private account
the balance. That to the firm was distributed among the
following accounts Voyage pr India, 5th voyage pr Paris,
ship pr 'Isabella', Ship pr 'Margaret Forbes', ship pr
'Diana', Voy pr 'Eugene' & Voy pr United States. All of
which I managed while in Europe.

Return to United States, Great Fire in New York, Neal & Co.

The year 1835 I spent principally at home, being engaged
part of the summer in making alterations in my house in
Washington Street. In the fall we had the Ship 'London' of
which Bej. R. Leech was supercargo arrived at New York from
Canton with a full cargo of Teas, etc. I and my brother
Nathan went on to manage her business. My brother was
absent in Philadelphia. On the 16th Dec. at sundown I had
just landed and stored in Osborn & Young's store 42 South
St. the last package of her cargo, and in the course of the
day had taken out the last fire policy, completing an
insurance of $220,000. That same evening while I was in my
room in building next to the corner of Wall and Broadway, I

204

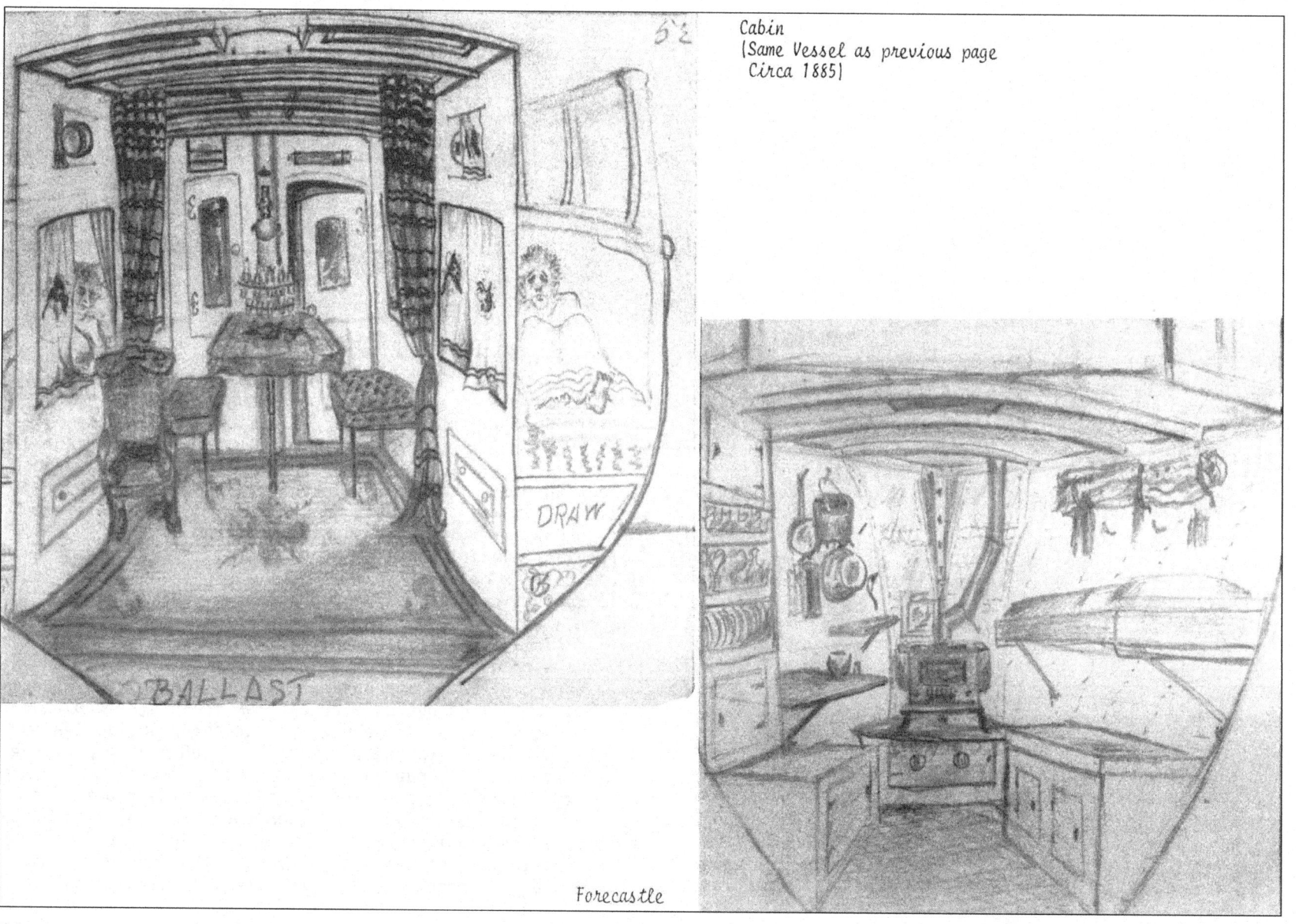

Cabin
(Same Vessel as previous page
   Circa 1885)

BALLAST

DRAW

Forecastle

discovered about 8 o'clock by the glare on the steeple of
St. John's church opposite, that there was a fire in the
direction of the East River, went out and found an immense
conflagration. The ship was lying at Coffee house slip -
fire was falling on her decks, and no one near her - cold,
tremendous, thermometer 12° below zero. Got the parts
off, and was shoving the ship off when Mr. Leach came to my
assistance - got her into the stream - but finding the store
where (our teas) we were and all our papers and policies
were taking fire shoved the ship in so as to get ashore,
leaving Mr. L. on board. I got into the store and saved the
papers and about 200 chests of tea were got out on the wharf
- five minutes afterwards the roof fell in, and the whole
cargo was a mass of flames - the ship drifted over on the
Brooklyn shore. This was the great fire of Dec. 16, 1835.
Several acres of the most valuable stores in New York - the
Exchange - and a vast amount of property estimated at more
than 20 millions of dollars were destroyed. All the
insurance offices were ruined, and we lost $70,000 of our
insurance. My brother Nathan was on his way from
Philadelphia that night, but the pipes of the locomotive
froze up, and they were detained till the next morning. So
this year closed gloomily enough.

On the 30th June 1836 the house of Jon'a. Neal & Sons was
dissolved by the retirement of my Father, the senior
partner, and a new firm instituted under the name of Neal &
Co. who assumed all the business and liabilities of the old
concern. It consisted of myself, the senior partner, and my
brothers Nathan, W. & Wm. H...

Death of H.C. Neal, Our Daughter & of My Father Crisis

...We entered into articles by which it was stipulated that
as heretofore we should under no circumstances become
responsible for any other party, that we should give no
notes, except premium notes, nor endorse any business paper
- that we should pay cash for all duties, and consequently
give no bonds or bond men at the C. House. To these
conditions to which we scrupulously adhered while I was in
the house do I attribute much of our success.

Harriet Charlotte Neal (II)   Margaret Maria Neal

In 1837 our dear little daughter Harriet Charlotte died of
dropsy in the head, and was buried on the 20th, her remains
being deposited in the tomb of my brother in law, Amos
Choate, on the Hill burying ground. They have since been
removed to my lot in Harmony Grove, and a monument of white
marble, representing a mound covered with flowers (the
morning glory opening where her birth and closed when her
death is inscribed) rests over her grave. She was 6 years 1
mo. 6 days old.

Same year July our third daughter was born at our house in
Washington Street and was named after the one we had just
lost Harriet Charlotte and as well as for her mother. Same
year Oct. 9th Monday at 4 p.m. my Father departed this life,
aged 78 years and 9 months and was buried on the Hill
burying ground, early on the morning of the 11th, agreeably
to his own directions without any ceremony, over the remains
of his two wives. A granite monument "erected by their
children" now marks the spot. His death was occasioned by
weakness arising from hernia of long standing and from which
he suffered, but he had not been confined to the house but a
few days. All his children were with him when he breathed
his last. His property just about $200,000 after some
legacies to his sister and nephews and for charitable
purposes and especially for supplying the poor with fuel the
coming winter, was divided equally by his will among his
four children 1/5 to each and the other 1/5 to his
grandchildren.

1838. This year will be recollected for the pecuniary
crisis, mainly occasioned by the difficulties and subsequent
failure of the United States Bank of Pennsylvania, under the
management of Nicholas Biddle. Of my Father's property
about $120,000 was invested in the stock of this bank and
the rest of us had about $80,000 more at par, and it was
appraised at his death I think at $120 per share.

GEORGE PEABODY
President of Eastern Railroad, 1836-1842
From a photograph made in 1848-9

DAVID A. NEAL
President of Eastern Railroad, 1842-1851
From a portrait by Southward in the possession
of Robert S. Rantoul

STEPHEN A. CHASE
Superintendent of Eastern R. R. 1838-1842
From a portrait by Osgood in the possession of
Mrs. Ellen C. Lord.

JOHN KINSMAN
Superintendent of Eastern R. R. 1842-1855
From a photograph made about 1885.

Eastern Railroad   Elected President of It

Shortly after my brother Nathan was in New York and got some
intimation that the bank would probably fail at their agency
in London and he sold out all there was in the family
commencing at $120 and in one week running it down to par.
The Bank got over the difficulty in London, but failed in
this country within 60 days, so that this large amount of
property was saved to us by this energetic action on the
part of my Brothers. It was also this year 1838, that we
met with a great loss in the death of Mr. Bej. R. Leach, who
was our very efficient and intelligent agent in the East
Indies. He was with me as clerk in the 'Active' and has
ever since been in our employ. He went out in the little
Brig 'Theodore' which we built for the convenience of the
E.I. Agency, and he had been trading from Manilla and Java
to China, where he died of a diarrhoea contracted by his
exertions and exposure. Mr. Wm. P. Pierce, having also been
an agent for us, took charge of the business.

1839. Mostly at home, engaged in conducting the business of
the house, and in settling up Mr. Leach's estate. His
effects arrived in Salem via New York from China in August.

1840. In May I was elected a director of the Eastern Rail
Road. This circumstance has no doubt had an important
bearing on my subsequent career, whether for good or ill, I
shall of course never know. Mr. Geo. Peabody was present
and Mr. Stephen A. Chase superintendant and the directors
were Amos Binney, John A. Thayer, Isaiah Breed, Col. Howes,
John Cooper ------- Wm. Sturges and perhaps others whom I
don't recollect. Benj. T. Reed was treasurer. The next
year, 1841, Mr. Peabody having resigned the presidency of
the Eastern Rail Road, I was elected in his place, and
accepted it on condition that I should not be obliged to
neglect my own business to attend to it. I had no
experience except what I had acquired during the past year
as a director. It was now deemed important that the road
should be extended to Portland, and a company was got up for
the purpose of which in 1842 I was elected the first

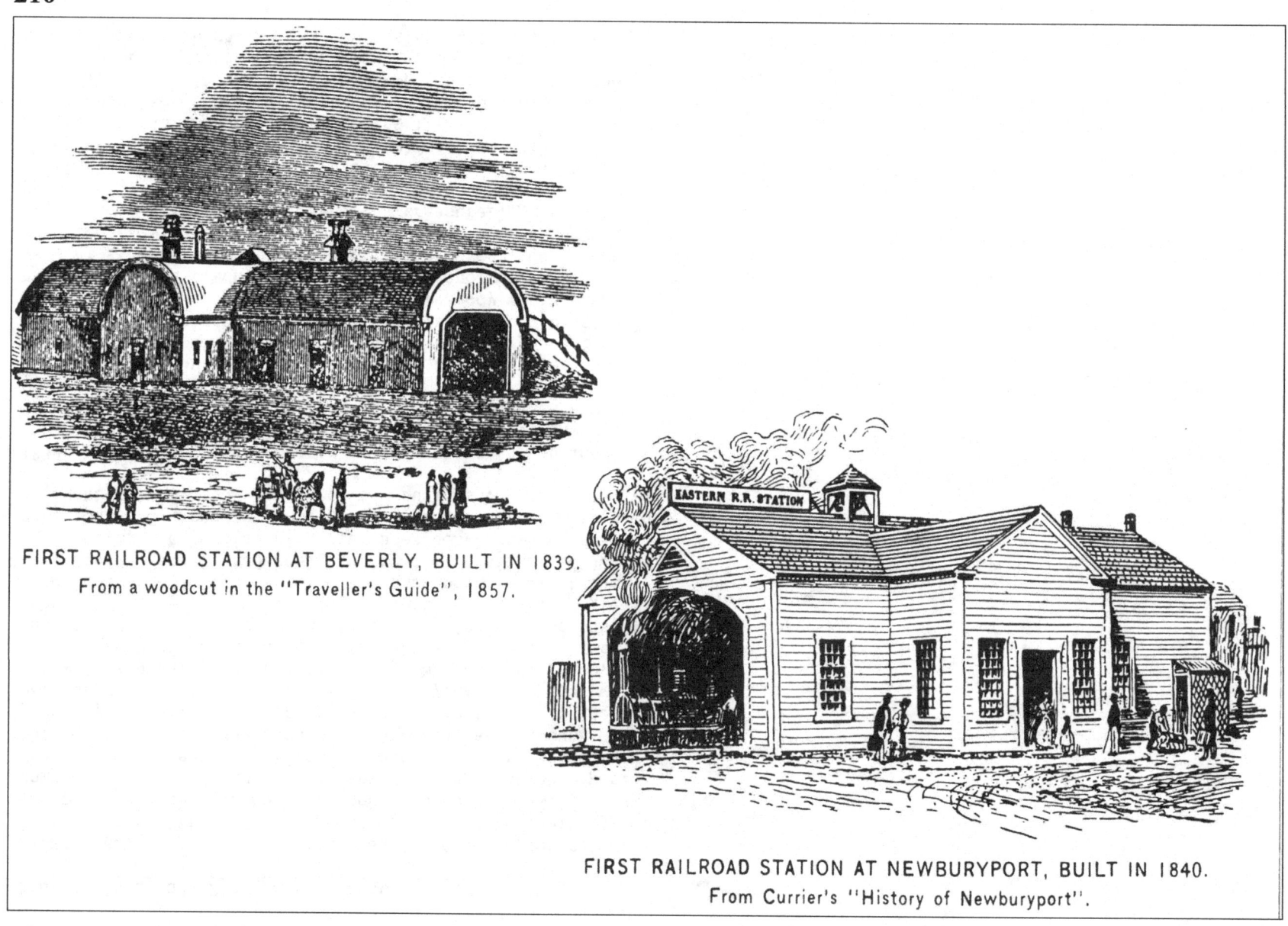

FIRST RAILROAD STATION AT BEVERLY, BUILT IN 1839.
From a woodcut in the "Traveller's Guide", 1857.

FIRST RAILROAD STATION AT NEWBURYPORT, BUILT IN 1840.
From Currier's "History of Newburyport".

211

president, and the work was placed in my charge, and in
April the contract for connecting the roads was signed. In
January of this year the new Ferry Boat was put on and same
day the new depot at East Boston was burnt. Same year
purchased ...

Barstow Trust - Eastern EXCH.- Hotel, Left Firm of Neal & Co.

...Wilkinson & Pratts wharf for a new depot on Boston side.

Nov. 21st opened the P.S. & P.R. Road for travel to
Portland. This road 51 miles has been completed in less
than 18 months at a cost including the equipment of less
than $22,000 per mile.

In 1843 Dudley L. Pickman, having resigned the trusteeship
under the will of Simon Forrester for the benefit of Mrs.
Andrews, Mrs. Barstow and Mrs. Coit, I accepted his place as
associate with Hon Leveritt Saltonstall. The third trustee
who was Hon. Nathaniel Bowditch (resigned) not being deemed
requisite, his place has not been supplied.

On the 17th June this year was held the great meeting for
the inauguration of Bunker Hill Monument.

Carried over 7,500 passengers over the Eastern R. Road.

October opened new track to Marblehead, the old tram rail
having been removed. Mr. J. Kinsman Supt. vice chase
resigned.

In 1844 commenced building a hotel on the Eastern R.R. wharf
under charter of Eastern Exchange Hotel Co.

Our Eastern R.R. Board of Directors chosen this year were
Binney, Breed, Hoper, Bryant, Thayer, Adams and myself. Mr.
Reed resigned as treasurer and his clerk Wm. S. Tuckerman
was appointed in his place. The superintendant Mr. Kinsman,
Conductor Bancroft, Thompson, Annable Davis.

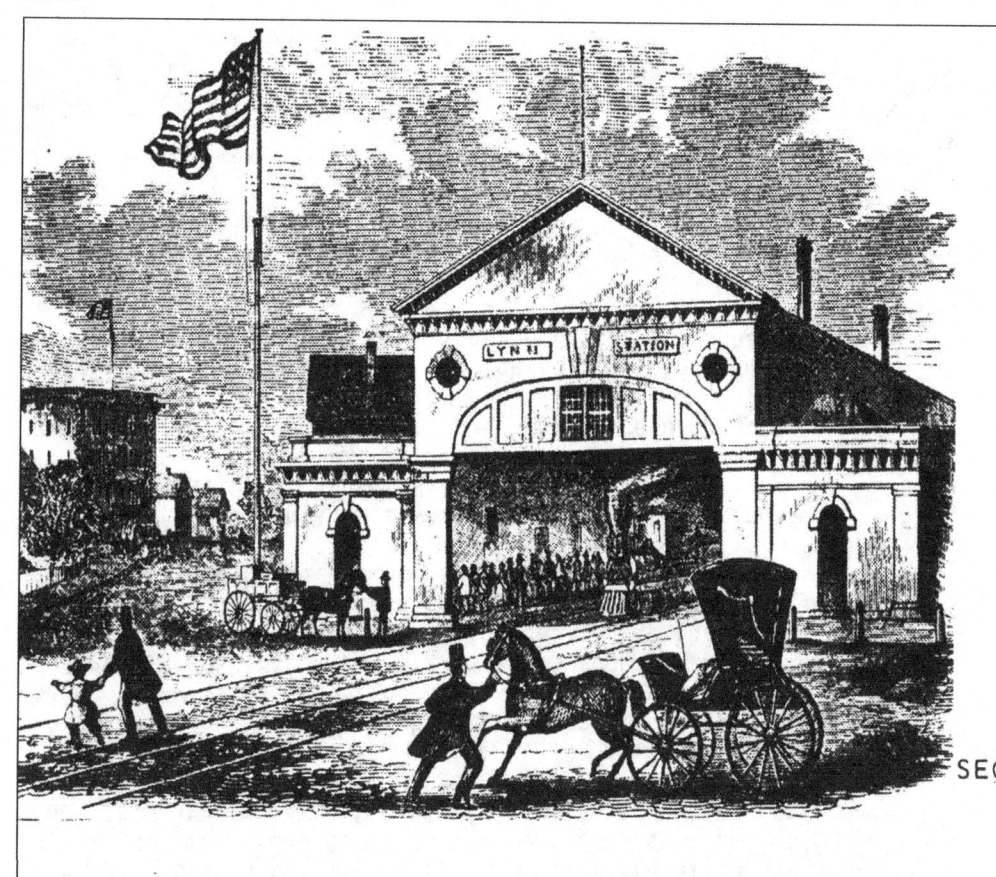

SECOND RAILROAD STATION AT LYNN, BUILT IN 1848
From a woodcut in Ballou's Pictorial, 1857.

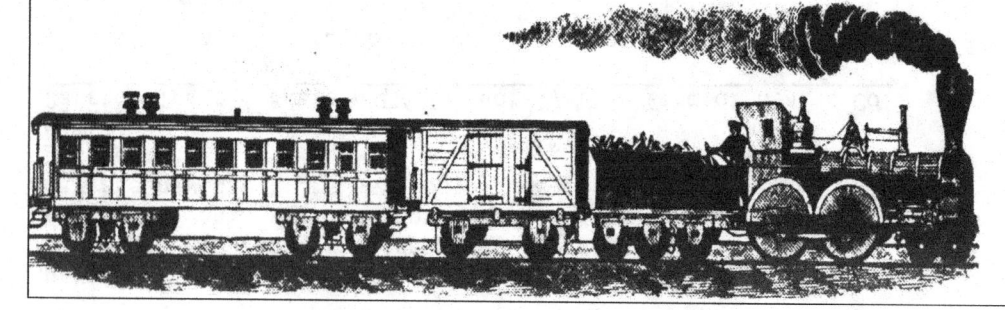

RAILROAD TRAIN OF ABOUT 1850 SHOWING THE
BAGGAGE CRATE

213

In the summer of this year visited Bath, Gardiner and
Augusta in reference to a road from Portland to the Kennebec.

In 1845 was engaged during the session of the Legislature in
contending against the charter of a rival road from Salem to
South Reading and subsequently I wrote a series of articles
on the subject that was published in the Salem Register, and
afterwards in pamphlet form for the use of the Legislature,
in which I replied to the objections made to the Ferry and
contended that the good faith of the state should forbid the
charter of parallel roads.

In 1846 the same contest continued. In June of this year,
finding my time altogether absorbed by my duties to the RR
companies with which I was connected, by mutual consent I
dissolved my connection with the house of Neal & Co. which
had now been in operation just ten years. When we formed
the partnership of Jona Neal & Sons Jan. 1, 1831, I
estimated my property at $31,459.33. When July 1, 1836 we
formed the new firm of Neal & Co. it was $37,375.68 and now
July 1, 1846 including my part of my father's property
$39,155.15 it is $125,000.00, having therefore cleared
beyond my expenses and exclusive of my inheritance from my
Father's estate $48,471.17 or an average of $4,847 per annum.

Gloucester Branch - Michigan Central RR - Visit to Michigan
& Illinois

In 1847 I continued fully occupied with the business of the
Eastern and the Portland Saco & Portsmouth Railroads. Made
a contract by which the latter was leased to the B & M and
Eastern RR Companys conjointly for 99 years at net 6% to the
stockholders. Also opened the Gloucester Branch on the 1st
Dec. Completed the new stone depot in Salem and moved the
offices there in November.

In June and July of this year, being a director and largely
interested in the Michigan Central R Road, went out to
Michigan with John M. Forbes and John C. Greene, and in
company with Mr. Brooks, the Engineer & Superintendant, went

LOCOMOTIVE "MARBLEHEAD, NO. 5" (SECOND OF THE NAME) AND THE
MARBLEHEAD TRAIN (PASSENGER AND FREIGHT) STANDING IN THE
SALEM STATION.

LOCOMOTIVE "CITY OF LYNN" NO. 28, BUILT IN 1854, STANDING IN
FRONT OF THE DANVERS STATION.
This locomotive won the celebrated race for the U. S. mails between Boston and Portland

on the road as far as completed, to wit from Detroit to
Kalamazoo, and thence in a carriage to St. Josephs and then
to New Buffalo to determine which of these points should be
selected as the western terminus of the road on Lake
Michigan. After a careful consideration of the matter we
decided in favor of New Buffalo where we concluded to
endeavor to build a harbour. From New Buffalo west to
Michigan City and thence by a Steamer to Chicago, being my
first visit to this place, and then made my first
acquaintance with Mr. Wm. B. Ogden, who was then engaged in
promoting the construction of the Chicago & Galena R. Road,
but had made but little progress.

At this time Chicago was a comparatively small place, having
about 5,000 inhabitants, real estate exceedingly low, and
its business with the interior being all carried on by
teams, very insignficant. One thousand dollars invested
then would now bring an hundredfold depressed as is real
estate at this time. Its population then may be multipled
now by a quarter of an hundred, and yet fall short of the
reality.

It was in 1847 that I bought the Estate I now own at West
Beach, Beverly Farms, Mass. with the view of erecting there
a summer residence.

In 1848 during the winter engaged in contesting before the
Legislative Committees the petitions for new roads from
Salem to Boston. Chas. T. Russel was employed as our
counsel.

In April visited New York, Philadelphia & Washington - got
propositions from Ketchum, Rogers & Grosnevor for locomotive
engines purchased coal in New York and Philadelphia, and in
Washington had some interviews with Hobler about mail
service.

Legislature passed bills for railroads from Salem to South
Reading, and from Salem to Malden, also increasing Capital
of the Eastern R. Road and allowing it to go into Boston
proper and this at a stockholder's meeting,...

The year 1848 marks the first serious accident on the Eastern Railroad. The presidential campaign of 1848 had nearly drawn to its close when, on Thursday evening, November 2nd, two large political gatherings were held, one at Salem and the other at Lynn. Daniel Webster was advertised to address the Whigs at Lynn, and Caleb Cushing the Democrats at Salem. Special trains were run to Salem from all the towns in the vicinity, including Marblehead. At that time, and until much later, the Marblehead branch train leaving Salem used the down track from Boston until it reached the junction at Castle Hill, nearly a mile from Salem. On this day the extra train for Marblehead left Salem just before midnight with over two hundred passengers on board. As it reached the junction at Castle Hill an extra train from Lynn, drawn by the locomotive "Huntress," No. 10, was seen approaching. The man in charge of the ball signals at this point became confused (there were those who said he was "under the influence") and hoisted the lights which gave the Lynn train the track. The result was a frightful collision. The Marblehead train was just entering the branch track and its locomotive, tender and forward cars were utterly demolished, six persons were killed and sixty-four on both trains were injured. The locomotive "Marblehead" was so badly damaged that it was broken up, and the locomotive "Sagamore" was rebuilt and renamed "Marblehead" to take its place. Engineer Glover jumped and was only slightly injured. Conductor Harris was standing on the platform and was thrown out at the side of the track, but not hurt. The coroner's jury at Marblehead, after an inquiry into the affair, severely censured the Eastern Railroad Company for carelessness in the management of its trains.

The inquest does not seem to have borne much fruit, however, for in the annual report of the next year (1849) the directors say "they have not felt themselves author- ized to accede to some demands, which they consider exhorbitant, in a case where all precautions, which had for so long a time been entirely successful, were taken, and where there seems to have been nothing but a fatal combination of circumstances that human sagacity could not have anticipated." . . .

It would be interesting to know the amount of damages the company had to pay on account of this accident, up to that time the worst in New England, but there is no way of ascertaining. Probably they were not as large as may be imagined, for in those days people were not as prone as they are today to sue railroad corporations.

Bradlee, Francis B.C., "The Eastern Railroad- A Historical Account of Early Railroading in Eastern New England" Historical Collections of the Essex Institute, Vol. LII, October, 1916, No. 4

Philadelphia & Reading R. Road, Appointed Commissioner,
Accident E.R.R.

...held in May - the directors were instructed to carry out,
but they raised no money and indicated no means of doing
so. In June and again in August visited Maine and the White
Mountains at Gorham, and then resigned the presidency of the
P.S. & P. R. Road, Capt. Ichabod Goodwin elected in my
place. Built new depot at Lynn. The affairs of the Phila.
& Reading R. Road in which I have an interest, and of the
stockholders a very considerable number resided in Boston,
being in a very depressed state the value of the shares of
$50 per having been reduced to $10 and even less. I was
invited to proceed to Philadelphia and act in behalf of the
N.E. stockholders and by a vote of the Board of Manager
adopted Dec. 13th, 1848, the invitation was confirmed and
full powers granted for a full investigation, and to present
any suggestions for the financial and mechanical arrangement
as might seem proper; making the salary $3,000 per annum, it
being understood that I was only to give it such time as I
could spare from my other duties. This brought me in close
connection with Mr. Tucker, the president, Mr. Bradford the
treasurer, Mr. St. George Tucker its counsel, Mr. W.H.
Fisher and Mr. Geo. Edwards, both of whom had been largely
interested in its management and with the directors Messrs.
Norris, Lejie, Loesser of Orangebune and Rutlands of Reading
- who with Mr. Fressper, Prest & Mr. Lee, one of the
directors of the canal between which and the road there was
existing a ruinous competition. Also had a good deal to do
with Mr. Nichols the superintendant and Mr. Steele the
engineer of the road, and subsequently with Mr. McCalmont of
the house of McCalmont Bros. of London, large holders of
stock and bonds and Mr. Cullen, their confidential agent in
this country.

In this way was fully employed between Boston and
Philadelphia. While I was in the latter place on the 3rd
November a very serious collision took place between two
extra trains at the Marblehead switch, by which 6 persons
were killed and 40 more or less injured.

May 24, 1848, the stockholders authorized the directors (an act of the legislature having been obtained May 9, 1848), to arrange for what was known as the "new route" into Boston, that is, the entry of the Eastern Railroad into the city proper, thus doing away with the ferriage across the harbor from East Boston. At first it was proposed to use for this purpose what was known as the Chelsea Branch Railroad (now the Grand Junction Railroad), then in course of construction, especially as the Eastern Railroad had an interest in the stock, but the plan was soon found impracticable. Several of the directors and a strong minority of the stockholders bitterly opposed the "new route" idea as unnecessary and entailing a foolish waste of money, and they were successful in postponing the project for some time.

A short description of the practical working and running of the trains which, except for minor changes, was carried on in much the same manner for over thirty years of the company's early existence, may not be out of place here. In the original rules used when the road was first opened it is stated: "No train will start from either Depot until the arrival of the train expected from the other Depot," and "When anything shall happen to a train to render assistance necessary, let a Brakeman be dispatched to the nearest point for assistance and let him get on horseback as soon as possible. Let no conductor leave his train." . . . "The head brakeman or baggage master will tend the brake on the car next the engine and will seat himself back to the engine, keeping a good lookout to the rear of the train. He will carry a whistle, which he will blow whenever it becomes necessary for the engine to stop or whenever he is notified to do so by the conductor. This signal will be answered by the engineer with his whistle, which shall be the signal for applying all the brakes." . . .

The first time-books for the employees giving rules, etc., for running trains were printed on single sheets of a size 10 inches square, to be folded up and carried in the pocket. Beginning in 1850 small pamphlets, about 7 1-2 x 4 1-2 inches in size and varying in contents from 12 to 38 pages, were used for time-books. These were in fashion until 1871, when the first type of folding time-books, like the kind now in use only much smaller, came into vogue.

From the time-sheet to take effect Monday, October 8, 1849, the following rules and directions are quoted as being most curious and out-of-date. "No train or engine to pass between the passenger depot and Sumner street, East Boston, at a speed exceeding five miles per hour. No engine, whether attached to a train or otherwise, will be used in the vicinity of any depot unless the engineer and fireman belonging to the same are upon it. No train to be shifted from one track to the other, unless a brakeman is upon the same. Depot masters will see that this rule is strictly adhered to. Engineers will be held responsible for the proper use of their engines and to see that water, fuel and oil are at all times provided. The fireman to be subject to the orders of the engineer. All trains coming into the depot must brake up so as to run in at a slow rate. A brakeman at all times to ride on the back of the train." Later this rule was changed to: "The engine must be made to assist in bringing up the train which must come into the depots at a slow rate." "Express, extra and merchandize trains will keep out of the way of the regular trains by not leaving a turn-out unless they have time to arrive at the next turn-out at least TEN MINUTES before the time noted in this table for the arrival there of the regular train—which MUST NOT LEAVE any of the stations mentioned in this table earlier than the time designated.

"In all cases of meeting of the trains at the turn-outs, each train must take the right-hand track, and must remain until the expected crossing train arrives; and no train must leave any depot, or turn-out, WHEN A TRAIN IS DUE AND EXPECTED, UNTIL IT ARRIVES. When any train is to pass a switch after any other train, and arrives at the switch too soon, it must wait for the arrival and STOPPING of the expected train, and pass the switch in proper order. On the double tracks each train will pass on the right-hand track.

"Enginemen will keep a good look-out to see that all is right before passing the switches of the Marblehead and Gloucester Branches, and also at the crossings of the Essex and Concord Railroads, which must be passed at a speed not exceeding 12 miles per hour.

"ON APPROACHING THE BRIDGE AT NEWBURYPORT, THE SPEED OF ALL THE TRAINS MUST BE REGULATED SO AS NOT TO EXCEED TEN MILES PER HOUR, AND THE BRIDGE MUST BE PASSED AT A SPEED NOT EXCEEDING THAT RATE. THE *BLACK BALL* AT THE DRAW SIGNIFIES THAT THE DRAW IS OPEN, AND TRAINS MUST STOP. IN FOGGY WEATHER, CARE MUST BE TAKEN TO SEE THAT ALL IS RIGHT AT THE DRAW BEFORE PASSING.

"Trains following each other must keep at least one mile apart, and in the evening a TAIL LANTERN must be used on the forward train.

Bradlee, Francis B.C., "The Eastern Railroad- A Historical Account of Early Railroading in Eastern New England" Historical Collections of the Essex Institute, Vol. LII, October, 1916, No. 4

In 1849 busily engaged in conducting the business of the
Eastern Road, rendered more complicated and difficult from
the necessity of settling with the persons who were wounded,
and the families of those who were killed in the collision
of the 3rd Nov. '48. Also in investigating the accounts and
regulating the connections of the Philadelphia & Reading
Railroad.

Philadelphia - Death of N.W. Neal

In May at a special meeting of the E.R.R. stockholders they
reconsidered their former vote, instructing the directors to
build the Road into Boston, but simply to have surveys
made. At the annual meeting of E.R.R. held July 9th in
Boston the following board of directors were chosen: Neal,
Breed, Reed, Goodwin, Philbrick, Thorndike, S. Heeper.

Nothing material occured during the last half of this year.

At the beginning of 1850 was in Philadelphia engaged in
various negotiations with Mr. Gardener of Gardener, Me.,
Ruel Williams of Augusta, Col. Stanley of d^o ('ditto'
meaning Augusta) respecting the Kennebec & Portland R.R. and
with Mr. Little of the At. & St. L. R.R. also with Mr. Lang
of S. Berwick, Capt. Patten of Bath, Capt. Goodwin Prest,
P.S. & P.R.R. - Mr. Howe & West of the B. & Me. respecting a
connection in Portland with the At & St. L. and the Kennebec
& Portland roads in front of the city with the P.S. & P.

This year imported 4,000 ton RR iron from England for double
track between Boston & Salem & renewals. In June I made a
visit to Ohio & Michigan.

August 5th. A collision occurred at the crossing of the
Salem & Lowell road with the Eastern, on the North River in
Salem between the down Gloucester train, and a coal train
from Philips wharf, by which the engineer Henry W. Knowles
was injured and lost his right arm.

<u>Obituaries</u> (glued into the family "Neal Record", paper unknown)

The late <u>Capt. JONATHAN NEAL</u>, of this city, who during the
war of the revolution was in the military service of the country,
and after ts close was remarkable for the energy of his character,
and his enterprize and success as a merchant, left behind him three
sons, distinguished for their skill and success in the mercantile
profession second to none in existence. Two of the brothers made
themselves accomplished naviagators. The eldest and only survivor,
is the great Railroad financier, who has so successfully conducted
the Eastern Railroad, and saved from annihilation the Read
(Pennsylvania) Railroad, and whose advice is sought throught the
Union in Railroad difficulties and embarrassments. The second,
<u>NATHAN WARD NEAL</u>, bearing for his middle name his mother's name, was
educated at Cambridge, in the class that graduated in 1816, was the
partner who conducted the outdoor business of the firm, and was as
well known on the exchange in New York and Boston, as any merchant
of those cities, and as universally respected as known. He died two
months since - And we have now to record the death of <u>WILLIAM H.</u>,
the third brother, on Friday last-Remarkable for the suavity of his
manners, his kindly feelings, and high sense of honor-an eminent
merchant and skilful navigator-for many years President of the East
India Marine Society-leaving a widow, the daughter of Joseph Ropes
Esq., who died less than four months since. Every sympathy must be
awakened, and every feeling heart bleed for the desolation of this
afflicted family.

"Insatiate archer! could not one suffice?
They shaft flew thrice, and thrice our hopes are slain."

Aug. 13 & 17. On a journey to Sodus Bay and town of Lyons in N.Y. state at request of Mr. J.C. Adams, to view his plan for canal there.

In September the Salem & South Reading R.R. began to run trains. Sept. 16th started with a party consisting of Messrs. Henshaw, Williams, Rice, Lombard, Reed, Andrews and others, over the Fitchburg, Cheshire, Vermont &'Mass. R. Roads to Bellows Falls, and next day by a special train to Brandon and Burlington, and returned to Boston the 19th.

In Oct. visited Philadelphia on business of the P. & Reading R. Road. November 17th. At 9:50 P.M. my brother Nathan died at the house of my sister Mrs. Choate in Chestnut Street, Salem, after a confinement to the house of six months, aged 53 years, having been born August 27th 1797. His disease was of the blood, called by physicians anehimia. It was first apparent about one year before. It disappeared in the winter, but came on rapidly after that and soon compelled him to give up to it. He graduated at Harvard in 1816, and has since been engaged in merchantile pursuits, first in company with Jos. S. Cabot, afterwards as partner in the houses of Jona Neal & Sons, and Neal & Co. of which last he had been the senior for the preceding three years.

Death of Wm. H. Neal, Illinois Central Railroad

He was buried on Wednesday the 20th November, being deposited in Mrs. Choate's tomb on the Hill burying ground. He was never married.

1851 January 17th. My brother William Henry died this morning at 5:15 of exhaustion in consequence of having been unable to take nourishment, not having been able to keep anything on his stomach, and also of excessive bleeding at the nose. He had suffered severely from rheumatic gout for several years. He was 51 years, 10 months old, having been born on the 8th March 1799 - leaves a widow, the daughter of the late Capt. Joseph Hopes, but never had any children. He followed a sea life for some years, and then engaged in

The rules concerning free passes were as follows:
"Eastern Railroad Company.
To the Conductors:
Dear Sirs:
"The following persons you will pass free on the Eastern Railroad and are not required to report them, viz:

1st. Directors, treasurer, superintendent, and clerk of the Eastern Railroad Company,

2nd. Directors and clerk of the Eastern Railroad in New Hampshire.

3rd. Directors, treasurer, superintendent and clerk of the Portland, Saco and Portsmouth Railroad Company.

4th. The members of the immediate families of the above.

5th. The directors, treasurer, clerk and superintendent of the Boston and Maine Railroad.

6th. The chief machinist, bridge inspector and road master of the Eastern Railroad. Freight agent, clerks in the treasurer's and superintendent's offices, and persons regularly attached to the engines or trains of the company.

7th. Special agents of the post office department, on the exhibition of their credentials. . . .

"Also: circumstances may occur in which you are authorized to exercise a sound discretion in regard to passing persons free. Such, for instance, as the officers of other roads occasionally passing over this road; of shipwrecked seamen; of persons entirely destitute, etc., etc. But in such cases, you will insert the name of the person passed in one of the tickets furnished you for that purpose, endorse your own name on the back of it and return it to the office at Salem.

"D. A. Neal, President."

Salem, Jan. 1, 1850.

Excerpt from the 1870 pamphlet compiled by David A. Neal, entitled "The Illinois Central Railroad, It's Position and Prospects":

"If to make two blades of grass grow where but one grew before, be worthy the high commendation of the philosopher and patriot, it will not be deemed an act altogether unimportant or useless to the country to open to the approach of industry, millions of acres of the most fertile soil the sun ever shone upon, and to make available at once the alluvial deposites of the ages..."

mercantile pursuits as partner in the houses of Jona Neal &
Sons and of Neal & Co. of which last he was the only
surviving partner after the death of my brother Nathan. The
settlement of the affairs of that firm now devolved on me.

The ferry boat of the Eastern RR having been burnt on the
8th to the Water's edge, made a contract with Mr. Geo. T.
Sampson to rebuild her. Having in 1850 agreed to become one
of twelve applicants for a charter for the purpose of
building a railroad in Illinois, under the terms of an Act
of Congress passed on the 20th September of that year by
which 2,595,000 acres of land was granted in aid of its
construction, and a bill in consequence having passed the
Illinois legislature on the 10th of February 1851 incorp.
Robert Schuylie, Geo. Griswold, Morris Ketchum, Jona Sturges
Jos. W Alsop, and granting them the aforesaid lands on
condition of their completing the work within a given time.
It was an immense undertaking for twelve persons to
accomplish, but it seemed to promise great results. Robert
Schuylie, whose reputation for skill, experience and
integrity was at this time not only unimpeached, but
unrivalled, was made President and he concocted a plan of
carrying it on mainly by loans, based on the granted lands.
The scheme was at least ingenious, and under different
circumstances would have proved more succesful than actual
results now exhibit it. Yet it has not been a failure.
More money has been called from the stockholders than was
anticipated. As much has been obtained on loans, but on
much less advantageous terms. The road has been built, but
it has cost a much larger sum than was estimated. The
original projectors have all lost money instead of making
it. In one item alone have the expectations been realized
and that is in the sales of the lands. These have brought
more money, and have sold more rapidly than anyone ventured
to predict. In the early part of this year 1851 I published
a small pamphlet at the request of the board, setting forth
the details of the plan, and the securities it offered. It
was believed that a loan could be negotiated in London and
the directors in New York make arrangements with Hon. Robt.
S. Walker, the late Secretary of the Treasury, to proceed

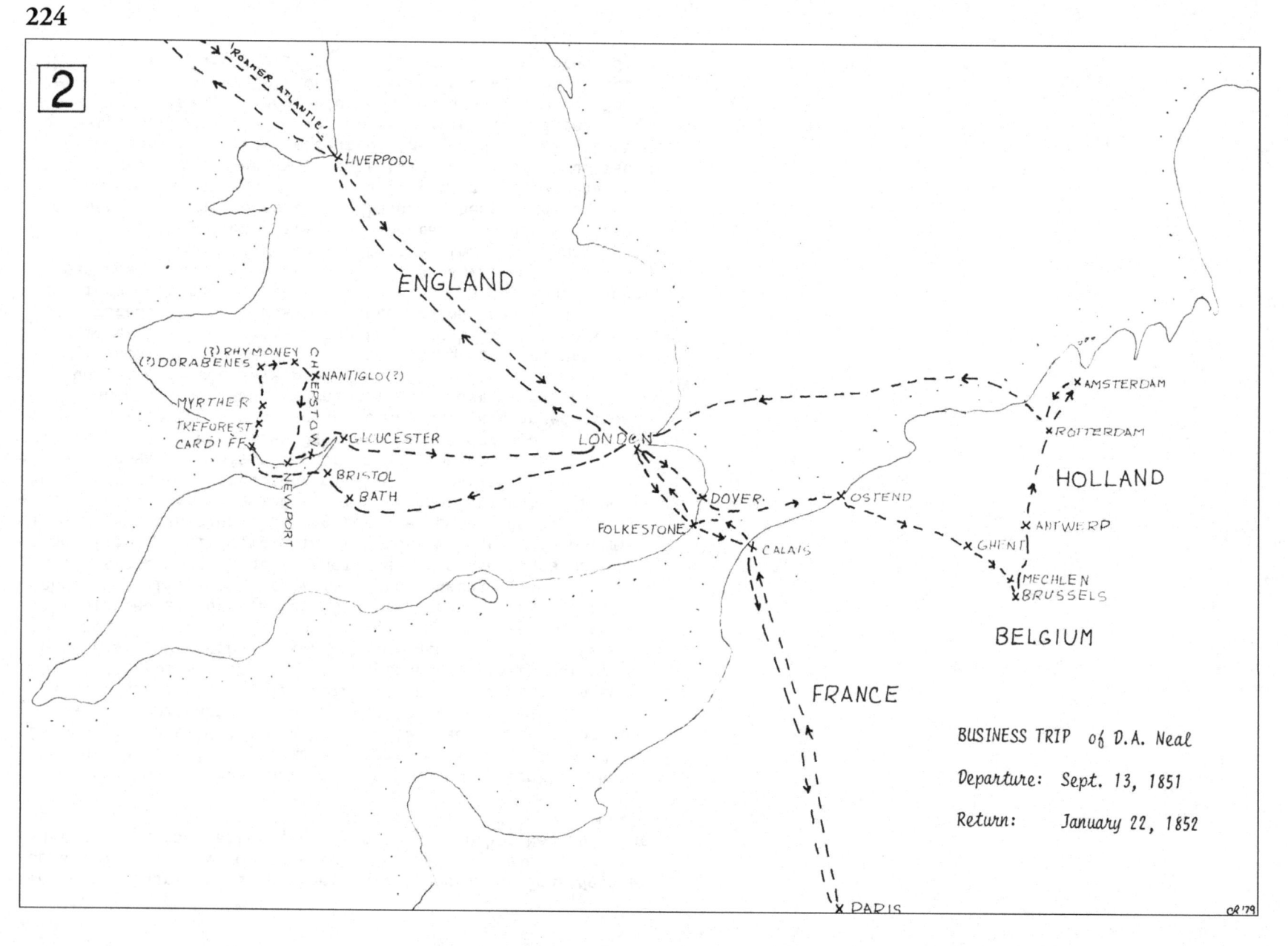

2

ROAMER ATLANTIC

LIVERPOOL

ENGLAND

(?) RHYMONEY O
(?) DORABENES
NANTIGLO (?)
CHEPSTOW
MYRTHER
TREFOREST
CARDIFF
GLOUCESTER
NEWPORT
BRISTOL
BATH

LONDON

AMSTERDAM
ROTTERDAM

HOLLAND

DOVER
OSTEND
FOLKESTONE
CALAIS
ANTWERP
GHENT
MECHLEN
BRUSSELS

BELGIUM

FRANCE

BUSINESS TRIP of D.A. Neal

Departure: Sept. 13, 1851

Return: January 22, 1852

PARIS

thither for that purpose. They felt however that some one
of the managers should accompany him, who could act for the
company in any emergency under full powers, and take up the
negotiation if Mr. Walker should not succeed within a
specified time. They urged me very much to go. I felt that
it was a great work which could be carried on only in the
way proposed. My eventual interest would be very large, and
decided to conform to their wishes, and confiding in their
honour I made no stipulation whatever for my own services,
beyond the payment in any event of my expenses. Accordingly
on the 20th August I resigned my office of President of the
Eastern Railroad. I had before resigned my place in the
management of the Reading Railroad, that company having been
now entirely extricated from its financial difficulties, its
arrangements with the Skuylkill Navigation Co. had put on
the most satisfactory footing and the market value of its
stock advanced from 80% discount to nearly par.

To give me a position abroad in relation to the business in
hand, I was chosen vice president of the company, and
invested with full powers to accept or reject any
arrangements Mr. Walker might make, and if he should not
have succeeded by the 20th November current, I was then to
continue the agency in his hands or assume it myself as I
might see fit.

On the 13th of September we embarked on board the 'Roamer
Atlantic', Capt. West, at New York for Liverpool. We
arrived at Liverpool on the 24th. Mr. Brown and some other
gentlemen called and the next day we took the railway cars
to London, where we took rooms at Hotel St. George, Hanover
Square, but a day or two afterwards, at the suggestion of
Mr. Corbin a friend of Mr. Walker, a Virginian but for years
a resident in Paris, we removed to rooms at No. 10 Half Moon
Street, Picadilly, where Mr. Corbin also had his lodgings.

Mr. Walker at once entered into correspondence with the
Barings & Rothchilds on the subject of his mission, but
found little encouragement. I did all I could to forward
his views. At Mr. Bates invitiation went out to his place

at Shene (Wimbledon Common) and adjoining the Park at
Richmond, and remained from Saturday till Monday. This
place ...

London, Amsterdam, Great Exhibition, Negociations

...formerly belonged to Mr. Hope of Amsterdam. In the
chamber in which I was lodged I found silver plates fastened
to the window shutters on which was engraved the names of
celebrated persons who had slept there. Among them I
recollect that of Louis Napoleon, the present Emperor of
France. I conversed freely with Mr. Bates on the subject of
our mission and he promised to give it his full
consideration.

At this time the Great Exhibition at the Crystal Palace or
Hyde Park was open and I visited it very often. It was a
thing not to be forgotten. On the 16th of October I
embarked at Folkeston for France, remained in Paris until
the 20th when I returned to London. Remained there until
the 19th Nov. when I embarked from Dover for Ostend, thence
by rail to Ghent, Mechlin, Brussels and Antwerp where I met
my old friend Mosselman and dined with him. Thence to
Rotterdam and Amsterdam, where I called on Mess. Hope & Co.
and visited M. Labercheus. Tried to interest them in our
project, but found they refered everything to London. In
Amsterdam I made an acquaintance with Mr. West Roff a sugar
refiner, in case I should get up a large refinery in Boston.

On my return to London on 26th found Mr. Walker engaged in
negotiations with the Rothschilds, but on the 2nd Dec. while
I was in the office of the Barings, Mr. Bates came in and
announced the coup d'etat in Paris, an event that gave Louis
Napoleon supreme power and eventually the imperial crown
that he now wears.

It however settled all hope of the negociations with the
Rothschilds. The fall of funds was immense and a stop was
at once put to all speculation. Mr. Walker now gave it up.
I resumed correspondence with Rothschild, but all I could

Land Department Illinois Central Railroad,

Chicago

229

get them to do was to forward under their own envelope a
circular which I had lithographed in English, French and
German to their correspondents on the continent and to agree
if anything could be done, to take the agency of the bonds
in London, but they would not head a subscription.

While on this visit to England I went with Mr. Baeller Toms,
an iron broker, into Wales to see the iron works in that
region - by rail to Bath and Bristol - thence by steamer to
Cardiff - thence by Taftvale railroad to Treforest where the
Abldare Co. works, owned by Mr. Fithergill, then to Myrther
a town at the terminus of the road containing 60,000
inhabitants. On the 30th October - here we took a team of
horses and visited the Penydaren works belonging to Thompson
& Laemore, then to Dorabenes where are the works of Sir John
Guest. Then we went to Rhymoney and from thence to the
Tredegau works of Mr. Thompson. Then we passed the works of
the Ebbuvale-Colbrook-Vale and other companies - stopped at
Nantiglo, then works of Mess Bailey Bros. & Co. and on the
31 inst took the Western Valley RR to Newport, the...

Return to U.S., Washington, 2ND Visit to England

...South Wales R.R. connecting with the Great Western at
Swinton, passed through Chepstow on the Wye, Gloucester, and
arrived in London at 6 pm.

Also while in England visited Mr. Lampson (the great fur
dealer) at his seat about 30 miles from London on the
Brighton R. Road, and Mr. Morrison (the richest commoner in
England) at his estate Basildoo Park on the great Western
R.R. near Reading, and spent two or three days there, during
which time witnessed the country hunt or fox chase on his
grounds.

Having furnished the Rothschilds with the circular and
arranged with Messrs. Fox Henderson & Co. paid them to send
out an agent to the U.S. to see if it would be worth while
for the, with Brassey, Pete and other contractors to make a
bid for constructing the Illinois Central R. Road. I

RAILROAD BUILT BY SALEM MEN

Played Important Part in Organizing Illinois Central; Capt. Neal, Robert Rantoul and William H. Osborn.

The University of Illinois has published, in a quarterly serial issued last year, a detailed 200-page History of the Illinois Central railroad putting on record, facts about a number of well known residents of this neighborhood, which cannot fail to interest News readers. Salem men, among whom were Joseph Francis Tucker and Joseph Linton Waters, formed connections with that great enterprise when it was struggling into life, as did also President Franklin Haven of the Boston Merchants bank, whose colonial estate at Beverly Farms has long been one of the landmarks of Southern Essex county. But the passages from the history quoted, relate to David A. Neal, Robert Rantoul, Jr., and William Henry Osborn. Captain Neal, with Mr. Rantoul and Mr. Haven were of the original board of directors. Mr. Osborn was president of the road for years, at a late period.

Captain Neal was president of the old Eastern railroad when it was a distinctly Salem affair, with its offices in the present Salem stone station. He carried it as far east as Portsmouth, if not beyond, and he extended the Rockport branch as far as Gloucester. The stone station was the third station built, following two wooden ones, and only came into being after the tunnel had been put through. It was built on a plan which Mr. Neal obtained in England of a station which he saw there. President Neal went from the Eastern railroad to the Philadelphia & Reading road, and from that became the executive vice president of the Illinois road while it was building. In 1851 he was sent abroad with an ex-Secretary of the United States Treasury, Robert J. Walker, as agents to negotiate for the road, its first great loan, and in this matter his railroad experience, as well as his life-long intimacy with George Peabody, the London banker, an almost townsman, served him and the Illinois road well. No rails were made in American then. American locomotives were a new thing. Between December, 1851, and February, 1852, they had placed a loan in London, on terms which enabled the road to pay in bonds, as these were preferred to cash by the English railmakers, from whom all the running material of the road had been purchased and shipped. Richard Cobden was among the leading English promoters of the enterprise, and so were the Rothschilds and Barings.

In December, 1850, nine memorialists had addressed a petition through Robert Rantoul, Jr., who was one of them, to the legislature of Illinois, setting forth the large experience of the memorialists in railroad enterprises, demonstrating their financial sufficiency, and asking for a charter from the State of Illinois which would enable them to build a road from Cairo in Illinois, at the mouth of the Ohio river to Galena at the northwest corner of Illinois, with a branch line to Chicago at the northwest. This was

Not a New Scheme

The plan was to extend the road through the country north and south from Cairo to Mobile bay, its connections making it for the United States a central avenue of transportation and travel, open all the year round, which was not true of the great river. The federal government had already made a princely grant of land. The memorial offered put a new face upon the enterprise and resulted in the granting of a charter, drawn by Mr. Rantoul and personally and successfully urged by him upon the legislators at Springfield. Next, after the president of the road, he is spoken of in the history as the most influential factor in the enterprise, and a growing city, 100 miles south of Chicago, at a junction with a cross-road, is named for him.

Of Mr. Osborn the History says:

"Although not one of the original directors, William H. Osborn soon became interested in the Illinois Central, and from the retirement of President Schuyler in 1853 to the acquisition of the Southern Lines in 1882, he was the dominant figure in the history of the company. A man of great ability and strong personality, with a broad grasp of affairs, he won the absolute support of stockholders, employes and shippers, and for over 20 years English and Dutch shareholders gave him their unqualified proxies, thus entrusting to him the complete control of the Illinois Central. So well did he execute this trust that even during the periods of deepest depression they did not condemn his management of the road. The company owes more to Mr. Osborn than to any other person connected with it.

"The remaining directors were prominent business men, but they did not exert such an influence upon the management of the property, as did Rantoul, Schuyler and Osborn.

"Fortunately at this time Mr. Osborn, who, more than any other person connected with the road, had helped to place its finances on the substantial basis of today, assumed complete control of the financial affairs of the company."

Mr. Osborn grew up in Salem where he was well known. Before he went to Illinois he had been a bookkeeper in the extensive and well managed livery establishment of Smith & Manning, and also had been a clerk in the counting room of Hon. Stephen C. Phillips. Later he lived in New York city.

The Salem Evening News
Wednesday August 23, 1916

concluded to return to the United States and therefore on
the 5th of January 1852 left London for Liverpool, having
previously made my farewell call on Baring Bros. & Co., W.M.
Rothschild & Co. - Mr. Geo. Peabody - Mr. Lamprier - Mr.
Chas. Fox - Mr. Brassey - Mr. Gilbert, and arranged with Mr.
Anthony to sell Michigan C. R.R. bonds and to look out for
the interst of the Illinois Central etc. etc. and on the 7th
embarked on board the Steamer 'Arctic', Capt. Luce, for New
York.

After touching on George's Shoal, as we suppose, once,
without damage, we arrived at New York, covered with ice on
the 22nd - the winter being very severe. Immediately made
my report to the Ill. Cent. R.R. Board of Directors and
tendered my resignation as vice president, but the latter
they declined to receive and begged me to hold it and take
especial charge of the lands and contract of the Co.

Shortly after went to Washington, and succeeded in getting
the selection of the lands completed, mainly through the
exertions of Mr. Griswold and other directors. Early in
March we had information that Mr. Gilbert and Mr. Billings
who had some sort of authority to see what could be done,
were in treaty in London for a loan, and afterwards that it
only required the presence of someone with the requisite
authority to complete it. I was urged on one day's notice
to go out for the purpose and did so, leaving New York in
the 'Asia' on the 25th and arrived in Liverpool about the
6th of April.

In London found the talk of the completion of a loan
amounted to nothing more than some indefinite talk with Fox
Henderson & Co. who had neither the means nor the intention
of doing anything of the sort. Subsequently however I
entered into a negociation with the House of Derean & Co.
who had been successful in the French rail roads and with
some assistance from Mess. Bilbert & Billings and Mr.
Hertellinson, an English broker, succeeded in getting them
to undertake the loan of $5,000,000 @ 6% at par or 202.6.8
per $1,000 of Bonds. I also purchased from Bailey Bros. &

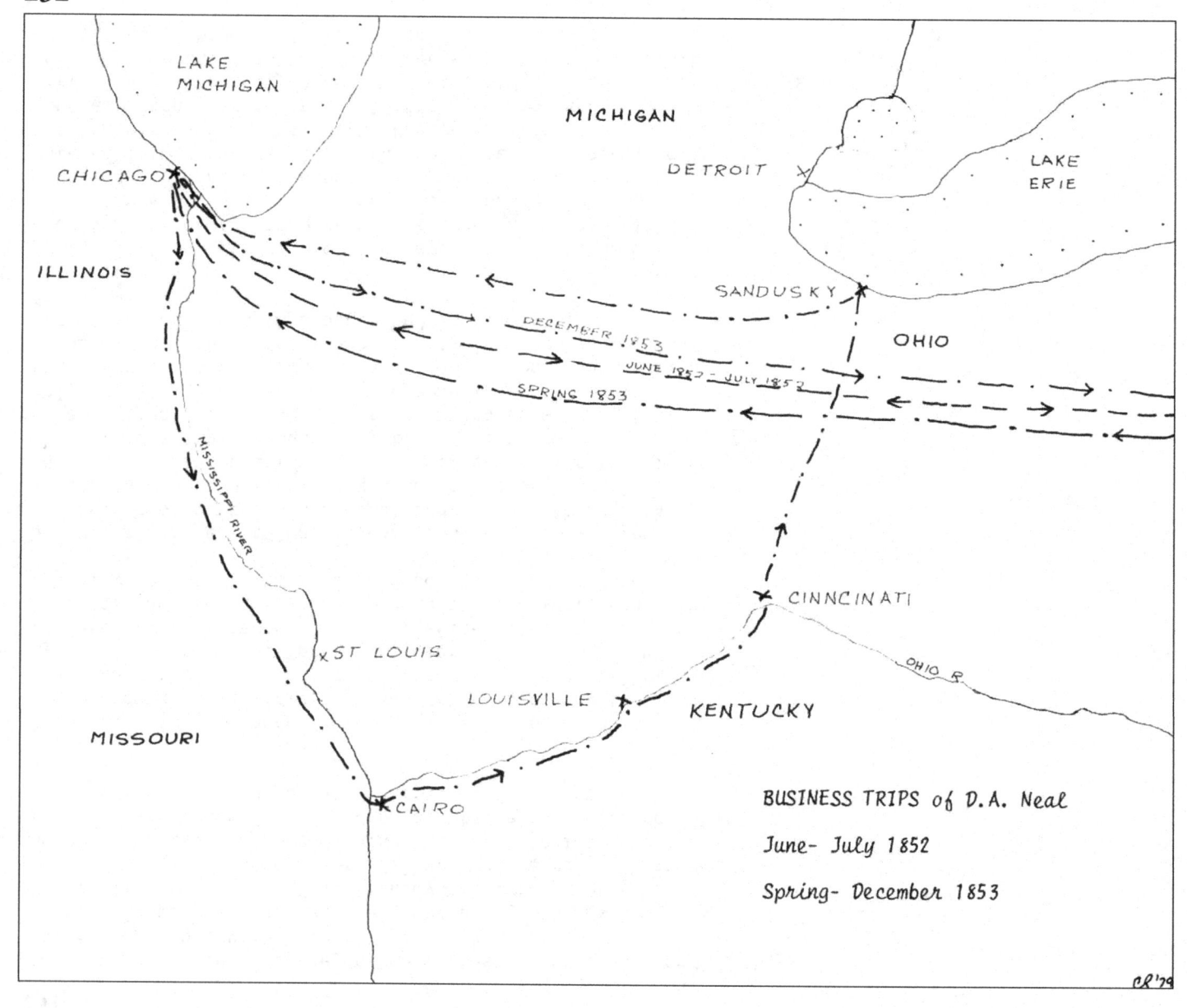

LAKE MICHIGAN

MICHIGAN

DETROIT ×

LAKE ERIE

CHICAGO

ILLINOIS

SANDUSKY

OHIO

DECEMBER 1853

JUNE 1852 - JULY 1852

SPRING 1853

MISSISSIPPI RIVER

CINNCINATI

× ST LOUIS

OHIO R.

LOUISVILLE

KENTUCKY

MISSOURI

× CAIRO

BUSINESS TRIPS of D.A. Neal

June- July 1852

Spring- December 1853

233

Co. and from Mr. Robinson of the Ebbervale work 2,500 tons
of rails at about an average of ₤4.18.6 per ton on board or
about $41 per ton delivered in New York or N. Orleans (at my
option) duty paid. By this purchase the Co. saved at least
half a million of dollars. The payment was to be altogether
in bonds of the Co. and I did it on my own responsibility.
I returned home in the latter part of May in the 'Atlantic',
Capt. West, and again offered my resignation which was again
declined. While in Europe this time I made a flying visit
to Paris with Mr. Hugh M'Celmart - visited Fontainbleau,
Versailles, St. Cloud, making my headquarters at Maurice's
Rue Richelieu.

In June I proceeded to Chicago, made a tour of the state,
fixed with Mr. Mason the chief engineer the contract for the
work and proceeded in the work of classifying and appraising
the lands for sale - came home in July - returned shortly
and remained in Illinois till November.

In 1853 spent the winter with my family in New York and
Washington being employed in correcting the land
selections. In the spring again went to Illinois and
returned via Cairo, Louisville, Cincinnati and Sandusky.
Then went again to Chicago, where and in New York spent the
balance of this year.

Loan - Purchase of 25,000 Tons RR Iron - NY - Washington

In 1854 was busily employed most of the time in the land
office in Chicago, arranging sales, accounts, etc.

In March 1855 - Mr. John Griswold being elected President of
the Illinois Central R. Road, and being willing to spend his
time in Illinois, could attend to the business there, I was
able to leave and resigned my office as vice president of
the Co. and employed myself in managing the Associate Lands
which were tracts in Illinois, in all about 19,000 acres
which I had bought in 1852 for a/c Geo. Griswold, Jon'a
Sturges, Ketchum, Rogers & Bement and myself, each one
quarter, on a/c of which business I made a journey to
Illinois in August & September.

Ten Chestnut Street
Choate Residence
(10 Cambridge St. is
 directly behind it, now
 part of the same residence)

Harriet Charlotte (Neal) Rantoul

During 1856 employed very much as in 1855 having visited
Illinois on the business of our lands during the summer. On
the 20th October at 1 a.m. my sister Mrs. Mehitable Choate
died at her house in Chestnut Street, Salem, after a long
and distressing illness, having been subject to a severe
catarrh but finally died without a struggle. She was
married to Amos Choate in 18-- and became a widow in 1844.
She left me her house in Chestnut Street and had prepared it
and put it in perfect order for my reception. Mrs. Choate's
remains were deposited in her husband's tomb on the Hill
burying ground on the 20th. She was 73 years of age, having
been born in November 1783.

Death of Mrs. Choate, Fire Washington - Saratoga Etc.

On the 1st November I removed to her house from Washington
St. house, and on the 6th the house took fire from the hot
air chamber in the cellar and great damage was done to the
western side of the house, but the house and all the
furniture was saved, the latter in perfectly good condition.
I moved back same day to our old residence fom which we had
removed nothing.

1857. Occupied in repairing the house in Chestnut Street.
Passed part of the winter with my daughters in Washington at
Willard's. Left a few days before the inauguration of
Buchanan as President of the U.S.A. In May visited Illinois
and went by rail all through the state.

1858. Theodore's affairs having become embarrassed by
reason of the Calcutta trade having resulted in such heavy
losses, arranged them so as to settle all his liabilities.
On the 13th May my daughter Harriet Charlotte was married to
Robert S. Rantoul.

In the summer made a visit to Illinois & Ohio and returned
via Montreal, Quebec and Portland.

May 10th purchased for my wife's account the estate No. 10
Cambridge Street and adjoining my estate on Chestnut Street
for $1,050.

Neal Property at 67 West Street, Beverly Farms, Massachusetts
The view on the left, facing inland shows the original House
but the view on the right, facing the Atlantic Ocean has in
the foreground a wing added during the early part of this
century.
It is the closest Beach property to the Beverly Farms Railway
Station, a short five minute walk.
Since the death of the youngest Neal Granddaughter, Harriet
Charlotte Rantoul on April 9, 1975 at the age of 96 yrs.,
the House has been radically renovated for modern occupancy.

1859. In January arranged to place the property for my daughters Harriet C and M. Marie by selling them 1/2 Bartlett Wharf Property, 1/2 my interest in Illinois Lands in Co and 1/2 my interest in the Duprey Contract at rates that I think will eventually give them a large profit, but with the understanding that if it shall prove otherwise, the property shall be taken back at cost and interest - this I have done to compensate in a measure for the large sums I have been obliged to advance for my son Theodore to extricate him from his pecuniary difficulties, and enable him to meet all his engagements.

In June and July made a journey with my daughter Maria to Saratoga, Lake George, Montreal and Quebec.

1860. This year established the Associate Land Co. and conveyed to it all the Associate Lands - Theodore made Secretary and agent. Did not go to the Beach (Beverly Farms) this summer. Rented it to J. W. Rogers. In June visited Illinois in company with my son, got sick there and subsequently with family went to Lancaster, Hollis, etc.

On the 6th Nov. the Presidential election took place throughout the United States, and the result was the election of Abraham Lincoln of Illinois as President, and Hannibal Hamlin of Maine as vice president, which has been followed by an intense excitement in the Southern States at their defeat and in consequence an attempt to secede from the Union is now being made, and in some of the states likely to be carried out. South Carolina is taking the lead.

Ending

At this present writing the year 1860 is just closing and I have got to the end of my book. I am now 67 years, 6 mo. & 23 days old. It is not probable that any events of much individual importance to me, except perhaps the loss of friends, can now occur between this and the closing scene of life. My health is in general good, being interrupted by occasional attacks of inflammatory rheumatism to which I

David Augustus Neal

Harriet Charlotte (Price) Neal

Portraits taken Circa 1858

have been more or less subject for 30 years. I may
therefore consider this autobiography closed. I have
written it for my own amusement, and have taken very little
pains to make it readable as I presume no one will think of
reading through it. I had one other object which was to
collect together in one volume the dates of the various
incidents in my life, as I have some times occasion to refer
to them.

In regard to my political and religious views, I have
embodied them on some sheets which I have tacked together.
The latter are somewhat peculiar, and if the ideas I have
suggested were put in a more demonstrative and readable
form, if in fact like Benton I had a Dumont to put my
notions into order, and my words into classical language,
the theories I have proposed and the suggestions I have made
might become worthy of some attention. I have however grave
doubts of the utility of discussions on the one subject on
which I suppose shadows, clouds and darkness will always
rest and about which therefore men's minds will always be
divided. This memoir and those papers have served to occupy
my hand and mind when otherwise the one might have been idle
and the other dimmed by ennui and inaction.

SALEM JUNE 8th 1861. I am this day 68 years of age for
allowing the day omitted in 1800 it is that time since my
birth on the 7th of June 1793.

Since I wrote the concluding pages immediately preceeding
the most important events that have ever occurred on this
continent have taken place, rendering the future of this
country too uncertain for the keenest mind to fathom. The
attempt to embody in a Southern Confederacy the Slave States
has so far succeeded that seven of them to wit South
Carolina, North Carolina, Georgia, Alabama, Louisiana
Tennessee and Texas have acceded to it, formed a government
of their own with Jefferson Davis as President, and embarked
in open rebellion to the United States for which the
inauguration of Mr. Lincoln on the 4th of March seems to be
the only plea, and was the signal for action. Fort Sumpter

Names of Accounts		Value of Holdings Dr Footing
1 Stock		
*2 Estate in Chestnut St		12.000 00
*2 Washington St Estate		6.500 00
5 Ackers Estate. 89.175 sq ft on Bright place, Brookline		1.783 50
*3 Land in Beverly 4¾ a. at W Beach with House & Barn		7.631 10
6 Estate in Brookline 212.781 sq ft		3.191 71
7 Bartlett Wharf Estate 110,000 sq ft ½ int in fee		30.800 67
8 Land in Illinois ½ int with H.A.H in 320 a.		1.284 00
9 Lands in Illinois in Co ½ int in ¼ certain notes		5.300 00
10 Lands at Amboy in Co ⅕ int in 200 a land & 150 lots		1.000 00
11 Bourbonnais Lands ⅕ int in certain notes		15.496 32
12 Dunleith Lands ⅕ of ⅙ in certain land & notes		6.821 36
13 Dupuy Contract ½ of ½ of ½ int in Contract		2.514 00
14 Associate Land Co Stock. 1000 sh #25 each full pd		25.750 00
21 S. D. & C RR 6% Bond	#35000-	2.226 00
22 M R O & E RR 7% "	#49.000-	15.729 00
23 SC & I RR 7% "	#24.000	20.618 00
24 Mich C. RR 8% "	#1.000	722 87
25 Ill. C. RR Debentures	paid	241 25
30 M R O & E RR Stock	1527 sh. par #50.	4.587 00
32 Eastern R.R Stock	36 sh. par #100.	2.358 00
33 Ill. Cent RR Stock	500 sh par #100. full pd	37.500 00
34 Phil & Read RR Pref Stock	100. #50.	2.000 00
35 Hous RR " "	100. #100.	3.500 00
35 Cancelled Bond Scrip	#7400.	5.350 00
36 Alt & St L. RR Stock	28 sh par #100.	2.044 00
37 Essex RR Stock	30. #100	30 00
38 S.C & I. RR Stock	525 #50	1.575 00
40 Mich C. RR Stock	80 #100	3.740 00
41 Mich South. G.P. 10% Stock	130 #100	4.247 50
42 Ch. Burl & Quincy RR Stock	60 #50	3.885 00
50 Kankakee Bridge Stock	24 sh. disposed of	156 57
51 Salem Marine Ins Co Stock	10 sh #100 p	960 00
52 Man Hap. Life Ins Stock	25. #100	2.750 00
53 Penobscot Boom Stock	140. #100.	9.310 00
68 Walter Arrington	Bal of a/c	10 55
69 Bills Receivable		14.149 26
70 Athenaeum	1 sh.	20 00
*71 House Furniture		5.750 00
*75 Barstow Trust	Bal of a/c	

		Dr	Cr	Net Value
75 Ill. Cent RR Co	" "		20 25	
*81 M. Maria Neal	" "	150 00	1.943 58	
93 Bills Payable		848 24	1.540 83	
97 Interest Acct		39 98	979 98	
99 Expense Acct		1.001 03		1.001 03
121 Ward & Co	Bal of a/c	8.499 01	7.396 07	1.102 94
127 I.C.RR optional Rights	unlisted, time expired	5 04		5 04
128 Ship Witchcraft	lost	5265 08	6.764 60	
129 Ship Cygnet	¼ of ship	2.755 09		2755 09
130 Ship Hamlet	⅛ "	7493 56	263 34	7230 22
131 Neal & Co. Texas Acct		10 00		10 00
131 Suspense Acct			1.010 00	
135 Merchants Bank	Bal of a/c	3.672 50	1.789 44	1883 06
137 Trusteeship	" "	516 97		516 97
139 Rents of Bartlett Wharves		157 96	2.000 00	
140 Illinois Land Dividends			599 67	
146 Cash		3.442 97	1.458 69	1.984 28
*148 Trust for F. J. Price	Bal of a/c	207 38		207 38
*149 Trust for H. Price	" "	42 00	69 28	
*156 Trust for H. C. Neal	" "		1.803 95	
157 Barstow Income	" "	1.000 00	1.696 00	
152 Reading Dividend Scrip	#1452. due Dec 31 1861	1.089 00		1.089 00
220 Profit & Loss		15.601 08		15.601 08
70 Pew in North Church		50 00		50 00
		#315.173 49	#315.173 49	#293,518.44

NUMBER COLUMNS ABBREVIATED DUE TO SPACE RESTRICTIONS CR.

E & O E. August 5th 1861

Balance Sheet for the Estate of D.A.Neal on Aug.5,1861. His ledgers, started by him in 1856 were maintained until 1906 at the death of M.M.Neal.

241

in Charleston harbour was shortly after invested and finally
attacked and carried by the troops of S. Carolina on which
Pres. Lincoln called on the several states for a levy of
75,000 men for the defence of Washington, and it was
answered by all the free states with the greatest enthusiasm
and alacrity. At this moment some 30 ro 40,000 men are
stationed in or near Washington, and 4 or 5,000 at
Baltimore, and 15,000 at Fortess Monroe. The particular
history of the last six months is too eventful not to be
recorded and remembered, so that any detail here would be
superfluous.

But during this period, when the country has received so
severe a blow, from which however it will in time recover, I
have personally been attacked with a disease that will in
all probability soon prove fatal, if that be the proper word
to apply to death. On Monday the 21st of January I was in
Boston on business and obliged to stand round on the icy
side walks for some hours and when I returned home in the
evening found my feet and knees affected with rheumatism.
This continued pretty severely for 3 or 4 weeks when the
pains abated but left me much emaciated and very feeble, and
my flesh continued to fall off, having little or not
appetite. Early in March I found from the pallor of my
countenance and the appearance of my skin that I was
suffering under the same disease of which my brother Nathan
died, anaemia or wasting of the blood, and at my age this
could hardly be expected to be remedied. Towards the end of
March Mrs. Neal, being alarmed at the sumptoms, called in
Doct. Stone as our family physician Dr. Cox was in Europe.
He prescribed a preparation of iron, the abstraction of
which mineral from the blood was the cause of the disease.
I have been taking it ever since, and I think with some
effect judging from the color of my skin and appearance of
my eyes. But my appetite has not improved in the least,
although I have rode out every fine day since the middle of
April and owing I think to some disarrangement of the organs
of the stomach and bowels which produces an oppression
whenever I attempt to eat. Still I am generally stronger,
can walk about better. The result however is not I suppose

242

<u>Obituary</u>("Salem Register", glued into family "Neal Record")

       Our obituary column contains the announcement of the death of
<u>DAVID AUGUSTUS NEAL</u>, Esq. in the 69th year of his age. Mr. Neal was
a man of extraordinary energy of character, and was well known for
his enterprise and zeal in connection with mercantile pursuits and
with the railroad business of the country. For several years he was
the president of the Eastern Railroad Company, and has since been
distinguished for the vigor which he infused into the mangement of
several of the most important of the Western roads. He belongs to a
family celebrated for mercantile enterprise, intelligence and skill,
his father and brothers, as well as himself, having done much to
give renown to the merchants of Salem as a class. In his earlier
years he was an active politician and not unfrequently wrote
political communications for the Register which were distinguished
for their acuteness, terseness of style directness and force.
Indeed, he always wrote well on any subject, and although he has not
figured much in the newspapers of late, we published a communication
from him in March last, we think, which showed that he retained his
interest in the political questions of the day and has lost none of
his gogency of expression or felicity of composition. During the
war of 1812 he was wounded in a daring adventure, and was also one
of the Dartmoor prisoners. As a shipmaster, merchant, railroad
President, his activity and energy were conspicious - indeed they
were marked traits in his character from his earliest youth-and
although he not unfrequently wore a rough exterior, and abrupt
address, yet he was a man of great kindness of heart, unusual
intelligence, and many and varied experiences, of which an
interesting and valuable record might be made. He will be much
missed in the marts of businesses.

243

doubtful, though it may be more protracted than I anticipated. But I am all ready. It is only taking a longer nap than usual. Nor do I fear what dreams may come when I have shuffled off this mortal coil. I am not conscious of ever having wronged a single individual, or of having now an enemy in the world. I may have had fewer nominal friends than most men, for I have always felt a delicacy in cultivating an intimacy with those who might help me or whom I could help. Friendship I considered too valuable to be exposed to the imputation of mercenary motives. In regard to my business it is reduced to the simplest form. I owe nothing, nobody owes me. I have no outstanding disputes. No one has any claims upon me, beyond those arising from daily transactions. My property is so situated that there will be little for my executor to do. The country is to be sure in a perillous state, but my living or dying can have no effect on its destinies. I don't see therefore but I am ready to go, and with the exception of parting with wife and children, which all must do once that there is anything to regret in doing so.

Such are my reflections on my 68th birthday, probably my last.

David Augustus Neal Died August 5, 1861

LAST WILL AND TESTAMENT OF David Augustus Neal

To repay as far as in my power the increasing kindness and affection of my wife I wish to secure to her if she should survive me and adequate provision for her declining years.

Happy in my children who have now attained a mature age without stain or reproach, I desire to make their future lives as free from contingencies as the fluctuations of property will permit.

With these views and being of sound health and mind, I hereby make, publish and declare this instrument or present writing, bu me subscribed, to be my last Will and Testament, hereby revoking each and every other will heretofore made by me.

First

I make and appoint Theodore A. Neal Sole Executor of this will.

Second

I hereby cancel all debts whether by book or note due me at the time of my death by either of my children and direct that all obligations therefore be cancelled.

Third

If my wife Harriet Charlotte survives me, I give and bequeath to her my Estate on Chestnut Street, Salem, geing the same bequest to me by my sister Mrs. Mehitable Choate and also my Estate at West Beach in Beverly. If the former should have been sold prior to my death, I give to her in lieu thereof the sum of Twelve thousand dollars ($12,000.00), and if the latter the sum of eight thousand dollars ($8,000.00). I also give to her all the furniture, plate, pictures, books, apparel, horses, carriages and generally all housekeeping articles of which I may die possessed to her and her heirs forever. If she should not survive me then I bequeath the same to my proper heirs above.

Fourth

If in the estimation of my Executor, my property, after deducting the preceding requests shall clearly amount to more than one hundred thousand dollars ($100,000.00) in value, I give and bequeath to my cousins, Stephen Osborn, Henry Osborne, Mrs. Hannah Roberts, Mrs. Harriet, wife of Iasic Allen and Jonathan Preston, and also to Mrs. Sarah, widow of my cousin John Preston, and to the brothers of my wife, Fitz James Price and Henry Price, each the sum of five hundred dollars ($500.00) to be paid in one year after my decease.

I also give, if it is the opinion of my Executor, there still remains, after paying the aforesaid legacies, the said sum of one hundred thousand dollars ($100,000.00) and not otherwise to the Mayor and Aldermen of the city of Saelm, in trust i.e. for the special purposes following and none other, the sum of five thousand dollars ($5,000.00) that the sum should be safely invested, and the interest or income thereof - from time to time, expended in the purchase of fuel, to be given or sold at low prices as may be deemed best by the Trustees, to such worthy and industrious poor

CONTINUED....

as are not supported, in which or in part at the
public expense but who may need some aid in addition to their own labour, to enable them to sustain themselves and families during the inclement
season of the year, such aid to be afforded in
the most private manner possible and the names of
the recipients to be witheld from the public.
In case of sales as above suggested, the receipts
to be reinvested in full, until the income of the
fund is exhausted, for distribution as before provided.

Fifth

I give to my son Theodore A. Neal, to be in full
for his services, as Executor of this will, my
Estate in Washington Street in Salem, or if it
should have been sold prior to my death, the sum
of seven thousand dollars ($7,000.00) in lieu
thereof and his heirs.

Sixth

All the rest and residue of my Estate, real person
or mixed I give and bequeath to my wife Harriet C.,
my son Theodore A. and to my daughters Margaret
Maria and Harriet Charlotte and to their successors,
as herein provided, jointly, in strict trust nevertheless and for the special purposes herein named,
to wit, that they shall hold and manage the same,
with full power in the consent in writing of a majority of their whole number, to each transaction,
to will, exchange or dispose of any part thereof
and to reinvest the proceeds in any safe and pro-
ductive property and to continue to do so during
the continuance of the trust and especially that

they cause my books of account to be continued in the
same form and manner as they have heretofore been
kept, employing if necessary an accountant for this
purpose and function that they will endeavour as soon
as it is conveniently can be done, so to dispurse
of the property as to pay off any liens upon the
Bartlett wharves in Boston or upon any other real
estate belonging to my Estate and that they will
commencing from the date of the Probat of this instrument (my Executor being hereby authorized and directed
to furnish them the means for the first year from the
Estate) pay from the net income and if necessary from
the principal of my Estate, as follows, for the term
of seven (7) years from the day of my decease,
annually and in quarterly payments to wit in the first
Tuesdays of January, April, July and October, to my
wife, Harriet C., if she shall survive me, the sum of
three thousand dollars ($3,000.00) and to each of my
children Theodore A., Margaret Maria, and Harriet C.,
the sum of fifteen hundred dollars ($1,500.00) and
after the expiration of same seven years, to my wife,
two fifths and to each of my children above mentioned,
one fifth of the net income of my estate payable as
the same may cause. In case of the death of either of
the above named, to wit my wife Harriet C. or my
children, Theodore A., Margaret Maria, and Harriet C.
the amount payable to her or him so decided shall
thereafter be first in such of my lineal descendants
and in such proportion as she or he may hence directed
by her or his last will and testament, or by any
instrument under her or his hand and Seal made in
presence of their competent witnesses and in default
of such will or instrument, to her or his children and
their descendant respectively and if there is none such
then to my proper heirs at leave.

If my wife shall not survive me, then the sum payable to each of my children, shall be for the said seven uears, twenty-five hundred dollars ($2,500.00) per annum and after than one third of the net income from my estate, and on their several deaths, in manner as above specified, But in one year after the death of my said wife and all my said children, such payments shall cease and the principal then in the hands of the Trustees shall be divided among the persons entitled under the preceding privisions of this will receive the aforesaid payments or income and in the precise proportion in which they are entitled, to them or their heirs forever and the conditions on which the aforesaid bequests are made ------------------- shall be in all cases free from the control of any persons or persons other than the parties shall have in property -- no right or power to abdicate or mortgage the same premises to the actual payment into their hands.

Seventh

If any one of the Trustees before named, to wit my wife Harriet Charlotte or either of my children, Theodore A., Margaret Maria or Harriet C. shall die or resign or let otherwise rendered incapable of holding said trust, the powers herein given to the four, shall develop in two then remaining, but any further vacancy shall be supplied by the Judge of Probat for the County of Essex as provided by law.

Eighth

It is my wish and will if the same bye confromable to law that my Executor shall not be required to give bonds except to pay debts and the legacies mentioned in #2,5, or 4th Sections and that the Trustees shall not be obliged to render any accounts except to the parties immediately interested.

In witness whereof, I David Augustus Neal, the Testator of Salem, Mass. have herewith set my hand and seal in the presence of the subscribing witnesses at Salem the twelfth day of May A.D. One thousand eight hundred fifty-eight.

Signed

David Augustus Neal

We, Robert S. Rantoul, Caroline Lovett, Henriette C.A.Price, whose names are herewith subscribed, do certify that David Augustus Neal, who is personally known to us did in our presence sign his name and affix his seal to the above instrument which he acknowledged to be his last Will and Testament and that he did so of his own free will.

In witness whereof we have hence named in his presence in the presence of each other at Salem, the twelfth day of May A.D. 1858.
Signed

Robert S.Rantoul, Caroline Lovett
Henriette C.A.Price

(Codicils not included in this translation)

Appendix A: Diary of James Price, August 10, 1792, Paris

-at 2 o'clock a.m. the inhabitants of the harbour St.
Antoine and St. Marceau began their march towards the
Palais of the Truillerie. the city in a great uproar.
At 3 o'clock a.m. 21 persons taken disguised in the Champs
Elise with Pistols, Dagers and other weapons of Defence.
Said to be the armed gard de corps of the King & confined
in the gard house & great preperations-making. the inhabitants to attack the palais. a great number of field fences
placed in the Different avenues of the Palais Arch,
the place de Carrousal, the Pont Royal, Place Louis
quinze & several other places - went myself at this time
& visited the Different Posts. the National Gards were
very strong in the Nabourhood of the Palais - the Whole
City illuminated - at 8 o'clock a.m. saw a head on a Pike
carried in the Palais Royale & was informed that of the King
gard de corps that was taken in the Champs Elise at 3
oclock were conducted to the Place Vedome to be beheaded.
I went imediately to the Place with Ingersol and Jarvis
and saw 6 fine followers that they were then sacrificing
one man's head being cut off previous to our arrival,
the rest cut off in our presence. the women expressed
their wish in having a revenge on the poor captives,
having armed themselves with swords & pikes which they
procured from the citisens they thrust their weapons in
the expiring bodies with such a Degree of revenge &
Satisfaction that it made my blood run cold. after satisfy-
ing themselves with the dead bodies they imbraced the
National Gards & gave them joy for the Sacrifice they had
met with & desired then not to fear that they would
carry their point that it was the only time to establish
their liberty upon the true Principals of equality.
at half past 9 oclock the Suise gards discharged 8 field
pieces placed in the end windowes of the Palais that looks
on the river Seine. one the Marseille National Gards &
citisens of Paris that were coming over the Pont Royale
to make the attack on the Palais & killed 200 Marsellois
at the first discharge who never brooke their line but

proceeded on regularly over the dead corps with
Double the fury to attack their then Declared
enemies & returned a Discharge of their cannon
immediately which was kept up on both sides very
warm for some time. the Suisse fired with great
vivacity the repetations of the cannon were so
rapid that it resembled the roaling of Thunder
in a great Storme. at 10 oclock the citisens
entered the Palais began their massacre on the
Suise & every other Person found in the Palais
- Set fire to the out building of the Palais
such as guard House & other buildings which extended round the Palais for the receptions of the
Suisse guards and demolished the whole. entered
above after the citizens after setting fire to
those buildings the National Gards to be entered
the Palais previous to entering. the King finding
how resolute the people were & his person in Danger for they would have killed him if they had
caught him Made his escape threw the Garden of
the Thuilleris to the National Assembly with
the queen the Prince & Princes Royalle and told
the National Assemblay as their persons were in
Danger that they had laft the Palais which was
besieged by the citisens & throwed themselves
under the protection of the Nation which they
represented with his family on his arrival busi--
ness was stopped imediately as agreeable to the
constitution the assembly cant proceed to business
whilst the King is on the flore. The Assemblay
provided a place for him & his family in the
back of the President Seat in a little room ad--
joining the National Assembly where the King &
his family could see in the assembley and hear
all the acts that were past against him During
his stay there which was 3 days had a small room
allowed him to lay in just big enough to contain
9 persons which his family consisted off & were
obliged to lay to-gether on matrass spread on

cotts- during their Stay the National Assemblay- the Swiss finding them selves over power'd asked for quarters but the people would not hear to their request for the Suises had began to Massacree the National Gards that was in the Palais to guard the King as decreed by the National Assembly imediately on the peoples entering the Palaise they <u>massacred every Suise that fell into their hands</u> & striped them stark naked every person that could provided himself with part of the Suisse uniform and carried it on the end of their pikes as a trofy of honor. there was near <u>half as maney women as men provided with cartouch boxes with powder & swords</u> who cut of the private parts of the Suises and carried them on the end of their Swords every person found in the Palais meet with the same reception & it was supposed that there were 4000 persons in the Palais consisted of 2000 Suise the remainder the Kings former Body Gards or Gard de Corps --- nobility & Priests disguised in Suise uniform. in one Single House was found 500 beds where the Suise quartered. they had beds even on the top of the House round the Palais which was set on fire. The Royal party that defended the Palais were mangled all to peases every man I suppose had not left then 20 or 30 gashes in his Bodey & Head. numbers of the Suŝie made a Sortie & tried to make there escape firing on the inhabitants as they were running but was massacred in their attempts. threw the streets the <u>Dead bodies laid in piles at the corner of every street</u> in the nabourhood of the Palais & streams of Blood running in the guters, the Dead on the part of the Citizens were carried off imediatley & throwed in the river that the numbers might not be known - 60 Suises who were killing the inhabitants in trying to make their escape were taken & carried to the Maison de Ville or Town House & their beged that they might be tried by the laws of the country that they were unarmed prisoners, the manusipalitee or officers who privided at that ime at the Maison de Ville order that they might be committed to the abbeye St. Germains & not be given up to the

people but in the Descending the Stairs of the Maison de Ville the populace who was waiting for them in the place de Greve cut every man of them to pieces as they came out and striped them as the otheres were in the Palais. Several persons on this Day was massacred because they had red coats some white Britches & others who was dressed generally supposed to be Suisse & aristocrats Disguised every gentleman here Dresses himself as mean as he can to appear like the <u>Sans Coulettes</u> or the Jacobine party. in Short there is no kind of Distinction to be seen at present in this city the etats major distroyed, crois de St. Louis are not worn for fear of being suspected & tortured. epolets are worn instead of gold ones they mean to establish true republican principal. at 5 oclock P.M. I visited the Palais of the Thuilleries & <u>was shocked at the sight of Dead Bodies Laying in heaps in every quarter</u>, in the garden they layed in ranges every man of them striped naked & cut in every part of the Body. the Palais crowded with people who were destroying the riches that had been collected for numbers of years which cost France large sums of money & let all the wine run out of the Butts in the Sellers after Drinking as much as they wished. no man was allowed to pilfer. between 20 & 30 who were caught in attempting to Steal was put to Death imediately in the Same manner of the Suisses except they were not Striped. the citisens are now imployed in carrying off the Dead filing the enjoint & examining the fire conductors to prevent the flames from spreading in the city.

* * *

Appendix B; Sails

Reference Abbreviations

Barnhart,C.L.,"The American College Dictionary"
  Random House, New York,1948...............ACD

Langer, Wm. L.,"An Encylopedia of World
  History" Houghton Mifflin Co.,
  Boston,1948...............................EWH

Kemp, P."The Oxford Companion to Ships
  and the Sea", Oxford University
  Press,London, 1976.......................OCSS

Fowler,H.W.&F.D.,"The Concise Oxford
  Dictionary of Current English"
  Oxford U. Press, London,1972.............OxD

****

Credits

Essex Institute, Salem, Mass.
Published Works

---------"A Green Hands First Cruise...."........116

Crawford,J.,"History of the Indian Archipelago.".158

Fracker,G.,"Voyage to South America..."..........170

---------"Three Years in the Pacific..."........174

Windsor,E.,"The Eastern Seas in the Indian
  Archipelago..."...........................159

Unpublished Works

Neal, H.C."Account Book of 1824".................182

Rogers,Wm. A.,"Journal....Voyage to India,
  A.D.1817".................................124

Photographs Only

Bickmore,A.S.,"Travels in the East Indian
  Archipelago" John Murray,London,1868
  Poultry Vendor............................132
  Water Carrier.............................159

Peabody Museum, Salem, Mass.
Published Works

Davis,C.G.,"Rigs of the Principal Types
  of American Sailing Vessels" Peabody
  Museum,Salem,1974
  Schooner.................................. 84
  Brig......................................168
  Ship...................................42,140

---------"Harper's Family Library-History of
  British India..."........................ 60

Harris,W.B.,"A Journey Through Yemen..".........142
  Man and Woman of Yemen...................142

---------"Marine Regulations.."................. 84

Mathison,G.F."Narrative of a Visit to Brazil..."..176
  Women of Lima............................173

Ward,Rev.W ."A View of...of the Hindoos.."......54,56

252

O'Meara,B.E.,"Napoleon in Exile or A Voice
        from St. Helena" W. Simpkin & R.
        Marshall,Vol. I & II,London,1822.........106

Roach,J.C."Old Ironsides-U.S.S.Frigate
        'Constitution'" U.S.Navy,Boston
        1976................................. 92,134

Robinson,B.R.,"American Naval Prints"
        U.S.Naval Academy Museum,Annapolis
        Maryland,International Exhibitions
        Foundation,1976....................28,30,34

---------"The Bodleys Afoot"Houghton
        Osgood & Co.,Boston,1880.............18,20,32

Wilkinson,R. "General Atlas of the
        World With Appropriate Tables"
        Robart Wilkinson,London,1809.........148,151

Unpublished Works

Neal,D.A."Journal of David Augustus Neal,
        1793-1861"..........................6,12,16
                                          22,44,52
                                          64,108,112
                                          118,128,138
                                          146,154,166
                                          226.

Neal,D.A.,"Last Will & Testament of
        D.A.Neal",1858...........................244

Neal,D.A."Personal Ledgers,1856-1906"............240

Neal,D.A.,"Letter to Wife from Chicago,1854".....228

Rantoul,C.N.,"Family Portraits,Washington
        St. House,Chestnut St. House,
        West Beach House & Contents
        from old photographs and existing
        buildings...............................10,24,80
                                          188,191,206
                                          234,236,239

Rantoul,R."School Journal,Beverly,
        Mass.,1814"..............................30

Rantoul,W.G.,"West Beach Sketches,1885"
        2 volumes........................196,202,204

Price,H.C."Assorted Letters,Floral
        Sketch,circa 1810"..................66,68,69
                                          74,78,80

****

Additional Reference Material

Essex Inst.,Salem: Eastern Railroad material
Harvard U.,Cambridge,Mass.:Dunn & Bradstreet
        ratings on the Neal companies
Library of Congress,Washington D.C.:
        D.A.Neal pamphlet for the Eastern
        Railroad,1851
Newbury Lib,,Chicago:D.A.Neal letters
        while involved with the Illinois
        Central R.R.,about 300.
New York Pub.Lib.,N.Y.: D.A.Neal
        pamphlet,Illinois Cent.R.R.,1854
New York State Archives:Neal documents
        from both the companies
Ohio Historical Society: D.A.Neal
        pamphlet for the Philadelphia
        and Reading R.R.,1849